LITERACY IN A DIGITAL WORLD

*Teaching and Learning in the
Age of Information*

LEA'S COMMUNICATION SERIES
Jennings Bryant/Dolf Zillmann, General Editors

For a complete list of other titles in LEA's Communication Series, please contact Lawrence Erlbaum Associates, Publishers

LITERACY IN A DIGITAL WORLD

Teaching and Learning in the
Age of Information

KATHLEEN TYNER

LAWRENCE ERLBAUM ASSOCIATES, PUBLISHERS
1998   Mahwah, New Jersey   London

Lawrence Erlbaum Associates, Inc., Publishers
10 Industrial Avenue
Mahwah, New Jersey 07430

Cover design by Kathryn Houghtaling Lacey

Library of Congress Cataloging-in-Publication Data

Tyner, Kathleen R.
    Literacy in a digital world : teaching and learning in the age of information /
        Kathleen Tyner.
            p. cm.
    Includes bibliographical references and indexes.
    ISBN 0-8058-2227-5 (hardcover : alk. paper). — ISBN 0-8058-2226-7
(pbk. : alk. paper).
    1. Computers and literacy. 2. Media literacy. 3. Mass media in
education. 4. Educational innovations. I. Title.
LC149.5.T96 1998
302.2'244—dc21   98-25290
                                                            CIP

Books published by Lawrence Erlbaum Associates are printed on acid-free paper,
and their bindings are chosen for strength and durability.

Printed in the United States of America
10 9 8 7 6 5 4 3

For my sister
Trudy Tyner

Contents

Acknowledgments

Literacy in a Digital World: Teaching and Learning in the Age of Information has been a long reflection on my relationship with media education. It would not have been possible without the direct contribution of many talented educators, publishers, and friends. I learned so much from teachers across the country about the art and science of teaching. This book also reflects valuable experience gained through my association with literacy and education experts Ruth Schoenbach, David Diepenbrock, Cynthia Greenleaf, and the teachers who participated in the Herald Project in San Francisco. They introduced me to the idea of cognitive apprenticeships and gave me an opportunity to connect media education to literacy in a public school setting. In addition, Lyn Lacy at the Minneapolis Public School District was very generous in sharing her experiences in the classroom, as well as sharing the standards development work of her colleagues. Irene Yamashita, a teacher on the island of Oahu, and Karen Webster of the University of Utah were only two of the many teachers who provided me with insight about the use of video in the classroom. Deborah Leveranz of Texas modeled for me the way to let go of the things I thought I knew in order to encourage my students to think for themselves.

Throughout the years I have benefited from the support of international media educators. Canadians John Pungente of the Jesuit Communication Project and Barry Duncan of the Association for Media Literacy in Ontario have been exceedingly generous with information and support and I have great admiration for their tireless efforts on behalf of media teachers. Roberto

Aparici of UNED in Spain; Cary Bazalgette of the British Film Institute in London; David Buckingham of the Institute of Education, University of London; Len Masterman, media education scholar and writer from England; and Robyn Quin and Barry McMahon, media educators and writers from Australia, have all proved to be generous colleagues and valuable mentors for my work in the United States. They are very busy people, but have always found time for me.

Because writing can be a lonely business, I am especially grateful for the generosity and warmth of my colleagues in the United States: All of the filmmakers and teachers at Appalshop in Whitesburg, Kentucky; Dr. Gary Ferrington, of the University of Oregon; Dr. Joellen Fisherkeller at the Department of Media Ecology at New York University; Steve Goodman and Karen Helmerson at Educational Video Center in New York City; Melissa Phillips of the Media Workshop in New York City; Marieli Rowe of the National Telemedia Council in Madison, Wisconsin; and the folks who collect student-produced work at Video Data Bank in Chicago. I am so happy to know they are out there doing quality work that helps so many teachers find useful ways to connect media and new technologies with school improvement. I want to thank Nanette Koelsch and Elise Trumbull of the Language, Culture and Equity program at WestEd in San Francisco. They provided important guidance on issues of literacy, linguistics, and English-language learning and I have great respect for their work.

I also want to acknowledge the editors and production professionals who made the publication of *Literacy in a Digital World: Teaching and Learning in the Age of Information* possible. The editors of the LEA media education series, Dr. Robert Kubey of Rutgers University and Dr. Reneé Hobbs of Babson College, gave me the opportunity to publish the book and provided advice and vital information along the way. Linda Bathgate, my editor at Lawrence Erlbaum Associates has been terrific, as has the production and copy editor, Sondra Guideman. The book and its author benefited from their vast experience and it has been a pleasure working with them.

Finally, this book would not have been possible without the contribution of my husband, filmmaker Scott Stark, who provided much-needed editorial assistance; technical and production guidance; and a wealth of knowledge about experimental film and new media. No one else would have taken the time or shown the patience. Bless him for steering my doubts and frustrations toward the brighter side of book publication.

Introduction

The fact is: I have a hard time describing the work I do to my own mother. I am an itinerant teacher, reluctant writer, and sometimes media producer. Since the late 1980s, I have migrated around the world to team up with collaborating teachers, usually local media artists, K–12 teachers, or community-based education groups, to teach and learn about the way that new technologies are changing education. This kind of collaboration is rewarding in a number of ways and provided the basis for much of the content in *Literacy in a Digital World: Teaching and Learning in the Age of Information*. The team-teaching approach integrates media analysis, media production, and pedagogy and it works for me for a number of reasons: It combines and expands the collective expertise of a team of teachers; it provides an opportunity for collegial reflection and critique on the teaching and learning experience; it prevents burnout and exhaustion because we can switch roles from time to time; and finally, students enjoy a change of instruction and a change of personality, especially if the instruction is intensive.

My longest and most creative collaboration was with media educator Deborah Leveranz, a native of the state of Texas. Deborah has a long history of teaching arts and media to kids in a variety of formal and informal settings, including public schools, public television, cable access trainings, juvenile justice settings, after-school programs, and universities. In 1990, we developed a week-long Media Literacy Institute for teachers by combining our experiences with media production and cognitive work. Either as a team, or separately, we have tested the boundaries of media education by conducting Institutes in California, Canada, Kentucky, states across the Midwest,

New York, New Mexico, Texas, Vermont, Washington, and so on. We have been invited to work in church basements, arts centers, film festivals, schools, hospitals, community centers, and one polka party. Teachers we have trained have taken it even farther, both geographically and conceptually. Over the years, we have collectively explored and discovered a number of strategies for integrating what we tend to call "media education" into an eclectic range of educational settings.

I wrote *Literacy in a Digital World* for myself, in an attempt to sort out and make sense of my experiences in teaching media and using new technologies. As part of this book, I have also attempted to reconcile some contradictions in my own thinking about the use of media and new technologies in the classroom. I hope that these experiences will also enrich the understanding and practice of others in similar circumstances. I would be very pleased if this book will spur other teachers, especially elementary and secondary teachers, to reflect on their relationship with media, to examine their educational practices and to write about their experiences. I say this with a good measure of self-interest. In order to really make progress with students, it would help to know more about the uses of media and technology within a much wider range of educational environments such as those found in informal settings, after-school programs, adult literacy programs, online, in the home, and in the street.

I feel comfortable when I can ground my teaching in research and I continue to seek a cohesive body of research from which to practice media education. After reading *From Memory to Written Record: England 1066–1307* by M. T. Clanchy (1993), a historian from Glasgow University, I began to seek out all I could find about the history of literacy, in the belief that new literacy technologies were both a product and a shaper of their times. Clanchy wrote about the overlap between the practices of oral literacy and the advent of alphabetic literacy and his book crystallized my thinking about the importance of literacy research and theory to inform my own teaching about media and new technologies. I am grateful to Clanchy for his scholarship, even though I must say, *From Memory to Written Record* caused me a great deal of anguish, because it forced me to rethink and scrap a great deal of initial work on this book. But for the better I believe.

Clanchy's research is a cautionary tale. For example, it indicates that the introduction of written legal and business records in medieval England did not contribute to efficiency in government, but was in fact counterefficient. The measurement of ownership, census, business transactions and the like, eventually in triplicate, gave way to monastic and monarchic bureaucracies that developed increasing complex systems to solidify and exert control over the populace. Ironically, posterity has been better served by these early written records than those who were polled at the time. Medieval written records, used in part as a mechanism of social control in their time, are the basis for the kind of historical analysis that enables scholars to study extant artifacts of literacy. In the advent of the Information Age, the increased use of paper, and conversely, the increased use of computers for monetary transactions in the advent of computers provided interesting parallels, although I wonder how we will study the artifacts of CPM machines and data punch cards in the year 2500.

The conversation about literacy and schooling takes on new urgency as teachers and parents are told—and children believe—that students' life chances hinge on their grasp of new technologies. Beyond simple decoding and keyboarding, the educational uses of new communication technologies has yet to be framed as a set of literacy skills. But the public is often reminded that computers are powerful tools and it is implied that with their use, personal power can accrue. In the broadest sense, history does show a fluctuating connection between new literacy tools and power, in that success comes to those who can understand and manipulate at least one of two main domains of information technologies: (a) the technical information infrastructure, that is, the physical properties and raw materials of literacy, including the tools, the technical personnel, the systems design, and the distribution mechanisms; and (b) the information itself, or more precisely, the discursive style that is peculiar to each medium and that shapes its content, succinctly summed up by Marshall McLuhan in the deceptively simple catch phrase, "the medium is the message." Both of these are skills having to do with the output of information, analogous to writing.

To control either infrastructures or media content is no mean task. A cynical popular saying goes, "Those who die with the most toys win." If power were assured by simply amassing communication "toys," a clean and unbroken equation for the uses of communication technologies for control would emerge throughout history. Although ownership and control of content and infrastructures is a formidable advantage, history shows us that it does not guarantee an unwavering power status in society. On the margins of history are dynamic examples of those who emerge from disenfranchised cultural sites to gain advantage by creatively exploiting the formal narrative structures of each medium to strike an alternative cultural resonance. Those who tell compelling and authentic-sounding stories then have an opportunity to attract sufficient attention to piggyback on communication systems owned by others. History is replete with examples of those who subverted the narrative approved by those in control. Socrates, Martin Luther, the Luddites, and contemporary culture jammers of many political stripes demonstrate that individuals can take advantage of cracks in the communication infrastructure.

As much as contemporary information corporations would like to corner the lucrative market share for new media—as newspapers did in the 19th century; radio and motion pictures did in the first half of the 20th century;

network television did in the 1950s; and Microsoft did at the end of the 20th century—history reveals too many exceptions to create a one-best formula for garnering power through even the most skillful control of literacy practices, information, and its infrastructures. One reason for this is that audiences use information and popular culture in unpredictable ways.

Advertisers are fond of saying that they know that 50% of all advertising works, they just don't know *what* 50%. Although information providers know a great deal about audience response to content, a predictable pattern of audience response to media messages remains outside their complete control. If it were, every prosocial public service announcement would translate into changed behavior in the public. But even the most elaborate media campaigns fall flat, or generate unintended meanings when they reach audiences. This element of surprise in the negotiation between audiences and information injects a sense of levity and randomness to the human communication experience that makes predictions about the future uses of literacy an amusing, if precarious, sport.

In this book, I investigate a third way to use literacy as a source of social power and that is the ability to decode information in a variety of forms, analogous to the reading of print, but also applicable to audio, graphics, and the moving image, a process that Paolo Friere and Donaldo Macedo (1987) call "reading the world." If citizens can also manipulate and understand the processes to create messages and distribute them, that is, "writing the world," then literacy practices accrue maximum benefit to the individual. It would be false to say that this vision of literacy would automatically translate into an equal distribution of social power. It is obvious that those who control both the channels of distribution and the skillful production of compatible content have access to the most favorable opportunities to influence social policy through sustained creative effort. Nonetheless, a sophisticated and powerful vision of literacy shows potential to enable each person to at least join the debate by skillfully negotiating within the existing power structure, as well as outside it. And this is why it is urgent that everyone has access to literacy in its most powerful forms. I wrote this book to capitalize on that observation and to encourage folks to use a wider variety of everyday information to their best advantage.

I have found it most rewarding to work on small media education projects, close to home, in the belief that these contexts will yield the most knowledge over time about new literacy practices in action, in specific contexts. For this reason, I include many examples of literacy practices from the Bay Area in California. Chapter 1 begins with a story about the San Francisco Public Library and relates it to a parallel instance in the history of literacy in order to explore relationships between oral, written, and digital modes of literacy. When viewed through a literacy lens, debate about the appropriate uses of literacy is very old, at least as old as the ancient Greeks. Literacy scholars

Walter Ong (1958) and James Gee (1991) are among those who have explored the connection between Plato's *Phaedrus* and modern attitudes toward literacy, reprised in chapter 1.

Chapter 2 continues on the premise that any analysis of the role that information technologies play in contemporary society and their relationship to complex social compacts such as literacy and schooling can best proceed by examining the way that communication tools contributed to the social landscape in the past. Of course, literacy, its definitions, and purposes are always in flux. Too much depends on the uses of literacy; which literacy, who uses it, who controls it, how it meshes with the power structure of the day; how widely information is disseminated; and how audiences receive it. Literacy scholar Harvey Graff (1979, 1987, 1995) has done both literacy and education a great service by revealing several dearly held assumptions about the power of literacy, as myths. Chapter 2 presents the case of ebonics, as the Oakland, California school district attempts to address pervasive problems in student performance with literacy theory. The Oakland District's advancement of the theory of ebonics met a wall of public opposition, in part created by prevailing conventional wisdom about the purposes of literacy and schooling. The story of ebonics in Oakland is an example of how the myths of literacy can contribute to the uses of literacy for both liberating and constraining purposes.

Because I work in a variety of mass media, I gravitated toward a mass communication theory base, with decidedly mixed success in connecting the research to the classroom. Chapter 3 attempts to make connections between theories of literacy and mass communication in an attempt to inform the role of electronic tools in schooling, especially in elementary and secondary schooling. Mass communication theory is frustrating to me, because it is divorced from some of the assumptions common to the study of literacy. Furthermore, it does little to inform teaching at the elementary and secondary levels of education. However, the study of mass communication does deal with electronic media. The major drawback of working from a literacy theory base is that the preponderance of literacy research is concerned with alphabetic literacy. I continue to struggle to find a coherent body of research that bridges mass communication with literacy theory and that can also prove useful to promising school practices.

It is tempting to follow the theoretical lineage of the technical determinists as a starting point for inference about the uses of new and emerging technologies, chief among them, Marshall McLuhan. McLuhan's ideas are simple, clear, and make definitive links between the uses of media and human affairs. The medium is the message, the global village, hot and cold media are all concepts that resonate on the brink of a highly touted Information Age. Furthermore, the technical determinists were the first to go beyond alphabetic literacy to address the uses of electronic forms of communication from an historical literacy perspective. On closer examination, the resonance of simplistic cause-and-effect reasoning about the way that communication technologies influence behavior in the real world ring hollow. Specific cases, rooted in the research on literacy within culture and social contexts, provide so many exceptions as to render cause-and-effect discussions about literacy moot. Nonetheless, many of the ideas of the technical determinists are seductive and contain enough substance to beg for more research in the uses of electronic literacy from an alphabetic literacy theory base. These are explored in chapter 3.

Chapter 4 continues the search for some consistency in research and practice by looking at the way that literacy is discussed in terms of "multiliteracies," such as technology literacy, information literacy, visual literacy, and media literacy. Chapter 5 expands the ideas behind a field of study known as "educational technology" in the hopes of informing the use of new technologies in literacy. The state of the research for three multiliteracies—computer literacy, network literacy, and technology literacy—is focused on the issue of equitable access to information tools, but the literature about the integration of information into schooling appears to be spotty. Chapter 5 concludes that it is clear that access to information is only the first threshold of literacy. In order to reach a more sophisticated notion of literacy in a digital world, schools must address the integration of new forms of information resources in educational settings.

Chapter 6 seeks some solutions to the integration of new information technologies through a discussion of three more multiliteracies: information literacy, visual literacy, and media literacy. This chapter focuses on media education from an international perspective and recounts some of the history of media education in England, much informed by the work of Len Masterman, a media education scholar from England. This history has particular resonance in the United States, where the field is relatively new and untried and where practitioners seem to be cycling through some of the approaches that have already been rejected by British media educators. There is much cohesion between information literacy, visual literacy, and media literacy, and the fields have the potential to go the distance beyond access to address the productive uses of information technologies for teaching and learning. The fact that these three fields of study do not join forces to link their research and findings is of significant interest. Perhaps a synthesis, under a different name, will come about in the future. At this point, it is too early to tell what nomenclature will emerge that unites the aims and principles of information, visual, and media literacies.

In the meantime, I often work under the banner of media education. Chapter 7 constructs a history of media education in the United States. In the process, several approaches and rationales for media education emerge. This chapter discusses the protectionist or "inoculationist" rationale for media education, an approach that is firmly rooted in the critical viewing campaigns of the 1970s. While writing this chapter, I began to see that I have been looking for a way to reconcile the word *media* with that of *education*. By this I mean that I can see the need to balance concerns about classroom content (media) with those of classroom process (education). It seems that many of the ideological splits and fissures in the field of media education occur when practitioners come down on the side of content over process. This is especially true of protectionists, who focus on the content of media, its representations, and its presumed negative effects. When classroom content is sorted according to the taste of the teacher, it is difficult to balance the needs of students to think independently about a wide range of popular culture and information, an essential element of process. But then again, one of the responsibilities of the teacher is to sort and select the appropriate content for learning events. This begs the role of pedagogy in media teaching. It is a thorny dilemma for teachers of media and I can say that I've stirred it up, but I cannot say that I have resolved it.

Chapter 8 reviews some approaches to media education that can be called an "asset model." An asset model for media teaching assumes that mass media and popular culture content can work as a benefit to literacy instead of as a social deficit. These include arts-based approaches to media education. The San Francisco Digital Media Center provided a useful example of the use of digital tools to further literacy from an arts-based approach. Chapter 8 also discusses a critical literacy approach to media education. The fact that critical literacy employs many of the inquiry-based teaching techniques of Socrates brings the discussion of literacy full circle.

In the early 1990s, I had the privilege of working with the Eastern Kentucky Teachers' Network, a group of Foxfire teachers from eastern Kentucky who are devoted to the study of pedagogy. In particular, these teachers modeled the value of experiential education in a process that continues to inform my own practice. Through Appalshop, a media arts center in Whitesburg, Kentucky, they experimented with the use of video to facilitate storytelling from a student-centered, cultural perspective. Appalshop offers the community a radio station, a world-class theater company, a recording studio, and a center for documentary filmmaking about the culture of Appalachians. This marriage of analysis and practice was a valuable lesson for me. I continue to try to reconcile the analysis of media with the hands-on practice of student production in my own teaching. This is a deceptively difficult task and I experience rare moments of exhilaration when analysis and practice click to create one of those "eureka" moments.

Chapter 9 takes advantage of my experience in eastern Kentucky and is one of the more practical chapters in the book for teachers. This chapter lays out the rationale for hands-on student production from a literacy perspective and attempts to link it to cognitive work. Chief among these rationales is the theory of literacy as discourse and the use of student-centered

education to achieve educational goals. I am particularly happy to have
found the work of Dr. Carol Lee (1995) of Northwestern University who
conducted empirical studies about "culturally based cognitive apprenticeships." Her research provided a much-needed bridge between literacy and
the pedagogy of media teaching. There are many examples of student work
in this chapter and recognition of the diverse needs and expectations of
students and teachers in the contemporary classroom. This chapter focuses
on the use of video, because I believe that video is a practical preliminary
tool for exploring the aesthetics and conventions of digital media and multiliteracies. Although digital media is currently dominated by the uses of
alphabetic literacy on networked computers, I also believe that it is only a
matter of time before the moving image becomes equally prolific in digital
media.

Chapter 10 also appeals to the practical side of teaching and learning. I
don't think that a profound vision of literacy can come about without drastic
and corresponding changes in the nature of schooling. Over the years, I
have come to see the value of standards-based education as a tool for reform.
By "standards," I do not mean the kind of high-stakes standards that politicians use to beat schools into submission. Instead, I see great value in
small, local efforts that lead teachers and communities into an ongoing
discussion about the nature and value of education. Chapter 10 provides
many examples of standards for elementary and secondary education, as
they pertain to the uses of technology and electronic media. I hope that
they prove useful for teachers and committees who wish to integrate critical
literacy practices with their uses of electronic communication tools.

After many interviews with teachers, I was convinced that it was not
enough to simply quote them throughout the book. I wanted their voices
to shine through in a sustained way. So I chose two interviews to print in
their entirety. I hope that the Afterword of this book gives a good context
for the concerns and struggles of teachers who work with students in diverse
settings. In chapter 10, I talk to Robert Gipe, who works with students and
media in rural settings, in both schools and arts-based spaces. I also talk
with Steve Goodman of Educational Video Center in New York City, an
urban program located in a high school in Greenwich Village.

In the end, *Literacy in a Digital World: Teaching and Learning in an Age
of Information* provokes as many questions as it answers. Since at least the
1960s, there has been a growing bifurcation between the literacy practices of
compulsory schooling and those that occur outside the schoolhouse door. The
literacy of schooling, based on a hierarchical access to print literacy, is
increasingly at odds with the kinds of constructivist practices necessary to
accommodate the more diverse, interactive, and less linear media forms made
available by digital technologies. In the absences of strong theory, literacy
practices are splitting into the kind of literacy practiced at school and the kind

practiced in the *real* world of home and community. As the educational system struggles to switch from the literacy appropriate to the Industrial Revolution to those literacies compatible with an Information Age, the tension for reform mounts: But for what purposes? Traditional compulsory public schooling is a worthy and well-intentioned idea that still has a fighting chance for survival if it can align theory and practice to accommodate the authentic literacy needs of students in a world awash in information. *Literacy in a Digital World: Teaching and Learning in the Age of Information* is an attempt to contribute to the conversation about the purposes of literacy and the nature of education in contemporary times. The book will not resolve the fissures, splits, and bifurcations that plague literacy and schooling, but I hope that it will begin to build bridges to some common ground.

Pause on Literacy
Fast Forward

The dedication of a new public library in San Francisco provided a unique occasion to witness the historical forces of literacy in action. The image of public libraries' place in the civic affairs of San Francisco is in keeping with the spirit of the city—energetic, forward-looking, and diverse, but tethered by a faint air of provincialism. The original library of the city was destroyed in the Great San Francisco Earthquake of 1906 and replaced by a magnificent Beaux Arts structure. This graceful edifice was the pride of the city until it was damaged by yet another earthquake in 1989. Each successive library building erected in San Francisco's civic center serves as a powerful symbol of cultural tenacity in the face of disaster. The latest library occupies its customary place in contemporary public affairs. It is the site where the culture of books collides with the emerging digital culture of the late 20th century.

In 1996, San Francisco dedicated a New Main Library to replace the old Beaux Arts structure. When funds were raised for the $140 million "New Main," its promoters promised to usher in library services that were unimaginable in the beginning of the century. One of the central goals for the 1996 San Francisco library was to align the library with the literacy needs for the Age of Information—to become a model "library of the 21st century."

On this count, the New Main delivers. The floor decks are wired for multimedia. Using microwave and satellite technologies, the New Main provides state-of-the-art videoconferencing. A large auditorium permits screening of prerecorded media. Six hundred computer terminals provide users with access to the library's holdings, including art, graphics, and special collections. An Internet connection allows users to access collections of other networked libraries around the world—even from their home computers. Microcomputers are available for projects and reference librarians access CDs to research answers to obscure questions posed to them by phone-in callers. Networked library patrons can access the Children's Electronic Discovery Center, a multimedia playground for children, through their computers.

But according to critics of the New Main, library *technology* came at the expense of the library *books*. Shelf space in the New Main does not match that in the old library and books that were readily available to the public at the old library are now shelved in closed stacks, or stored in an underground warehouse. Furthermore, in preparation for the move to the New Main, wholesale culling of the collection assigned tens of thousands of books to the city dump. The new state-of-the-art, mechanized sorting device mangled several thousand more (Baker, 1996, pp. 50–62).

The old card catalog contained 3 million index cards in 2,520 wooden drawers, replete with exquisite carvings of Greek figures, flora and fauna, and other 19th-century symbols of high art and culture. Too beautiful to discard, the old card catalogs were warehoused as antiques (Wiley, 1996, p. 224). Replacement of the old cabinets by a computerized referencing system had already begun in the 1980s, to some initial grumbling by the public. But the New Main of 1996 went one step further. It completely eliminated the card catalogs, calling them "predigital records," in favor of a state-of-the-art indexing system located completely on computers (Delgado, 1996, p. A-12). In the process of inputting the index cards to a computerized database, the handwritten notes from librarians who interpreted the works and cross-referenced them to other contexts over the years were lost. Even worse, clerical workers, who were in the position to choose and discard, sometimes missed a card altogether—relegating books to the limbo of non-indexed materials.

The computerized system became the main gatekeeper between reader and text, and patrons had no choice but to learn to navigate an unfamiliar, cumbersome, and complicated high-tech system. Although critics conceded that the computer-savvy librarians were supportive, they demanded the return of the card catalogs. With the computer interface as the primary reference tool, the experience of book selection had become less a matter of leisurely perusal and more of a direct, sterile transaction. No longer were library patrons able to browse the catalogs haphazardly, or to inspect the cards, or even to wander the stacks. To its detractors, the computerized indexing system was a relatively bland and frustrating experience, devoid of the joys of random intellectual discovery.

Instead, the old catalog cards were culled for an "art wall." The installation, designed by artists Ann Hamilton and Ann Chamberlain, was intended to simulate the "accidental juxtapositions that users of the old system experienced while thumbing through the catalog." Rendered dysfunctional, the cards were reduced to the quaint curiosities of an Industrial Age, when typewriters were manual and librarians still used mechanized date stamps and cursive handwriting. For a one-dollar donation, San Franciscans were invited to "embellish" the cards with their own naïve artwork for the artists to embed in the art wall (Wiley, 1996, p. 216).

Needless to say, the technological changes designed so proudly in the New Main in San Francisco created tremendous uproar from those citizens who resented the intrusion of technology into their library experience. The card catalog became the rallying post for their collective ire. To the lovers of the card catalog, the demise of physical card catalogs was a loss of tremendous proportion that went far beyond mere inconvenience. Digital records represented an irretrievable loss of knowledge, an obliteration of the past. The catalog became the focal point for resentment and anxiety about the encroachment of technology in all walks of life. Charging that library administrators were more interested in creating a technological show-place than a place of learning, the card catalog argument became a digital vs. print confrontation (Adams, 1996).

The criticism took supporters of the high-tech library—many of them librarians—by surprise. They patiently pointed to the efficiency of the computerized library system, to its accuracy and convenience. Librarians noted that prior to the computerized system, the index cards were often lost or inaccurate. Librarians scoffed at the romantic notion that the cards contained historical annotations, reminding patrons that the originals had, in fact, burned in the fires of 1906. In anticipation of their storage, cards had not been updated since 1991, leading users to believe that books were available that had, in fact, disappeared. Approximately 1.5 million books obtained since 1991 were not even listed. Under the circumstances, many librarians found the continued storage of all those little squares of card stock to be pointless. They were aghast to think that anyone would want to go back to the old method of referencing the library holdings by index cards.

Nonetheless, local library commissioners, responding to the hue and cry of the public, agreed to develop plans to save the old card catalog. Preservation plans ranged from binding the cards into books as is done at the New York Public Library, to storing the card catalog in the basement of a remote annex for use by historians (Ginsburg, 1996; Minton, 1996). By early 1997, the New Main's most vocal champion and chief designer, San Francisco's Chief Librarian, Kenneth Dowlin, resigned under fire.

The card catalog was the metaphor, if not the sole reason, for Dowlin's demise. Supporters of modernized library technology were shocked by the loss of Dowlin, a well-regarded librarian with a national profile, and exasperated by the arcane arguments put forth by those who wanted to return to the days of low-tech access. Again and again, they reminded detractors that the card catalog was no longer functional—to no avail. Again and again, supporters of the computerized library missed the point. They were under the mistaken impression that the card catalog argument was about the most efficient way to locate library materials.

Instead, opposing arguments about the card catalog at the New Main in San Francisco are illustrative of a unique window in history when the influence of technology in all aspects of public and private life raises questions about the rapidly changing uses of literacy and its tools. Literacy has been called a "technology of the intellect" (Goody, 1973). For centuries, these tools have been the purview of the printed word:

> Literacy is . . . above all, a technology or set of techniques for communications and for decoding and reproducing written or printed materials. (Graff, 1995, p. 10)

Just as oral traditions were both changed and incorporated by the printed word, electronic communication technologies seem to give with one hand and take with the other. Contrary to the concern that print culture will be eroded and obliterated by electronic forms, history demonstrates that literacy technologies ebb and flow, depending on the circumstances. They overlap, coexist, and change in symbiotic ways. Print culture did not eliminate oral traditions. Radio, television, and computers incorporate both print and oral conventions, but have yet to wipe out the book. In fact, book sales are at an all-time historical high. Instead, historical shifts in the tools of literacy change conceptions about what it means to be literate—a much more vexing and complicated question.

Digital communication forms are unique because they have the potential to collapse oral, written, print, and electronic codes and conventions into malleable nuggets of data, enabling diverse media to converge gracefully into a unified audiovisual schema. But if the transition from one form to another in times past is any indication, the mixing of media is bound to trigger unanticipated social tension. The introduction of new literacy tools raises intriguing questions about the way people pick and choose from the elements of a text—form, content, and context—to navigate and make sense of an increasingly mediated world. An historical long view of literacy helps to inform these questions and to put contemporary anxiety and hyperbole about new communication tools into perspective.

REWIND TO REFERENCING PAST

The San Francisco card catalog's demise is only one example in a long line of pitched battles over literacy. It contains echoes of a similar turning point in literacy history—the obliteration of a reference tool called *tally sticks,* or *tallies.* Tallies were a literacy technology that grew out of the shift from oral to written culture in England during the Middle Ages. Just as modern-day computer users do not yet trust financial transactions over the Internet, medieval citizens did not trust the veracity of the printed word. Medieval deeds, charters, receipts, and other accounts were written on parchment and the potential for the fraudulent use of seals and wax, or ink on parchment was great.

Tally sticks were simple wooden rods, but they became the answer to trust and security issues around the printed word—the carbon paper of their time. The names of the interested parties were coded onto the tally stick in ink and the wood was notched with a knife at differing widths, depths, and intervals to represent the amount, times, and length of transactions. After the transaction was recorded with the knife, the tally stick was then carefully split down the middle and each party got to keep one half of the stick. If a dispute arose, the interlocking halves were proof of authenticity and the method was widely trusted as a safeguard against forgery. Tally sticks became a clever and efficient way to ensure secure records of contracts and financial transactions, such as bills of sale, monies owed, and payments made.

Literacy historian M. T. Clanchy, in *From Memory to Written Record,* studies the shift from oral to print culture in England, from the time of the Norman Conquest to the death of Edward I, or roughly between the years 1066 and 1307. Clanchy argues that the tally sticks provided the accounting technology necessary to launch the financial system in England during the 12th century. They were adopted by private accountants during the 13th century as reading and writing became more widely used by an increasingly print literate populace (Clanchy, 1993). The technology of the tallies symbolized the shift from the culture of the spoken word, to that of reading and writing.

Tallies were easier to store and preserve than the bulkier, fragile parchment that was also used to record transactions. In the case of the tallies of the royal Exchequer, these relics of medieval transactions were stored in London at Westminster, as documents of public record. As the Industrial Age took root in the public imagination, "things medieval" had become not only anachronistic, but pejorative. Caught up in the spirit of reform that held the Middle Ages in contempt and promised more enlightened times, a statute was passed abolishing these receipts of the Exchequer, in 1834. The tally sticks stored at Westminster were piled into bonfires and burned. According to Clanchy, the documents made of parchment were carefully preserved, but tally sticks "were deliberately destroyed because they were in a medium, wood, which was too uncouth for scholars to appreciate. . . . People at the time believed them to be medieval because doing accounting with sticks looked so primitive, and even shameful, to nineteenth century reformers" (p. 124). Ironically, the bonfire of tallies spread to the House of Parliament, providing a sardonic footnote for contemporary literacy researchers.

Millions of these literacy records, made during a time of great historical shifts in literacy, were lost. Only a few hundred tallies survive in the late 20th century and are the basis for a rich body of literacy scholarship (Clanchy, 1993, p. 124). Unlike their card catalog counterparts, no one has yet thought to embed the last of the tallies into a work of public art.

LITERACY THROUGH A GLASS DARKLY

The attempt to comprehend literacy is probably an exercise in hubris—but it is one that continues to intrigue and lure scholars nonetheless. French literacy historian Henri-Jean Martin begins his book, *The History and Power of Writing*, by commenting on the vexing complexity of any study of literacy: "All history is first chronology. And anyone imprudent enough to risk study-ing the chronology of writing alternates ceaselessly between vertigo and myopia" (Martin, 1994, p. 1). Although comparisons are useful, literacy resists and refuses all attempts to pin it down into simple, definitive categories that transcend history. The form, content, and contexts of literacy records sprawl, overlap, and defy isolation.

The historical study of literacy was conducted in earnest in a time after World War II when the overall tone of both arts and humanities scholarship rejected the idea that one culture could truly and objectively understand another, due to the inability of researchers to completely transcend their own cultural and historical orientation. Contemporary literacy scholarship reflects the trend away from a psychoanalytical theory toward one that is more anthropological, or at least sociolinguistic, in nature. In the place of definitive conclusions about the nature of literacy and its effects on indi-viduals and societies, are various readings of social texts and signs within specific contexts, from a variety of perspectives.

It is fair to say that there are vocal critics to the widespread assumption among literacy scholars that cross-cultural and cross-historical objectivity is ultimately illusive. Art historian E. H. Gombrich (1960, 1992), who conducted landmark studies of the psychology of pictorial representations, vehemently dismissed the idea that "one age or culture can never truly understand another, or is even obliged to try." Gombrich attacked this perspective, calling it "cultural relativism," for the same reasons its proponents embrace it: "because it denies the existence of any objective standards of truth" (Baker, 1992, p. 9).

In a review of Gombrich's work, art critic Kenneth Baker suggests that:

> Objectivity is denigrated in the humanities these days because it is seen as the tacit philosophical excuse for Western imperialism and the technological "conquest" of nature. Those who possess objective truth are implicitly entitled

to impose it on those whose truth is shown to be merely poetic, mythic, or local. . . . The only proof against such arrogance, the "relativists" argue, is to break the spell of objectivity and its implicit pragmatic morality, and so lose our supercilious senses of intellectual access to other times and cultures. (Baker, 1992, p. 9)

It is against this backdrop of dominant "relativist" interpretation and rapid social and technological change that historical literacy scholarship came into its own. By recognizing that literacy cannot be viewed in isolation from other social factors, the discussion of the uses and purposes for literacy can provide deeper insight into its uses and purposes as a complex set of social practices. However, it is important to caution that an understanding of the history of literacy in this framework provides very little of practical use for those who want quick and easy mobilization of mass literacy campaigns. This kind of "one-size-fits-all" literacy goes decidedly against the tide of evidence that suggests an eclectic and idiosyncratic relationship between individuals, social groups, and literacy practices.

Literacy historians patiently collect evidence about how institutions such as churches, schools, states, social groups, workers, and families act on the practice of literacy over time—swinging the pendulum of history between control and freedom. Conversely, just as society shapes literacy practices, literacy historians also document evidence that new modes of literacy change social institutions.

Social expectations for new literacy forms give rise to the appropriate institutions to support the literacies *du jour.* Evidence abounds that the reorganization of institutions to accommodate new communication technologies, among them schooling, work, and recreation, is generally considered radical in its time. The adaptation of business practices to accommodate a proliferation of networked computers is a stunning case in point. But as literacy practices become established, what once seemed extreme becomes staid and routine, until the next wave of change transforms the radical into the status quo, threatening older forms and boxing them into a reactionary position.

As changes in contemporary literacy practices accelerate and converge, social agencies are attempting to incorporate them with a speed equal to their availability, in the hopes that state-of-the-art practices will revitalize existing institutions. In such a continuous change process, it is difficult to say which agent drives the change: the communication technologies, the literacy practices, or the institutional need for renewal in response to larger, historical factors.

For example, it is abundantly clear that the uses of literacy in the 20th century, as well as their technologies and records, are not the same as the uses of alphabetic literacy in the previous centuries. A full understanding of contemporary literacy is impossible without a complementary under-standing of 20th-century wars, postcolonialism, postindustrialism, human rights movements, social institutions, and hypercapitalism that have intervened to change the way that literacy is used in the 20th century. In order to make comparisons between the uses of literacy in the past, these kinds of sweeping historical movements must also be factored into the analysis—a daunting, but necessary prospect.

Once a literacy shift is set in motion, it gathers its own momentum. Questions about whether the changes in literacy practices are for the better or for the worse depend on the loyalties and vantage point of the questioner. Authorship, authenticity, appropriate content and form are open to debate. Who has a voice, what content is available, who receives it, how is it interpreted, and how information is used are questions that ebb and flow throughout the history of literacy.

Debates about card catalogs and tally sticks demonstrate that discussions about literacy readily crystallize into obsessive fixations with the tangible by-products of literacy, that is, tools and records. Understanding about the essence of literacy, that is, its social and cultural uses in specific contexts, is easily sidetracked in discussions about technologies. Literacy artifacts—the alphabet, the pen, the book, the computer—become metaphors for the diverse uses of literacy and its vague promise of "enlightened progress." The term *literacy* is shorthand for cultural ideals as eclectic as economic development, personal fulfillment, and individual moral fortitude. To be "illiterate" is a powerful social stigma.

The use of "technology" is similarly problematic. In fact, *literacy* and *technology* are often interchangeable in the lofty discourse of government and industry. Current ideals that promote technology as a panacea for social and economic instability echo literacy's grandiose promises—this time obtainable through the use of computers. Just as literacy embodied the ideals of an Industrial Age, technology is positioned as a symbol of enlightened progress in the Age of Information.

In fact, reading and writing are also a technology. They commodify thought and speech into records. Clanchy (1993) concurred that "literacy is primarily a technology of which records are the end products" (p. 20). Beyond that, literacy scholars make no other promises for literacy and eschew the notion that the concept of literacy can be divorced from its complexities. The question of *what* technology or literacy can actually deliver, beyond the ability to access massive amounts of information, remains open. Placing undue scrutiny on either the content or the form of literacy records will not help to answer this question. Instead, if we are to make sense of digital, print, and oral literacies in the context of our time, it is useful to focus on literacy as a series of social events, with contrary and diverse uses, in particular contexts. How mediated information might contribute to the social good, or what people actually do with all the information once they receive it, are questions that intrude on the rah-rah promotion of technology like uninvited guests at the party. Perhaps the questions go unanswered because they are inherently philosophical, contradictory, and unreconcilable. Too many assumptions get in the way and there are no pat answers. Literacy scholar Carl F. Kaestle (1991) noted:

> Literacy is discriminatory with regard to both access and content. Problems of discrimination are not resolved just because access is achieved: there is a cultural price tag to literacy. Thus, whether literacy is liberating or constraining depends in part on whether it is used as an instrument of conformity or of creativity. (Kaestle, p. 30)

Historical comparisons of literacy practices shed some light on our current dilemma about the appropriate uses of new and emerging communication technologies. Just as the comparison of library index cards with tally sticks provides tantalizing clues to the uses of literacy across time, to isolate and juxtapose historical examples of literacy can create a rich continuum of understanding that spans generations, echoes the past, and informs the future. But to rely on historical comparisons for neat answers to complex questions, or to put store in these comparisons as a way to make a comprehensive taxonomy about the nature of literacy and its future uses is to miss the point. Although similarities can be found between technologies, records, and uses across time, each event and each artifact is unique. When the records of literacy are isolated from their original historical conditions, the sense they make to modern audiences becomes distorted over time. Tallies, hieroglyphics, kinescopes, viewmasters, 78-rpm record players, and 8-track cassette players are relatively irrelevant information tools for modern literates. Nonetheless, these technologies and their records are important and valuable keys to understanding literacy's place in history.

LITERACY AND SCHOOLING

Attempts to analyze literacy's place in contemporary schooling offers a good example of the complexity of historical literacy scholarship. If it weren't enough that the confluence of literacy and technology issues makes an understanding of literacy complicated, the intertwining of literacy issues with those of schooling adds to the confusion.

During the 1800s the symbiotic relationship between schooling and literacy became inextricably entwined in the United States. Literacy, institutionalized in the context of schooling, became the tool to accomplish a wide variety of purposes. An understanding of the religious roots of the common school movement in the 19th century is essential in order to comprehend the state-directed nature of public schooling in the 20th century.

Literacy and its relationship to 19th-century schooling in the United States represents a familiar, yet unique version of the convergence of political, social, and religious events that sought to enfranchise working-class people into a cohesive view of the nation.

> In the nineteenth-century United States, the rapid spread of literacy served similar purposes of religious propagation, maintenance of political order, and the formation of a national character. According to Stevens [1985, pp. 65–81], "the process of becoming literate was itself a process of socialization promulgated by those interested in using the school to resolve social, economic, and political tensions arising from a culturally pluralistic and emerging industrial society. The process of schooling and hence the process of becoming literate are seen in relation to nation-building, a fervent evangelical Protestantism, and technological innovation." What is of special significance in the U.S. case is that the reformers advocated a republican form of government, based on more active citizen participation in political governance. (Graff & Arnove, 1995, p. 275)

In addition to its influence on schooling in the United States, the influence of the religious sector on widespread alphabetic literacy from the 16th to the 19th centuries in Europe offers a related case in point. The confluence of literacy technologies, uses, and content is obvious. Historical evidence demonstrates that although the printing trade spread rapidly in the 1500s, because the demand for books was high for the few people who could afford them, literacy on a mass scale did not automatically follow (Levine, 1986, p. 72). Literacy campaigns were not yet institutionalized in the form of church, trade guild, or school efforts to disseminate the technology of alphabetic literacy. The invention of movable type around 1440 was itself dependent on advances in the science of metallurgy (Martin, 1994, pp. 216–226). It took more than a century after mass printing technology with the mass literacy campaigns of the German Protestant Reformers of the 16th century to create a significant population of readers who could take advantage of the pictures and texts that the printing press made available to them. In other words, although the printing press was invented in the 15th century, it took events in the 16th century to provide a critical mass of users to make significant use of the invention.

But even then, the technology of book printing did not readily destroy the old culture of handwritten manuscripts. The religious aesthetic of medieval manuscript culture, at least the "look and feel" of hand-rendered manuscripts, was appropriated by printers. Gutenberg's 42-line Bible is barely distinguishable from that of a master scribe. It took several generations before the look of the book changed from that of the manuscript and it wasn't until at least the mid-17th century that page numbers began to appear at the bottom of a printed page, offering a way to reference documents beyond the idiosyncratic memory schemes of the first librarians—the medieval clergy—thus giving rise to modern libraries (Bolter, 1991, p. 3; Clanchy, 1993, pp. 154–162; Febvre & Martin, 1990; Levine, 1986, p. 72; Martin, 1994, pp. 302–303).

The religious movements of the 16th to 19th centuries in Europe also provide important historical evidence that informs contemporary discussions about *who* should have access to information. The printing press was important to mass literacy, but of equal importance was an Augustinian monk, Martin Luther, and the budding philosophical interest in individual liberties that seeded such monumental events as the French Revolution and the spread of democratic governance. The emphasis of the Reformers on the right of each person to read the Word of God for himself—and even more radically, for *herself*—was in sharp contrast to the literacy practices of the 16th-century Catholic Church. Catholic officials of the time took a hard line against laypeople interpreting the Bible without the benefit of a specially trained clerical class (Levine, 1986, p. 73). This denominational difference is one of the factors reflected in the initial spread of literacy throughout Europe. As Protestantism spread from Germany to the north of Europe, so did literacy. In contrast, the spread of literacy to the Catholic south of Europe was much slower.

But even though Luther preached the right of each person to read the Word of God, the responsibility for the interpretation of texts was still a question in his own mind. When widespread literacy was blamed for a peasant rebellion in 1525, Luther, too, turned against unsupervised book learning (Graff, 1995, p. 278). By then, of course, the spread of literacy took on a momentum of its own. It is said that Luther's *Ninety-Five Theses* spread the length of Germany in two days and to all of Europe within a month (Eisenstein, 1979, p. 204). The genie was out of the bottle.

ON THE HORNS OF PLATO'S DILEMMA

The problem with reconciling differing, sometimes polarized uses of literacy is at least as old as Plato, arguably the first literate. Plato found that using the technology of literacy was a relatively minor problem compared to what people did with the information that literacy made available to them.

Plato was a student of Socrates. Both men condemned the shift away from speech to writing, objecting that writing would disrupt the routine social arrangements—both public and private—of the time. In Plato's *Phaedrus*, Socrates uses the parable of King Thamus, a story of writing's introduction in Egypt, to extol the social virtue of memory:

> The fact is that this invention will produce forgetfulness in the souls of those who have learned it. They will not need to exercise their memories, being

able to rely on what is written, calling things to mind no longer from within themselves by their own unaided powers, but under the stimulus of external marks that are alien to themselves. So it's not a recipe for memory, but for reminding, that you have discovered. (Hamilton & Cairns, 1989, p. 520, 275a)

Literacy scholar James Paul Gee (1991) referred to the inherent contradictions in literacy as Plato's Dilemma. Gee explained that as a student of Socrates, when Plato charged that writing was inferior to speech, he meant that writing was neither immediate, spontaneous, or interactive enough to stand up to the question: "What do you mean?" Gee (1991) explained:

Such a request forces the speaker to "re-say" . . . what he or she means. In the process he sees more deeply what he means, and responds to the perspective of another voice/viewpoint . . . writing can only respond to the question, "what do you mean?", by repeating what it [the text] has said. (p. 269)

The alphabet was born in ancient Greece, but communication in Plato's time was still dominated by the cultural trappings of a traditionally oral discourse. As such, speech was considered essential for holding the body politic together (Martin, 1994, p. 92). Building on the ideas of Socrates, Plato extended his criticism of the technology of writing to include specific oral modes of communication, namely the nondialogic speaking methods of the politicians and poets. In the *Republic*, he slammed the poets, especially Homer, because he felt the oral conventions used by master poets created a passive acceptance of messages in the epics and did not afford listeners the ability to interrupt with the question, "What do you mean?" Politicians and other rhetoricians were thought by Plato to be hopelessly ambitious and corrupt because, like the poets, they used an uninterrupted flow of rhetorical flourish, meter, rhyme, and timing that created a passive role for the audience. Plato's tactic was to break the spell of rhetoric and to force rhetoricians into prose by asking "What do you mean?"

Plato's criticism of the rhetoricians is similar to the one leveled at television and other electronic media by modern critics. Televised politics, dramatic representation, video games, Internet chat rooms, and the evening news are all accused of using form over substance to sway media users. Like the ancient Greeks, contemporary critics of electronic technologies denounce media's ability to corrupt social institutions (Healy, 1990; Pearce, 1992; Postman, 1992; Winn, 1987).

Plato was an extremely sophisticated political animal. Literacy scholar Eric Havelock (1963) provides some insight into Plato's ambition. As Havelock sees it, Plato's disdain for the rhetoricians was an elaborate ruse to solidify the philosopher's own power base—a brilliant maneuver in his mission to wrest control from those who skillfully used the traditions of oral culture to sway the public. In the *Republic*, Plato sarcastically declares his hostility to the "inspired" poet, a glitzy rhetorician in his mind. He much preferred the legislator or the warrior to the poet. If poems were the most popular media of his day, Plato hoped to drain a certain pleasure out of them—for the listening public's own good, of course:

> If a man ... who was capable by his cunning of assuming every kind of shape and imitating all things should arrive in our city, bringing with himself the poems which he wished to exhibit, we should fall down and worship him as a holy and wondrous and delightful creature, but should say to him that there is no man of that kind among us in our city, nor is it lawful for such a man to arise among us, and we should send him away to another city, after pouring myrrh down over his head and crowning him with fillets of wool, but we ourselves, for our soul's good, should continue to employ the more austere and less delightful poet and taleteller, who would imitate the diction of the good man and would tell his tale in the patterns which we prescribed in the beginning, when we set out to educate our soldiers. (Hamilton & Cairns, 1989, pp. 642–643, 3.398)

Instead, Plato considered dialogic speech to be the most exemplary oral mode. With its "give-and-take" ability to engage both audience and speaker, he extoled dialogic speech as spontaneous, authentic, and liberating. It would follow that Plato would have looked favorably on modern progressive methods of education or that he might have embraced contemporary models of critical literacy, with their emphasis on literacy's relationship to reflection, liberation and political empowerment. But, decidedly, not so. Herein lies Plato's Dilemma about literacy and the seeds of its controversial nature.

It is useful to keep in mind that the ancient Greeks were not known for an egalitarian approach to governance, especially one that promoted the rights of every individual. Besides, both Socrates and Plato had their own political ambitions. They thought of themselves as "philosopher-kings" who were equipped to rule in the best interest of those in social classes below them. Literacy, to Socrates, was definitely intended for those elites who had the vested authority and the assumed wisdom to rule. Writing was not meant for everybody:

> And once a thing is put in writing, the composition, whatever it may be, drifts all over the place, getting into the hands not only of those who understand it, but equally of those who have no business with it; it doesn't know how to address the right people, and not address the wrong. (Hamilton & Cairns, 1989, p. 521, 275e)

Like Socrates, Plato wanted to be sure that the intended meaning of the text was "correct" and this was why he favored speech. Speech gave the author the immediate ability to correct any misinterpretation, as discovered through dialogue with the audience. Unlike the written word, speech did not lie around and grow ripe with each distortion. James Paul Gee commented:

> Plato wants the author to stand as a voice behind the text not just to engage in responsive dialogue, but to enforce canonical interpretations. And these canonical interpretations are rendered correct by the inherently higher nature of the philosopher-king, backed by the advantages (which the *Republic* ensures) of socially situated power and state-supported practice in verbal and literacy skills. (Gee, 1991, p. 271)

Like Kaestle (1991), Gee saw "Plato's Dilemma" as the crossroads where literacy for personal freedom and literacy for social control meet:

> In Plato, we see two sides to literacy: literacy as a liberator and literacy as a weapon. Plato wants to ensure that a voice behind the spoken or written "text" can dialogically respond, but he also wants to ensure that this voice is not overridden by respondents who are careless, ignorant, lazy, self-interested, or ignoble. (p. 272)

Contemporary sentiments, saturated by Western intellectual emphasis on individual rights, would lean toward more diverse interpretations of texts over fewer, controlled interpretations, but the balance between the two-horned uses of literacy is more delicate and contradictory than it first appears. Who is to say what a text means? The author? Audiences? Individual readers?

Recent debates about protecting children from Internet and television content demonstrate that questions about the power of the reader to interpret content are far from resolved. The response to these questions has as much implication for teaching and learning in a digital world as it did in ancient Greece. In fact, as a torrent of information flows through diverse media channels, the question of interpretation posed by Plato is a hydra in an Age of Information. Furthermore, as the egalitarian ability for anyone to create—as well as receive—information increases, questions of information veracity and interpretation intensify. Traditional gatekeepers of information—media professionals, clergy, librarians, teachers, parents—are increasingly ineffectual in their ability to provide interpretive frameworks for information. In an article on the use of new technologies to disseminate conspiracy theories, writer Tim Dougherty (1996) commented:

> The Internet's capacity to blur distinctions between the factual and the fanciful is, by virtue of the medium's growing prominence and the increasing fractiousness of our society, a troubling turn of events. (Dougherty, p. A-21)

Although many literacy scholars have tried, there is no easy way out of Plato's Dilemma. Gee (1991) remarked:

If all interpretations (re-sayings) count, then none do, as the text then says everything and therefore nothing . . . if it takes no discipline, experience, or "credentials" to interpret, then it seems all interpretations *will* count. If they can't all count, then someone has to say who does and who does not have the necessary credentials to interpret. A desire to honor the thoughtful and critical voice behind the text . . . leads us to Plato's authoritarianism. In fleeing it, we are in danger of being led right into the lap of Plato's poets, speech-writers, and politicians. For them, all that counts is the persuasiveness or cunning of their language, its ability to capture the reader, to tell him or her what he or she wants to hear, to validate the status quo. (p. 272)

Ironically, writing is the very means by which Plato records Socrates' condemnation of it for posterity. Plato reveals that at least since the first literates conducted a metacognitive analysis of the ideal uses of literacy, it has been a never-ending balancing act between control and liberty:

The uses of literacy are various. As a technology, it gives its possessors potential power; as a stock of cultural knowledge within a given tradition, literacy can constrain or liberate, instruct or entertain, discipline or disaffect people. Princeton historian Lawrence Stone once remarked that if you teach a man to read the Bible, he may also read pornography or seditious literature; put another way, if a man teaches a woman to read so that she may know her place, she may learn that she deserves his. These are the Janus faces of literacy. (Kaestle, 1991, p. 27)

As society shifts from the culture of the printed word into one dominated by the electronic confluence of image, audio, and text, studies about the uses of literacy in the past provide fascinating glimpses of the many faces of literacy. Literacy in contemporary contexts can only benefit from comparisons to historical transitions of similar magnitude, such as the transition between oral and written modes, or when manuscript practices gave way to printing. At the very least, an understanding of past literacy practices offers a welcome balance to the buoyant optimism, as well as the dire pessimism, about the uses of new and emerging literacy tools in any age of change.

CHAPTER TWO

Expanding Literacy

The study of the history of literacy is relatively new, gaining prominence and amassing a body of theoretical work after World War II, with the over-heated optimism of the Cold War era as a backdrop. The first generation of literacy historians were theory builders. European researchers (Cipolla, 1969; Goody, 1968; the late-1960s work of Stone, 1969; Webb, 1955) and others built on evidence collected from an even earlier group of literacy scholars as diverse as Eric Havelock (1963, 1986); the French Lévi-Bruhl (1910); and the Russian, Vygotsky (1962, 1978), who wrote in the 1920s and 1930s about literacy as a tool for transforming higher psychological processes.

Literacy historian Harvey Graff (1995) credits first-generation literacy his-torians with gathering evidence about the course of literacy over time, "its dynamics, distributions, impacts and consequences" (p. 302). Although many of their conclusions were sweeping, and certainly the researchers went in several, sometimes conflicting, directions, the first generation of literacy his-torians identified literacy as a legitimate and important subject for historical study. Evidence that literacy was conditional to historical forces began to emerge early on. Literacy apparently meant different things to different peo-ple, depending on economic and historical conditions and their own unique cultural and social perspectives.

A second generation of scholars went deeper into the diverse uses of literacy through field study and other techniques (Finnegan, 1988, p. 7). They began to provide evidence that tempered the conclusions of the early literacy historians and to refine some methodologies for gathering evidence, borrow-ing heavily from the fields of anthropology and sociology (Cressy, 1980; Houston, 1985; Lockridge, 1974; Soltow & Stevens, 1981; and Stephens, 1987).

According to Graff, whose own work can be counted as building on the earlier theory base, second-generation scholars provided information about the epistemology, practices, and interpretation of literacy practices over time. They added details about the uses of literacy by individuals and societies, as well as its patterns of distribution and use. In the 1960s, the anthropological work of Kathleen Gough (1988), who studied literacy practices in India and China, and that of pioneering social psychologists Scribner and Cole (1978, 1981, 1988), who conducted field studies with the Vai in Liberia in the 1970s, are examples of second-generation literacy historians. These researchers tested, challenged and revised the sweeping hypotheses from first-generation researchers—especially those who brought a morass of value judgments to their assumptions about literacy. These included conclusions about the superiority of "literates," as well as a prejudice in favor of alphabetic over oral forms of literacy.

The elevation of print over oral cultures was a serious misstep in the continuum of literacy research. Particularly specious were theories postulating that those societies marked by oral literacy practices—many of them native or migratory cultures—were intellectually inferior to those societies marked by alphabetic literacy practices—often of Western cultural origins. The early theories of the brilliant French scholar Lévi-Bruhl (1910), who wrote a book entitled *The Mental Functions of Inferior Societies*, are a case in point. Later in his career, Jack Goody, influenced by the work of second-generation literacy researchers, edged away from his own contributions to the elevation of cultures who were print-literate over those who practiced oral literacy modes:

> Although we must reject any dichotomy based upon the assumption of radical differences between the mental attributes of literate and non-literate peoples, and accept the view that previous formulations of the distinction were based on faulty premises and inadequate evidence, there may still exist general differences between literate and non-literate societies somewhat along the lines suggested by Lévi-Bruhl. (Goody & Watt, 1988, p. 13)

Subsequent generations of literacy scholars have finally amassed the evidence to put the myth of alphabetic superiority to rest. As Scribner and Cole (1988) found in their field study, it does not necessarily follow that "an individual who writes clearly thinks clearly" (p. 58). With this, Jack Goody eventually concurred, presenting several examples of how "writing is not a monolithic entity, an undifferentiated skill; its potentialities depend upon the kind of system that it obtains in any particular society" (Goody & Watt, p. 3).

Second-generation researchers questioned other totalizing assumptions about literacy. They found no links or weak links to connect literacy with large-scale social practices or cognitive consequences such as democracy, habits of mind, or logical modes of thought. In short, the second wave of literacy historians took a closer look at an astonishing range of conditions for literacy practice. They looked for evidence of literacy practices with specific groups of people, across time and cultures, in formal schooling situations and outside schools—sometimes refining earlier conclusions and sometimes changing theories altogether.

Since that time, literacy historians have seen patterns that have potential to inform the uses of future forms of literacy:

> Literacy appears to be . . . an *enabling* factor, permitting large-scale organization, the critical accumulation, storage and retrieval of knowledge, the systematic use of logic, the pursuit of science and the elaboration of the arts. Whether . . . these developments will occur seems to depend less on the intrinsic knowledge of writing than on the overall development of the society's technology and social structure. . . . The partial supersession of writing by new communications media will no doubt throw into relief more and more of the specific implications of literacy. (Gough, 1988, pp. 55–56)

In the late 1970s, the historical study of literacy shifted from compiling quantitative evidence of literacy practices to its meaning and uses in ever more specific social contexts. The blending of qualitative and quantitative methodologies through small-scale, field-based studies proved particularly fruitful. Quantitative evidence used to inform the field includes the various numbers and qualities of such records as signatures, tax roles, wills, deeds, charters, census data, and other legal documents, such as marriage licenses, voting records, school documents, and so forth. Inventories of business records, personal books, and public libraries also proved useful.

Studies began to refine both data and methodologies and to look at the linkages between literacy and other variables in historical contexts. The enormity of such a task is reflected in the still huge gaps in literacy research data. Even when literacy artifacts exist, researchers have not yet found time to attend to them. Literacy theorists are still faced with the daunting task of establishing the parameters, baseline measures, and dynamics between literacy practices and related variables, and then with applying them to specific demographic, culture, economic, and historical contexts. The contextual interpretation of literacy findings was impressively established by literacy historians of the 1970s and 1980s. Comparative studies methods initiated at the time provided important methodologies for discovering patterns of literacy across meanings, cultures, and contexts.

In the late 20th century, literacy researchers used both quantitative and qualitative methods, across the academic disciplines, to look at literacy in ever more particular settings. Looking for authentic literacy practices in action, they investigated literacy in schools, homes, workplaces, and recreational activities. They looked at a wider range of social groups, especially those who may have been marginalized from dominant literacy practices because of language, culture, or social circumstances. The particular cases provided by microlevel field work in literacy offer exciting potential for deeper understanding about the uses, traditions, practices, and acquisition of literacy and literacies of the past—and the future.

LITERACY AS DISCOURSE: THEORY AT THE TURN OF THE 21ST CENTURY

Since the 1980s, a generation of literacy scholars increasingly positioned literacy as discourse—one of many discourses in a multicultural, multilingual society. Scholars such as Delpit (1995), Fairclough (1989), Gee (1996), Giroux (1988), Kress (1985), Macdonnel (1986), and McLaren (1989) represent just a few of the many scholars who study literacy from a perspective of social linguistics and multiple discourses. Giroux and McLaren, in particular, attempt to reconcile the theory of discourse within the parameters of contemporary schooling. Discourse theories make the study of literacy more precise—and more complex.

Anyone who has ever studied a second language can readily grasp the concept of "discourses." A second-language learner soon finds out that language acquisition takes much more than fluent vocabulary and grammar. Instead, a full range of cultural knowledge is needed to fully participate in the culture. Furthermore, there are appropriate ways to speak and to "be," according to particular times and places, that is, public, private, formal, informal, and so on. This full range of understanding, including not only particular linguistic structures, but subtle delivery and style cues, make up particular discourses. A culture's dominant language, in the case of the United States, Standard American English, more often than not shapes the rules for its dominant discourse. A very particular, narrower form of standard English is the discourse most often found in schooling. This belies the fact that there are many other discourses, and that children in diverse, multicultural societies are initiated into both mainstream and non-mainstream discourses. The theory of literacy as discourse offers these students the tools to switch fluently between the wide range of discourses available to them in order to apply communication in strategic ways. In that way, people can appropriately use a discourse to their own best advantage—"putting their best face forward," according to the situation at hand.

James Gee (1996) takes a sociolinguistic approach to define literacy as "mastery of a secondary Discourse" (Gee, p. 143), a learned discourse that is distinguished from the discourse of primary, first language acquisition. He identified two broad kinds of discourses:

(1) Primary Discourses are those to which people are apprenticed early in life during their primary socialization as members of particular families within

their sociocultural settings . . . our first social identity . . . and (2) Secondary
Discourses are those to which people are apprenticed as part of their sociali-
zations within various local, state and national groups and institutions outside
early home and peer-group socialization—for example, churches, gangs,
schools, offices. (p. 137)

Discourses go far beyond language. They display, through word, deed,
style and manner, membership in particular social groups. People choose
to employ a certain discourse in order to further common interests, goals
and values.

A Discourse, then, is composed of ways of talking, listening (often, too, reading
and writing), acting, interacting, believing, valuing, and using tools and objects,
in particular settings at specific times, so as to display and recognize a particular
social identity. Discourses create "social positions" (perspectives) from which
people are "invited" (summoned) to speak, listen, act, read and write, think,
feel, believe and value in certain characteristic, historically recognizable ways,
combined with their own individual styles and creativity. (Gee, 1996, p. 128)

As Foucault (1966, 1969, 1985) notes, all discourses are the products of
history. Gee (1996) builds on Foucault to outline some basic points about
discourses:

1. Discourses are inherently ideological. . . .
2. Discourses are resistant to internal criticism and self-scrutiny since uttering
   viewpoints that seriously undermine them defines one as being outside
   them. . . .
3. Discourse-defined positions from which to speak and behave . . . are stand-
   points . . . in relation to other, ultimately opposing Discourses. . . .
4. Any Discourse puts . . . forward certain concepts, viewpoints, and values
   at the expense of others. . . .
5. Discourses are intimately related to the distribution of social power and
   hierarchical structure in society. . . . Control over certain Discourses can
   lead to the acquisition of social goods (money, power, status) in a society.
   . . . Discourse that lead to social goods in a society [can be called] *dominant
   Discourses* . . . those groups that have the fewest conflicts when using them
   . . . *dominant groups.* (p. 132)

THE DISCOURSE OF SCHOOLING

The problem is that children learn about discourses in an *ad hoc* and informal
way that is seldom made explicit to them in formal schooling. Furthermore,
the range of acceptable discourses in schools is too narrow to accommodate

their growing awareness of the possibility of mastering a broad range of discursive styles. Without structured practice, it is questionable whether students can learn to recognize, master and apply a range of discursive styles to particular events, in order to foster their own success in a variety of social situations.

The extensive body of literacy scholarship by Brazilian educator Paulo Freire, who died in 1997, reflected the belief that the constrained discourse of schooling was created to perpetrate social inequity. He and coauthor Donaldo Macedo (Freire & Macedo, 1987), commented on the failure of school-based literacy to connect the culture of school, which Freire refers to as the "schooling class," to the social realities that students face outside the classroom:

> Educators . . . fail to understand that it is through multiple discourses that students generate meaning of their everyday social contexts. Without understanding the meaning of their immediate social reality, it is most difficult to comprehend their relations with the wider society. (p. 154)

They see the kind of literacy promoted in schools as a potential trap for students who do not operate from mainstream cultural perspectives. According to Freire, the dominant culture defines literacy, and therefore the reading and writing skills that are acknowledged by mainstream society and sanctioned in the schooling process are only those that reinforce the social status quo. Relatively speaking, this is a very narrow set of competencies that can force many students to leave knowledge of their homes and neighborhoods—the discourse they know with confidence—at the school door. If the discourse of home and the discourse of school are mismatched, the student is at a significant disadvantage—unless a formal and structured intervention helps them to understand: (a) that there are many discourses; and (b) when each discourse can be used appropriately and successfully. While offering the hope of enhancing a student's life chances, the narrow, mainstream view of school literacy as the one, "correct" and all-purpose way to communicate does not equip students to take full advantage of opportunity inside and outside the school. Although some students may squeak by and succeed nonetheless, Freire would say that literacy of this kind creates a passive acceptance of the dominance of some social groups over others.

Freire sees more potential in critical literacy, a deeper kind of literacy that he and Macedo call "reading the world." Critical literacy implies a questioning stance, an analysis of both the form and the content of mediated communication. According to Freire, critical literacy has some potential to balance social inequalities and is a fruitful way to put the mechanisms of democracy into motion, but, he says, critical literacy is not generally encouraged in the "schooling class." Furthermore, according to Freire and Macedo, when literacy is defined in service of the competitive marketplace, some children must lose in order for others to win, thus perpetrating social inequity.

The function of schooling, then, can become a way to weed out the losers from the winners, before they enter the labor force. Although forced and arbitrary "tracking" programs are on the wane, Freire recognizes that literacy can be used to accomplish subtle, *de facto* forms of tracking, even when students are grouped together in the same diverse, mainstreamed classroom. Clanchy (1993) has voiced a similar concern: "Modern readers are conditioned by their own schooling to believe that literacy is the measure of progress and that those who use documents less are less civilized" (p. 20). Freire and Macedo (1987) commented on the use of literacy—to separate "literates" from "illiterates"—as a serious and sinister threat to democracy:

> This large number of people [in the United States] who do not read and write and who are expelled from school do not represent a failure of the schooling class; their expulsion reveals the triumph of the schooling class. In fact, this misreading of responsibility reflects the schools' hidden curriculum. (p. 121)

LITERACY MYTHS AND THEIR CONSEQUENCES

As more refined and focused data about literacy were amassed, literacy researchers became circumspect about the grand theories of the past—theories that sought to pin down the exact nature and correct uses of literacy. The evidence—both qualitative and quantitative—that emerged from the study of literacy over time and place just did not square with conventional wisdom about the importance, meaning, and power of literacy. Research confirmed that literacy was a valuable technology that enhanced participation in society. It did not confirm that the technology of literacy, by itself, was necessarily a predictor of success in modern life.

> *Nothing* follows from literacy or schooling. Much follows, however, from what comes *with* literacy and schooling . . . namely, the attitudes, values, norms, and beliefs (at once social, cultural and political). (Gee, 1991, p. 280)

Literacy historians may be no closer to a definitive response about what literacy *is*, but at least there is some consensus about what it is *not*. Literacy historian Harvey Graff (1979, 1987, 1995) has provided leadership in examining some of the most common misconceptions about literacy and proclaiming them "myths." Through patient, case by case analyses, he has made a significant contribution to a greater understanding about the role and uses of literacy in society. Graff demonstrated through numerous historical examples that little historical evidence exists to justify the contention that the powerful effects of literacy lead to:

> logical and analytical modes of thought; general and abstract uses of language; critical and rational thought; a skeptical and questioning attitude; a distinction between myth and history; the recognition of the importance of time and space; complex and modern governments . . . separation of church and state . . . political democracy and greater social equity; economic development; wealth and productivity; political stability; urbanization; and . . . lower birth rates . . . [or] to people who are . . . innovative, achievement oriented, productive, cosmopolitan, politically aware, more globally . . . oriented . . . more liberal and humane . . . less likely to commit a crime . . . more likely to take . . . duties of citizenship seriously. (Gee, 1991, p. 267, in a review of Graff's 1987 book, *The Legacies of Literacy*)

Graff contends that research about the history of literacy simply does not support linear, direct links between literacy and "the social good." There is too much conflicting evidence to the contrary. When a causal connection does exist, literacy is only one of a confluence of intertwined factors. Even then, numerous historical examples contradict the notion that literacy is directly tied to economic and social development, individual moral fortitude, citizenship, and other social responsibilities. The research reveals no one formula for mass, universal literacy and no common effect of such literacy.

According to Graff, this is true for both individuals and for societies. He puts forth the history of literacy in Sweden as a prime example. Even when mass literacy is achieved in a society, as is demonstrated by several centuries of near total literacy in Sweden (Graff, 1995, pp. 22–23), it does not necessarily translate into the development of corresponding institutions associated with modernity such as schooling, full employment, or other economic and cultural changes. Graff asserted that:

> [Some research] has labored under the specter and shadows of *modernization theories* with their strong assumptions of literacy's role, powers and provenance—an issue that must be confronted critically. Some students have chosen to challenge the assumptions of modernization's links to and impacts upon literacy (or vice versa); others have assimilated their work within the traditions of modernization theories, suffering conceptual and interpretive difficulties. . . . In some cases, the assumption of modernization actually substitutes for empirical, as well as critical research. . . . Problems also include the persisting presence of obstructive dichotomies such as literate versus illiterate, print versus oral, and the like, none of which are interpretively rich or complex enough to advance our understanding. (p. 304)

Despite a shift in academia toward more complex and sophisticated viewpoints about literacy, the public's image of literacy still belongs in the little red schoolhouse of long ago. To the average citizen, the purposes of literacy are practical and applied: to get a good job, vote in an informed way, and understand the labels on consumer products. Every cultural group desires the kind of literacy that will open wide the doors of opportunity to their children to at least accomplish those three things. It does not seem too much to ask. The problem is that even this narrowly conceived version of literacy eludes too many people.

In his review of *Literacy: Reading the Word and the World* (Freire & Macedo, 1987), literacy theorist Peter McLaren (1988) commented:

> Mainstream theories of literacy conceive of being literate as possessing only that requisite fund of knowledge—that privileged form of linguistic currency— necessary for students to succeed materially in an industrialized capitalist society . . . the nonstandard literacies of minority groups and the poor (that is, different dialects, nonstandard English) are regarded as deficits or deprivations rather than differences. (p. 214)

Under the hothouse conditions of schooling, devoid of the culture and day-to-day experiences of students, linguistic- and ethnic-minority students continually came up short on routine measures of school performance. McLaren (1988) noted, "Mainstream approaches to literacy, which too often concentrate on the sheer mechanics of reading and writing, fail to take seriously enough the learner's sociocultural contexts—his or her own social reality—in which meaning is constructed" (p. 220).

Such a view of literacy fuels the debate about the teaching of reading, that is, the merits of a phonics approach versus those of a whole language approach. When literacy is envisioned as a relative, situational, social act, instead of as a monolithic, standardized commodity, it shakes the foundation of literacy teaching and learning. Such a concept is a sharp divergence from past ideals of literacy as the key to national unity, social order, good character, and economic progress.

WHEN PAST AND FUTURE COLLIDE

In December 1996, the school board for the Oakland Unified School District in California announced that all public schools would institute a new literacy program to improve education for African American students in the school system. There was consensus that improvement strategies were urgent. Although African American children made up over 53% of the student body, their grade point average was lower, as a group, than any other group's scores: 1.8 out of a possible 4.0 grade points. The school drop-out rate for African American children was almost 20%. Their representation in competitive student enrichment programs was low and the children were overrepresented, by 71%, in special education classes (Hatfield, 1996, p. A-5). Clearly, the school board was hard-pressed to come up with innovative educational interventions that could turn the tide from school failure for large numbers of the district's children.

School officials recommended the institution of ebonics, a combination of the words *ebony* and *phonics*, a form of African American speech that traces its grammar, syntax, and linguistic structure to roots in Western African languages such as Ibo, Yoruba, Ewe, Fula, Mandinka, and Mende. The Oakland school board recommended training that enabled teachers to recognize ebonics as the home dialect of many African American students in the District, in order to enhance their learning of standard English, the English they need to function at school and in other public forums outside the classroom (Hatfield, 1996, p. A-5).

The recognition of ebonics has been integrated as a part of teaching in Los Angeles since 1990, based on the belief that the negative attitudes of teachers toward the home language of African American students set up low expectations. Noma LeMoine, Director of Language Development Program for African American Students in Los Angeles said:

> We recognize that mainstream English is the language of instruction. It's the gatekeeper to post-educational opportunities and careers. But that doesn't mean that mainstream English is a superior form of language. It is the language of the dominant class in America. (Wagner, 1996, p. C-7)

The Oakland proposal to conduct workshops for teachers in ebonics created a nationwide media frenzy, generating so much controversy that the Oakland school board hired a public relations person to explain their position to the public. The plan was denounced across the political spectrum, from conservative talk radio hosts such as Rush Limbaugh to progressive African American artists and intellectuals, including poet Maya Angelou and writer Ishmael Reed. Although he subsequently tempered his remarks, The Reverend Jesse Jackson was initially outraged:

> While we are fighting in California trying to extend affirmative action and fighting to teach our children so they become more qualified for jobs, in Oakland, some madness has erupted over making slang talk a second language. (Seligman, 1996, p. C-7)

The controversy revolved around the actual wording of the Oakland ebonics proposal, which positioned it as a distinct language and insinuated that there was a need for translation between black English and standard English. It read in part that "numerous validated scholarly studies" have demonstrated "that African Language Systems are genetically based and not a dialect of English" (Oakland Unified School District, 1996). School board members hastened to clarify that the word "genetic" was used to refer to genesis or origins, "cultural and historical," and was not a reference to human biology. Critics of Darwinist tracts, such as the *Bell Curve* (Herrnstein & Murray, 1994), were not appeased.

The board should also have worried about their assertion that ebonics was a widely recognized language. By all accounts, the debate about whether ebonics was a language or a dialect was not nearly as settled as the Oakland school board implied. Although scholars weighed in on both sides of the issue, most linguists recognized black English as a distinct dialect of English—not a separate language per se, and not a dialect that was in need of translation. But linguists also acknowledge that the distinction between a language and a dialect often hinges on politics. The running joke in linguistic circles is that "language is dialect with an army." The arcane remark emphasizes that the boundary between language and dialect is usually drawn by politicians, not scholars. In Oakland, language is dialect with a school board.

Critics charged that labeling ebonics a language was a cynical attempt by the board of education to make a grab for federal bilingual funding. The U.S. government, in a federal law called Title VII, draws the line by recognizing only *foreign*, not domestic languages. Certainly, the U.S. Department of Education, in charge of channeling funds for bilingual education, was unwilling to recognize ebonics—or any other form of nonstandard English—as a second language. A bilingual teacher commented that it was important to teach Standard American English to African American students in a culturally sensitive way. But, she said:

> What I find abhorrent and divisive is the blatant opportunism they display in labeling the dialect that these students speak as a bona fide language simply as a ploy to secure bilingual funding. . . . They are doing a disservice to the students by telling them it is a language, an assertion the board has made without any empirical support. (*San Francisco Examiner*, 1996, p. A-2)

School officials were completely unprepared for the negative and vehement response to the decision. Print and broadcast media, notoriously simplistic in their reporting of educational issues, just did not "get it." The public was left with the impression that Oakland schools would now teach nonstandard forms of English. Weary school officials stated, again and again, that the action did not mean that the District was going to teach black English over standard English. It meant that the home language of children would be valued, recognized, and used as a bridge to move children to standard English. School officials issued a statement, clarifying their objectives:

> . . . to build on the language skills that African American students bring to the classroom, without devaluing students and their diversity. We have directly

connected English language proficiency to student achievement. (DelVecchio, 1996, p. A-21)

The fact that the school board had good intentions for the success of Oakland school children was lost—drowned out in withering public denunciation of the proposal. Given the simplistic wording of their proposal, the Oakland school board was naive to think that it could be otherwise.

The ebonics controversy serves as a classic illustration of the complexity of literacy, as well as an example of how poorly educators communicate what they do to the public. Educators, immersed in the esoteric details of new educational theories, forget that laypeople have not kept pace with the field of literacy and language learning. Decades-old ideas about literacy that educators might consider *passé* are still firmly engrained in the mind of the public. The ebonics debate demonstrates that it takes much more than a hastily wrought policy, no matter how well-intentioned, to inform the public about new theories in English language learning. Issues of literacy are always hot buttons for controversy—never value free.

In contrast, schools from Wisconsin to California have introduced programs that use ebonics with little fanfare. Los Angeles educators amassed evidence and patiently explained to stakeholders—step by step—their plan to improve school gains for African American children by using the children's home discourse as a springboard for standard English learning. Had Oakland bothered to explain the policy to their stakeholders before going public, the ebonics plan may have received a more positive response. Or not. It takes time and patience to move the public away from old myths about literacy and schooling. In the meantime, the opportunities of too many students are stunted by school failure. It is no wonder that the subject of literacy can make educators cagey. It is hard to reconcile what the public expects from literacy with educational experiences that educators know their students deserve.

ERASING THE MYTHS OF LITERACY

As previously noted, literacy is only one of myriad social variables that interact to shape, and are shaped by, historical events. For example, at the end of the 20th century, it is assumed that high birth rates are correlated with low levels of literacy and that by raising female literacy rates, birth rates will decline accordingly.

But one need only go back 50 years, to the close of World War II, to find the opposite logic at work—high literacy rates were correlated with *high* birth rates (Graff, 1995, pp. 114–145). Similar anomalies appear to debunk any direct cause-and-effect relationship between literacy and criminality; literacy and morality (Graff, 1995, pp. 200–225); literacy and employment (Berg, 1971); and literacy and social equality (Fry, 1981). Specific cases of literacy throughout history drive home again and again the lesson that literacy practices, in isolation, are so dependent on other social contexts as to be relatively useless to predict isolated social behaviors. It is no wonder that literacy historians are cautious about predictions for literacy. Those who overpromised the social benefits of literacy and technology in the past were forced to eat their words.

By weeding out those ideas that are not supported by historical evidence, it is possible for researchers to establish some principles for literacy, based on concrete findings, which can serve as hypotheses for future generations of literacy study. Certainly such guideposts are useful in the uncharted territory of electronic literacy forms. Graff has provided significant leadership in his effort to debunk literacy myths from a solid research base. In the 1995 edition of *The Labyrinth of Literacy*, Graff outlined some common conclusions that have emerged from research evidence that he used to mitigate the most virulent public myths about literacy.

1. *Literacy is inextricably rooted in history.* In other words, it cannot be properly understood in isolation, outside the other powerful forces of its time. Graff said that "concrete historical circumstances . . . mediate in specific terms whatever supposedly general or 'universal' claims are made for literacy." He urged academic disciplines with an interest in studying literacy, for example, anthropology, the humanities, sociology, and so on, to take an historical view of literacy. Graff stressed that "present-day conceptions, arrangements, and practices of literacy, as well as schooling, are historically founded and grounded" (pp. xviii, 323).

2. *"Strong theories of literacy fail."* Graff said that "many common notions about literacy are rather fragile when probed or tested" and stresses the complexity of literacy, both practically and theoretically. He warned against simple dichotomies that attempt to explain it through false comparisons, "from literate versus illiterate, literate versus oral, print versus script, and so on" (pp. xix, 323–325). The competing purposes for literacy and the institutions set up to accommodate it, such as schooling, are always problematic and difficult to reconcile.

3. *Literacy is not value-neutral.* "No mode or means of learning and communicating is neutral: they all reflect and incorporate the assumptions and expectations, the biases and emphases of their production, acquisition, use, maintenance and preservation, even as they vary from culture to culture and time to time . . . [they] tend to interact dynamically and complexly in specific practices and specific contexts" (pp. xix, 325–327).

4. *There are many literacies.* Here, Graff makes clear that alphabetic literacy, that is, reading and writing, is extremely valuable and a highly desirable skill. But he cautioned that it is "one exceptionally valuable set of

competencies among others with which it interacts." He went on to say that "potentially revolutionary remaking of elementary and even higher adult learning and of concepts of literacy . . . may follow from serious recognition of the many, if not infinite forms of literacies." Graff found some of these literacies more plausible than others: "the alphabetic to the numeric . . . geographic, or spatial . . . many of them silly or worse" and he warned that "care in designation and description is an obvious mandate here" (pp. xix, 326).

5. *One set of literacies is not superior to others.* Contemporary literacy scholars seldom use the word "illiterate," in the belief that unless there is a profound physical or mental hindrance, every person can possess some degree of literacy. Instead of illiteracy, then, people fall somewhere on a continuum between more or less literacy, and even the boundaries of such a continuum are arguable.

And since there are many literacies—in the broadest sense, oral, print, and electronic modes—there are several continuums of literacy that should count. Because print has so dominated the ideal of what it means to be literate, Graff contends that "massive damage to individuals and societies [have] paid high prices for their presumed lack of literacy or failures to learn" (pp. xix, 327–328).

6. *Alphabetic literacy is not easy to learn.* Graff pointed to the awareness of "the difficulties regularly, perhaps normally experienced by those attempting to gain, practice and master the elements of alphabetic literacy. . . . Recognition of the 'many literacies' may contribute to this reconfiguration and reevaluation" (pp. xix–xx, 328).

Partly in the belief that reading and writing are so easy that even a child can do it, Graff pointed out that the last 200 years of schooling has served to enforce "expectations and common practices [that] equated literacy learning with elementary education." He said, "Coupled with the suspect conclusion that once one had those 'basics,' then building upon that foundation—using literacy and advancing—was easy, led to the equally easy presumption that failure to learn and advance was primarily the fault of the individual learner, not the schools or society" (pp. xx, 329–330).

7. *There are multiple paths to literacy.* The assumption that the methods prescribed by formal schooling are the only way to become literate is contradicted by historical evidence that shows literacy being learned at the mother's knee, in churches, by trade guilds, and so on. "The irony is that a history of learning at many ages in fields, workshops, factories, dame schools, class and ethnic and gender associations, among other informal and formal, integrated and segregated locations, was obscured in the triumph of one correct path. The costs are inestimable, the losses irreplaceable" (pp. xx, 328–329).

8. *Societies take multiple paths to literacy, just as individuals do.* Graff pointed out that "research demonstrates that there is no one route to near-universal literacy and . . . no one route with respect to literacy to economic development, industrialization, democratization, and the like" (pp. xx–xxi, 330–331). Along these lines, Resnick and Resnick (1977) have outlined at least three major historical models for literacy development before the 20th century: the Protestant-religious; the elite-technical, best exemplified by trade union and guild efforts; and the civic-national (pp. 370–385). There are doubtless many others as digital literacies proliferate alongside widespread economic and social change.

9. *Literacies co-exist.* One form of communication does not automatically displace another. As Marshall McLuhan noted, each literacy technology has unique aesthetic form that influences content and these same elements are adapted by each medium in unique ways. For example, it has been argued that the book owes much to illustration, since the woodcut blocks used to create pictures inspired Gutenberg to experiment with type (Manguel, 1997). Generalizations about codes, conventions, and aesthetics for each medium abound and are based as much on subjective personal taste as on objective observation: comic books are iconic; television is immediate and favors close-ups; in-depth information is more compatible with print, which enables reflection on content over time; wide shots look better in cinema; digital media enable more user interaction; etc. These forms coexist as they borrow and swap genre, style, codes, and conventions—with mixed aesthetic success, of course. The ability of digital tools to collapse sight, sound, and motion with relative ease accelerates experimentation with the convergence of aesthetic form and structure from different media.

Although Graff teaches caution about making historical comparisons between the uses of literacy, these comparisons abound to intrigue the researcher. The advent of print did not replace writing, although the uses and institutions for writing may have changed because of the printing press. Signatures are still important tools for purposes of authentication, just as they were in 11th-century Europe, although the technology may change—the signature of the future may consist of a digital fingerprint. And, just as 13th-century peasants proudly attached their signature seal to their belts so that everyone could see that they were literate, 20th-century businesspeople swap cards that prominently list their e-mail addresses, to signify that they are Internet savvy.

Nor could print culture dislodge the traditions of oral communication. The courtroom call to order, "Oyez! Oyez! Oyez!" demonstrates that many of the conventions of formal oral speech, such as repeating a promise three times, can be found in the text of modern contract law and court proceedings.

Individuals switch between old and new ways of speaking, writing, reading, viewing, and listening every day. Digital literacy practices, and the social institutions that support them, only add to the range of available literacy choices. Some literacy technologies atrophy from widespread disuse, but the conventions they foster in form and content may linger for centuries.

AVOIDING FALSE DICHOTOMIES

A survey conducted by the Benton Foundation (1996) found that there is significant correlation between heavy library use, frequent bookstore patronage, and home computer use. Of those who had visited the library at least once in the past year, 88% went to a bookstore at least once. Of those who own home computers 79% went to the library at least once and 90% frequented a bookstore at least once. Those who did not have a home computer used neither bookstores nor libraries as much. Only 60% went to the library at least once that year and 69% to the bookstore (Benton Foundation, pp. 21–22). Clearly, electronic forms of communication have yet to supplant print—quite the contrary. Book sales in modern times have soared, although the print literacy acumen of the outward literacies of privileged, industrially developed countries is deceptive. In fact, most people have always read for very applied, utilitarian purposes and only read an average of one book per year for pleasure (Manguel, 1997).

The Internet borrows extensively from the conventions of alphabetic literacy and is extremely dependent on the printed word. Static Web pages look like billboards. Interactive Web pages mimic radio, telephone and live speech. The way that pictures and texts work together in multimedia interfaces is reminiscent of the visually stunning illustrations of Biblical texts seen in the illuminated manuscripts of medieval times. E-mail has revived letter writing. In some ways, digital media has the potential to revive and refresh oral and print communication forms, by making new juxtaposition of image, text, and sound possible.

Nonetheless, the proliferation of electronic media raises intriguing questions about the future of books. Although the printing press made print far more available and less costly, it did not fundamentally change the relationship between writer, reader, and text.

> The electronic revolution now in progress will, on the other hand, generate mutations in every aspect of writing and reading—indeed, in the fabric of meaning itself. CD-ROM, the Internet, the miniaturization on microchips of whole libraries, immediate access to vast bibliographies, the as yet incalculable facilities offered by virtual reality are set to dwarf the impact of moveable type . . . each special domain interrelated with all others via electronic synapses

of recognition, classification, and translation (as in the human brain?)—is no longer a science-fiction fantastication. (Steiner, 1997, p. 120)

In many ways, uncertainty about the future of literacy fuels a burgeoning interest in the history of reading. In the last two decades, scholarly work in the field of historical literacy has accelerated. The results of such research offer some solid principles and guideposts for scholars who want to forge ahead and study literacy in the brave new world of electronic communication. At the very least, the study of literacy in the Age of Information can avoid the gross errors of the past.

Chief among these misconceptions is the tendency to elevate one form of literacy over another. Jack Goody (Goody & Watt, 1988) coined the phrase "The Great Dichotomy" and Ruth Finnegan (1988) "The Great Divide" to characterize the separation of oral and print literacy and the contrived elevation of print over oral forms. Contemporary literacy research has dispelled the notion that such divides and dichotomies exist between literacy practices, calling them "false dichotomies" and worse. As new communication tools emerge on the social landscape, it will take some scholarly vigilance to temper the tendency to isolate them from other forms of literacy into new, equally false dichotomies that position the technologized world as superior (or inferior) to print-based cultures. A powerful lesson in the history of print and orality demonstrates that electronic communication also has the potential to be used for either human liberation or human oppression—depending on the circumstances.

The scholarship on the uses of electronic and digital communication forms for literacy purposes is abysmally weak. The only clear statement that can be made from the disjointed and uneven research available about the uses of new and emerging communication technologies for purposes of language and literacy learning is that no one can say with authority the direction that digital media will take. Based on the history of alphabetic literacy, digital literacy is probably headed for both good and bad purposes, all at the same time, at the speed of the electrical current that carries it.

CHAPTER THREE

Divergence and Convergence
on the Electronic Frontier

If literacy is a technology of the intellect, hi-tech versions of digital pen and paper are the new mental prosthesis that promise to dissolve the line between thought and communication. Contemporary computer scientists have begun to make small contributions to the development of technologies that link brain processes to hardware. Medical interfaces and even a "thought-controlled" cursor have been prototyped. But scientists differ on exactly when commercially available devices will allow users to "jack-in" to cyberspace. Their responses run the gamut: David Nagel, president of AT&T Labs, thinks that a brain–computer link "reflects a naive view of the term *brain* and an unwarranted optimism about technology." Nicolas Negroponte, founder of MIT Media Lab, is characteristically enthusiastic, pointing to "kidney and heart computer interfaces, as well as bionic arms that tap into the human nervous system." Mark Weiser, principal scientist at Xerox PARC, believes that the perfect brain–computer interface is already here. He remarked that the most effective communication interface is "called language, and it enables us to effectively communicate with other meat computers [humans]" (Pescovitch, 1996, p. 80).

As digital technologies coexist in the territory previously claimed by alphabetic literacy, it would be refreshing to see the lessons learned from research about alphabetic literacy applied to new and emerging electronic forms of literacy. Unfortunately, although technologies are converging at breakneck pace, research about them has not followed suit. Barriers between academic disciplines are formidable and this isolation must be overcome in order to leverage the theory base for alphabetic literacy for insight into the potential uses of new literacy tools.

The body of research that does attempt to inform the uses of digital communication forms is scattered across disciplines, disjointed, and only tangential to studies that explore alphabetic literacy. With relatively few major exceptions, such as Walter J. Ong (1982) and his theories of mediated communication, it is as if alphabetic literacy scholars stopped at the threshold of electronic communication, but were reluctant to open the door. The challenge for the next generation of literacy researchers is to conduct and support work that crosses the threshold to explore the social uses of electronic literacy tools. In order to extend the principles of literacy research so that they apply to electronic media, problems of integration and conceptual order within the field of historical literacy study must still be resolved, chief among them, an alliance between literacy researchers and mass communication scholars. Furthermore, both fields would benefit by including the relevant concept and theory related to a third discipline—the study of education.

There are some useful models for disciplinary cross-pollination. As early as the 1950s and certainly by the 1970s—about the time the second generation of literacy historians were busy working on models, methodologies, and approaches for refining the field—literacy history was "discovered" by scholars from a number of other disciplines. These researchers began to add literacy as an incidental, independent variable to their studies of culture, economics, demographics, literature, and so forth. Some delved into the electronic universe and some stuck with the study of alphabetic and oral modes. In addition to adding to the body of knowledge, their cross-disciplinary work provided a model for collaborative research across disciplines.

The work of Shirley Brice Heath (1978), who explored the social history of reading and its relationship to sociolinguistics is one example. Raymond Williams (1961), who used the history of literacy as a component in his economic and political theories of cultural materialism, is another. As part of his cultural criticism, Williams addressed electronic forms and popular culture, as well as the ideology of print. Canadians Harold Innis (1951), a mentor to Marshall McLuhan, McLuhan himself (1962; McLuhan, Fiore, & Agel, 1967) and Walter Ong (1958, 1982) were some of the first to attempt to broaden the historical study of literacy to address both print and electronic modes of communication across disciplines. English and Canadian researchers grafted literacy studies onto research in the fields of literature and mass communication, specifically those that related to new theories of audience–reader response.

The inclusion of literacy as a research variable across such a wide range of disciplines was not without its problems. Although it broadened the acceptance of literacy history as an object of study, juggling all of the conflicting theories and personalities interested in literacy also proved exhausting for researchers who were devoted to the more focused history of alphabetic literacy. Although the attention was welcome, it was difficult for the burgeoning investigators of literacy history to retain enough focus to provide a cogent analysis that could inform the future direction of the field. Just as the second generation of literacy historians were poised to refine the theory base for the study of literacy in historical contexts, a cacophony of analysis about literacy trends and practices, from diverse corners of academia, provided enough background static to make the task of unifying the field all the more cumbersome. Kenneth Levine (1986) commented on interdisciplinary attempts to synthesize the linguistic and social practices of literacy over time:

> Part of the price of opening the door to insights from a variety of social, historical and critical perspectives is a lack of conceptual order and integration. Out of the disorder no overarching theoretical system has yet emerged which can be presented with any confidence to the reader, and moreover, the possibility of a unified theory of literacy, dealing with its comparative development in different societies and (necessarily) with interactions between written and non-written channels of communication, itself remains contested. (p. 183)

Levine contained his remarks to address the difficulty in unifying oral and written forms of communication. When digital and other electronic forms of communication are added to the mix, the task of finding "conceptual order and integration" between the various strands of literacy is exacerbated.

MASS COMMUNICATION STUDY AT THE CROSSROADS

Inasmuch as the study of alphabetic literacy is now established across disciplines, it is at least possible for a cross-disciplinary approach to flourish. In particular, alphabetic literacy's centrality to schooling provides a sturdy bridge between the theory and practice of both literacy and education.

In comparison, the study of electronic media grows out of a relatively narrow theory base—one that is parallel to, but never seems to intersect with, similar work in either literacy or education studies. In the main, the body of research that addresses the forms, institutions, and social uses of electronic communication has been the purview of communication study, and in particular *mass* communication study. The bulk of mass communication research has focused on analog media, especially broadcast television, although lately postsecondary departments have been dropping the "mass" from their name (and the *s* from communications) in order to acknowledge that new and emerging communication forms take on narrow, as well as mass, strategies for dissemination—and that communication is both interpersonal and intrapersonal. The study of mass communication began as a practical field, ginned up quickly to make sense of the astonishing growth and penetration of broadcast media.

In spite of timely efforts (some would say "past-timely") to acknowledge digital media in communication studies, and in spite of the strong presence of print journalism as a traditional topic of study, there are few examples of high-profile, collaborative research between contemporary literacy scholars and mass communication scholars. Because digital media borrows many of its forms and conventions from both print and broadcast media, there is some potential to bridge the body of evidence about alphabetic literacy with that of mass communication. Such an interdisciplinary look at digital media offers a rich context for fresh theoretical and practical understanding about the uses of new technologies.

Unfortunately, finding the common threads between literacy research and mass communication research poses several problems. One problem is that the two theory bases are only tangentially compatible. Another is a difference in the emphasis placed on the importance of qualitative research methodologies by each field. Finally, because mass communication is offered in public elementary and secondary schooling only in an elective, or *ad hoc* manner, the rationale for bridging communication and education studies as a branch of educational theory and practice is also problematic.

Both oral and alphabetic literacy researchers, with their emphasis on complexity and historicity, would be resistant to, if not appalled by, the simple communication models and decontextualized variables that dominated mass communication literature of the past. Furthermore, although literacy studies have a long association with educational theory, mass communication studies have not been similarly tied into educational theory and practice. In such a context of irreconcilable difference, a coherent theory base that can be used to inform the uses of an expanded kind of literacy for teaching and learning still proves illusive. Because theory building has traditionally originated from university scholars, it would help if postsecondary researchers would drive the convergence of literacy with communication research toward a more unified approach that could offer some assistance to their colleagues in the field of education. But in matters of literacy, things are never simple.

SCANNING THE FAULTLINE

The study of "educational technology" is one attempt to reconcile research about new literacies with that of education. Although it holds promise for integrating diverse bodies of research, educational technology is still finding its way as an approach to teaching and learning. It remains to be seen whether it will add more or less clarity about promising uses of digital literacy in education.

It is the increasing use of educational technologies that brings differing assumptions about the purposes of education into stark relief. Joshua Meyrowitz,
in his essay, "Instructional Technology and the Bifurcation of the University"
(1995), claimed that arguments about the uses of technology in schooling
obscure a faultline between vastly different assumptions about the definition
of knowledge and the role of the university in an information society.
According to Meyrowitz, there is inherent tension between traditional scholarship, associated with the "academic cloister" ideal of Plato's Academy and
the modern, "relevant university" that serves as "the research center for society,
discovering, testing and *applying* [information in efficient ways]" (p. 75):

> More and more, the university is becoming a neo-vocational school, not en-
> gaged in generating new knowledge, but in packaging available information
> as sets of specified skills. . . . Relevant education is primarily concerned with
> transmitting current information over space to as many people as possible.
> In contrast, traditional education is concerned with the progress of knowledge
> over time. (p. 78)

Meyrowitz said that the ideal of the cloistered, medieval academy fosters
an attitude toward information based not upon the quantity of information
obtained, but upon the attainment of knowledge in the pursuit of an ultimately unattainable truth. Information content and approach are virtually
inseparable. The quality of the teacher–learner relationship is central; the
focus is on exploring weaknesses and contradictions in the body of knowledge; students are responsible for making sense of the information; and all
students are not expected to do equally well.

> Traditional education is a continuously meta-communicative process proceed-
> ing up the ladder of abstraction until only a few strong and willing minds
> cling to the rungs . . . students are not expected to emerge with uniform
> information, but with sharpened reasoning, critical skills, and the knowledge
> of how to develop new knowledge. (p. 79)

The relevant university, on the other hand, strives for efficiency of information transfer, that is, results-driven, "just-in-time" information packages.
It relies on the belief that texts are authoritative and, when framed in relation
to information needs for critical literacy, the relevant university represents
the worst of all possible worlds: Texts are assumed to have fixed meaning,
yet there are fewer opportunities to approach information in a dialogic way.
The process of obtaining reflective knowledge over time is "largely irrelevant"
and the content, as well as its applications, are planned in advance by
"content specialists."

Rather than knowledge growing from the collision of independently developed ideas, educational information will be structured through collaboration and consensus. Rather than students learning from, and joining in, the debates among adherents of incompatible philosophies, they are likely to become the audience for expressions of conventional wisdom . . . to the extent that teachers become anonymous and authoritative "experts," so do students become passive receivers of "approved" information. (p. 81)

According to Meyrowitz (1995), it is a wonder that "traditional" and "relevant" education have worked in harmony for so long. He attributes this to the fact that until relatively recently, the range of available educational technologies was limited. Thus, although their objectives were different, both traditional and relevant schooling approaches were forced to handle information in much the same way: "Many of the fundamental differences between these two forms of education have been masked by the surface similarities in their forms of instruction: book, talk and chalk" (p. 82). By any account, the adaptation of other classroom technologies has heretofore been too glacial to register. As California futurist David Thornburg quipped in an Arizona Town Hall Meeting about educational technology, "It took twenty years to get the overhead projector from the bowling alley to the classroom" (Thornburg, 1997).

But the use of technology for purposes of schooling is accelerating, and the introduction of systematic instructional technology offers relevant education a form of instruction compatible with its own goals. Instructional technology serves to decentralize the university beyond the cloistered environment, offers access to packaged education to vast numbers of people, and introduces a mediated, machine-to-person relationship into the learning equation that offers efficient transference of information/knowledge. In contrast, the ideology of instructional delivery is antithetical to the goals of traditional scholarship. According to Meyrowitz (1995), although both reflective and applied forms of instruction have their place in schooling, technology is the wedge that forces the bifurcation of the university—driving competing theories about the purposes of education even farther apart.

Meyrowitz's ideas about the bifurcation of the university provide a plausible explanation for why clear and unified bodies of theory about the uses of electronic literacy in education are so hard to find. Scholars who want to study the nature of digital communication forms and their uses begin their search in one of two likely areas of study: literacy or communication theory. Nowhere is the difference between the traditional and relevant university, envisioned by Meyrowitz, more obvious than in these two divergent fields of study.

It doesn't take long to see that literacy scholars proceed in their pursuit of knowledge on a long timetable, patiently testing hypotheses and making cautious, frequently revised statements—adding one study to the next to test and re-test long-range theories. When quantitative data about literacy records is revealed, alphabetic literacy scholars look for qualitative field studies to support it, in an attempt to methodically move toward an understanding of literacy's contribution to historical events.

Communication scholars, on the other hand, operate from the assumption that media have powerful effects on society—many of them harmful. Their research is marked by a sense of urgency and recommendations for action. The body of research in the field is rife with aggressive conclusions and timely, opportunistic theories. A disproportionate number of the conclusions from mass communication study are based on decontextualized, quantitative methodologies.

Researchers who want to make sense of new technologies soon find themselves bouncing back and forth between the conflicting paradigms, assumptions and data provided by communication and literacy studies. There is little "conceptual order and integration" here that can be used to alleviate the daunting "vertigo and myopia" inherent in the study of literacy (Martin, 1994, p. 1).

IN SEARCH OF DIGITAL LITERACY

Both literacy and communication scholarship have much to offer the hapless researcher of electronic literacy. The ideological and methodological "disconnect" between literacy and communication research, makes reconciliation of the two bodies of research confusing, to say the least. This results in creative, eclectic, and idiosyncratic research conclusions across the disjointed research base, such as those advanced by educational technologists, McLuhanists, and other technical determinists. It seems that as rapidly as literacy researchers back away from strong effects models, mass communication scholars embrace them.

As argued in previous chapters, alphabetic literacy historians have become increasingly tenuous over the years about creating cause and effect relationships between literacy and other social acts such as behavior, crime, employability, family life, and values. Research on alphabetic literacy combines both quantitative and qualitative research, but of late, literacy scholars have attentively filled in gaps in the qualitative side of the research. Researchers increasingly enhance the quantitative information about literacy records with cautious, meticulous and complex research characterized by field-based work and the study of the uses of literacy in specific contexts. Literacy researchers use the quantitative data to move closer and closer to the ground—to look at literacy in action in ever-more-minutely contextualized situations. This combination of quantifiable numbers with descriptive information is vital to a deeper understanding of the practices of literacy.

As contemporary literacy scholars call for more qualitative field-based work, to back up their quantitative data, mass communication researchers are still apparently compelled to present ever more quantitative methodologies to back up their observations. To be sure, since the 1980s, the field of communication study has also moved toward the simultaneous investigation of content and contexts through the use of qualitative methods such as those employed by "uses and gratifications" theory (Lull, 1985; Silverblatt, 1995; Wartella, Heintz, Aidman, & Mazzarella, 1990). However, in the main, mass communication study fails to place an emphasis on contextual factors equal to those seen in the study of alphabetic literacy. It continues to expend a disproportionate amount of effort in the quantification of data about media (hours of media used, acts of representation in content, acts of violence, numbers of media users, etc.). Content analysis methodologies are particularly prominent. With an emphasis on the naming, counting, and classifying of media content for purposes of inference, content analysis decontextualizes content from media in a way that diverges sharply from contemporary studies of literacy. The use of content analysis in communication study does little to acknowledge and inform literacy as a complex collection of social events, inseparable from their contexts and manipulated idiosyncratically by users to create meaning.

Finally, there is little research to differentiate form (e.g., television, film, Internet) from content (representation, narrative, genre). Researchers often lump form and content together indiscriminately, for example, the "effects of television," or "TV shortens attention spans." In many cases, conclusions about media effects, derived from a hodgepodge of methodologies are used to bolster hypothesis. Such an analysis, devoid of its cultural and historical contexts, does little to inform the uses of digital literacy tools. Moreover, the lack of coherence in theory and practice across such a diverse body of communication research leads to confusing, simplistic, and highly speculative hypotheses about the effects of electronic media on users' brains, behaviors, or attitudes.

In contrast, the effect that alphabetic literacy has on its users is, at best, a marginalized concept in scholarship about the history of literacy. For example, although mass communication scholars link mass media with crime, violence, immorality, and other social ills with a tone of great authority, comparable conclusions about the effects of print reading and writing on the same social problems is far more tentative—almost nonexistent—in the current crop of alphabetic literacy research. Only when literacy is discussed as "discourse," from a critical literacy perspective, are popular culture and mass media even brought into the discussion (Giroux & Simon, 1989). Even then, literacy scholars demonstrate a characteristic reticence to attribute totalizing effects to media. In an article about the uses of media for learning about multiculturalism, literacy scholar Carlos Cortés commented:

Many analysts have treated the media as virtually all-powerful forces that inculcate audiences with their beliefs . . . this common trap of media determinism . . . remains popular in protest-group proclamations and political pontifications about media impact. While most media content analysts present only sporadic concrete evidence of media impact on the construction of audience knowledge, some content analysis scholars suggest or even categorically assert what viewers learn from the media, inappropriately using media content (teaching) to proclaim audience impact (learning). (Cortés, 1995, p. 175)

Cortés went on to say:

Other analysts have viewed the media as having limited power to influence audiences, treating the media as a reflector of social consensus . . . emphasizing the audience's activist role in constructing meaning. . . . In the middle stand scholars who agree that media . . . do teach . . . but argue that research to date has generally failed to identify the precise content of audience learning. (p. 175)

As Cortés noted, in spite of the fact that the results of the media effects studies are controversial, the conclusions of individual mass communication studies can be bold. Bold statements get attention from policymakers, but such statements make alphabetic literacy scholars cringe. Media scholar Elihu Katz (1988) commented on the dilemma faced by media effects researchers:

There are many conflicting views of media effects. We researchers get rewarded in various ways for saying the media are totally ineffective and we get rewarded—sometimes even by the same people—for saying that the media are omnipotent, they're to blame for everything. (Katz, 1988, pp. 361–374; cited by Davies, 1996, p. 9)

The assumption of effects, or even conversely of *no* effects, is rarely a hypothesis in studies of alphabetic literacy. The literacy scholar would want to know much more about a host of social variables. For example, it is doubtful that a contemporary scholar of alphabetic literacy could be found who would claim with conviction that books incite aggressive social behavior; or that reading makes children fat; or that the format of the written page disrupts children's attention spans.

The point here is not to elevate the study of literacy over that of mass communication, but to try to examine points of divergence and reconciliation. It is true that equivalent statements were made about print literacy as either a social and moral virtue, or as a harbinger of social demise, by literacy researchers of the past. But modern literacy scholarship has taken great pains to address and recontextualize such totalizing explanations of literacy's effects. In contrast, sweeping claims are often made by those who study the use of television and, by far, television is the most dominant electronic medium studied by mass communication researchers.

The tendency toward effects studies can be partly explained by looking at the dominant theory strands for communication study. As humanities scholars moved away from psychoanalytical theories of interpretation, mass communication researchers revived them as a primary analytical tool for the study of media effects audience's cognition, behavior, and attitude. Psychological theories used in communication research include cognitive social psychology models that suggest almost direct effects of media on behavior (Gantz, 1993) to those that are less behaviorist, such as the social learning theories of Bandura (Bandura & Walters, 1963). In addition, the far more contextualized and sociological hypotheses of Meyrowitz (1985) and Postman (1982) incorporate the perspectives of social psychology in the investigation of media's culpability in the breakdown between adulthood and childhood, as well as in public–private life.

Other social psychology studies have grown out of cognitive development theories detailed by Anderson and Collins (1988); enculturation theories (Gerbner & Gross, 1976); and effects of media on racial or gender role stereotyping in both print and electronic popular culture (Allen, 1993; Brabent & Mooney, 1986; Guerrero, 1993; Kilbourne, 1989; Powell, 1982; Seidman, 1992; Takanishi, 1982). In fact, researchers who looked at the effects of media and gender stereotyping were some of the first mass communication scholars also to explore computer effects (Ware & Stuck, 1985).

Semiotics, the study of signs, is another mass communication theory that attempts to deconstruct the elements in the frame in order to explore the symbolic nature of media and popular culture (Altheide, 1974; Real, 1977; Seiter, 1987). Just as semiotics further decontextualize form and content "within the frame," uses and gratifications theories attempt to recontextualize media use by studying the array of social and cultural factors "outside the television frame" (Rosengren, Wenner, & Palmgreen, 1985; Real, 1989). Uses and gratifications studies attempt to examine the way that media are used and thus get at some of the purposes of literacy for users of electronic media and popular culture.

Other theoretical approaches to the study of media effects take on quasimedical hypotheses to prove behavioral, attitudinal, and even physical effects, generally from a psychological theory base. Because they work from strong hypotheses about media's power to inculcate, they are the most difficult to reconcile with alphabetic literacy studies. Studies on the relationship between television and violent–aggressive behavior, many of them behaviorist, dominate mass communication research (Pearl, Bouthelet, & Lazar, 1982; Singer, Singer, & Rapaczynski, 1984; UCLA, 1995), but others include television as addicting or habituating (Winick, 1988; Winn, 1987); television and its relationship to weight gain and overall mental and physical health (American Psychological Association, 1993); the arousal hypothesis that media can be an affective factor in sexual behavior and aggression (Zillman, 1991); and the belief that television shortens a child's attention span and reflectiveness (Singer & Singer, 1976) and can condition the brain to change at the expense of concentration (Moody, 1980) and perceptual salience (Wright & Huston, 1983).

With the strong focus on media effects studies, communication study has provided little room for topics of mutual interest to literacy scholars. But "uses and gratifications" study has some compatible points of interest, as do semiotics and various audience response theories. There is also some hope that cultural studies approaches to new media will prove beneficial as a bridge between print and digital literacies (Bazalgette & Buckingham, 1995; Buckingham & Sefton-Green, 1996; Kubey, 1997).

Until these bridges are established, literacy researchers will remain reluctant to entertain the brave new world of digital communication tools. The majority of communication scholars who do study the way that alphabetic and electronic forms work together invoke the technical determinist theories of Marshall McLuhan and his contemporaries (Carveth, 1996; Ferris & Montgomery, 1996; Metz, 1996; Negroponte, 1995). To the staid literacy crew, who believe that a strong, simple theory about literacy is worse than no theory at all, the iconoclastic theories that Marshall McLuhan formulated about electronic forms of literacy are beyond bifurcation—almost beyond the academic pale.

WHATCHA DOIN' MARSHALL McLUHAN?

Blame Marshall McLuhan for the perception that researchers of electronic media have a tendency to play fast and loose with the evidence. He had brilliant ideas and bad ideas, but it is not always clear that he could tell the difference between the two. Furthermore, McLuhan was notoriously lax about supporting his theories with research or challenging them through debate. He seldom bothered with the simple follow-through it took to apply his theories to actual projects. When challenged about some particularly audacious remarks, tossed off in typical bombastic fashion during a 1955 lecture at Columbia University Teachers College, McLuhan responded, "You don't like these ideas? I got others" (Marchand, 1989, p. 132).

This is the man who was prescient enough to foresee a "global village" and coined catch-phrases such as "the medium is the message." McLuhanist concepts gain currency as the convergence of form and function in new media accelerates. He foresaw the invention of videotapes, calling them "television platters" (p. 101). Not all of his ideas resonated with the public.

One of his business ventures was to patent ProhTex, a product designed to take the telltale smell of urine out of underpants (p. 230).

McLuhan was enamored with simplistic bipolar theories about the workings of the brain (right brain–left brain), and his theories about the characteristics of media tended to emphasize each medium's sensory effects. He rarely bothered to bolster these highly physiological theories with rigorous scientific evidence. Building on the earlier work of Innis (1951), who took a much more measured approach in his own theories about the characteristics of each medium, McLuhan attempted to analyze and classify human response to media. One such example was McLuhan's notion that the photoreceptors of the retina were more "tactile" than its outer edges.

> Color TV will mean more involvement. . . . We see color with the cone of our eye, black and white with the edges . . . color is more in demand in a primitive society. So are spiced dishes. I predict a return of hot sauces to American cuisine. (*New York Times*, June 14, 1966, cited in Marchand, 1989, p. 185)

McLuhan provided little factual evidence to back up his pronouncements. He saw media as a technological prosthesis that extended sensory experience and assigned a confusing array of characteristics to each medium: Television was cool, but radio was hot. The telephone was cool, and so on. Only McLuhan could definitively remember which was which.

The open secret is that McLuhan was highly contemptuous of electronic media. The British literary critic, F. R. Leavis, was his mentor at Cambridge and under his tutelage, McLuhan learned to apply the analytic powers of the literary critic on the cultural environment, especially the world of popular culture. Leavis believed that:

> Practical Criticism—the analysis of prose and verse—may be extended to the analysis of advertisements . . . followed by comparison with representative passages of journalese and popular fiction. (Leavis & Thompson, 1933, p. 6)

For Leavis, popular culture suffered from comparison with classical literature, and that was decidedly the point. Inspired by D. H. Lawrence, Leavis lamented the demise of the "organic community" of rural folkways and crafts. He believed that media were to blame and attempted to engender a moral panic about the insurgence of popular culture in society. With his moral outrage about the erosion of values from a Golden Past, Leavis was to British cultural conservatism in prewar England what critics of television, advertising, and other popular culture have become to the postwar United States.

Leavis' ideas resonated with the deeply religious and politically conservative McLuhan. Although McLuhan was as playful as Leavis was pedantic, they both believed that unless people understood the encroaching nature of media, they were in danger of losing the values of literacy essential to the traditions of Western civilization (McLuhan, 1964). There is ample evidence that McLuhan was appalled by popular culture. This fine point is lost on modern-day advocates of new technologies, who tend to embrace McLuhan and to see his theories about new media as not only prophetic, but optimistic.

Like Leavis, McLuhan believed in the superiority of print. Of television, he said, "To resist TV one must acquire the antidote of related media like print" (Marchand, 1989, p. 170). He held comics in contempt and in a Playboy interview from the 1960s, McLuhan said, "I find most pop culture monstrous and sickening. I study it for my own survival" (Marchand, p. 43). He saw the study of media as the ultimate revenge for their destructive force. In a 1960 report to the National Educational Broadcasters Association, McLuhan said:

> Instead of scurrying into the corner and wailing about what media are doing to us, one should charge straight ahead and kick them in the electrodes. They respond beautifully to such resolute treatment and soon become servants rather than masters. (McLuhan, 1960, cited in Marchand, p. 148)

In a letter to the editor of *Life* magazine, McLuhan wrote:

> Recognition of the psychic and social consequences of technological change makes it possible to neutralize the effects of innovation. If we maintain lively dialogue with, and among, the technologies, we can enlist them on the side of traditional values instead of watching those values disappear while we play the helpless bystanders. (McLuhan, 1966, cited in Molinaro, McLuhan, & Toye, 1987, p. 334)

More troubling to literacy theorists, some of whom might share his distaste for popular culture, were McLuhan's sweeping and totalizing claims about the presumed power of communication technologies. He approached media study as a technical determinist with a modernist bent. In *The Gutenberg Galaxy* (1962), he explained that tribalism was natural to humanity and that the phonetic alphabet had disrupted this ideal state of grace. Many of McLuhan's ideas for *The Gutenberg Galaxy* were derived from his former student, Walter Ong, who often agreed with McLuhan, but in the main was a much more meticulous academic who thoroughly documented his hypotheses. It was McLuhan who pointed Ong to Peter Ramus, an obscure Renaissance theologian. Ong's study, *Ramus, Method, and the Decay of Dialogue* (1958), contained the basic ideas for *The Gutenberg Galaxy*, that is, that during the Renaissance, the invention of the printing press shifted Western culture from oral to visual modes with resulting shifts in supporting social institutions.

Embellishing on Ong's research, McLuhan credited the invention of the printing press with the rise of rationalism, science and industry, capitalism, nationalism, and logic. He believed that the printing press favored the visual and, characteristically, linked sweeping historical shifts to the rise of the visual over the oral. Such a theory promotes the notion that there is a clean divide between oral and print culture—the kind of dichotomy that literacy theorists have come to abhor.

Over the years, McLuhan lost some of his moral earnestness and even occasionally did reveal optimism about new media's contribution to the social good. For example, attesting to the ability for technological prosthesis to enhance humanity, he predicted that tiny computers, about the size of a hearing aid, would allow people to share their experiences by jacking into the wired brain of the outer world (Marchand, 1989, p. 170). Although literacy theorists still do not quite know what to do with McLuhan's work, he is extremely popular with the public. To the lay person, McLuhan's brash theories contain a grain of truth, and there is no question that many of his predictions about the nature and uses of electronic media have come to pass. Like the cult of Elvis, the cultural resonance around McLuhan takes on a life of its own.

McLuhan cannibalized ideas all around him and tried to jam them into his systems for classifying media properties. In addition to Leavis, Innis, and Ong, he also re-worked ideas from his Canadian contemporary, Edmund Carpenter, who took a similarly sweeping anthropological look at media (1972). As he echoed his contemporaries, McLuhan sometimes distorted the original ideas, truncating them before they could run their course through the gauntlet of academic scrutiny. Like Plato, he skillfully used the very medium he decried.

Contemporary scholars are still sifting through the flotsam and jetsam that McLuhan and his contemporaries left in their wake. Caught up in the buoyant enthusiasm and cultural hyperbole of the 1960s, many of the ideas of the technical determinists have proven to be vastly overstated. But many display spectacular insight and some, for example, the way that each medium shapes content, have proven promising for informing contemporary scholarship about the uses of new and emerging communication forms.

FROM ORAL TO PRINT TO ELECTRONIC
AND BACK AGAIN

In *Orality and Literacy* (1982), Ong advanced a theory about the way that literacies converge that he called "secondary orality." In his comparison of oral, print, and electronic modes of communication, he said:

> The electronic transformation of verbal expression has both deepened the
> commitment of the word to space initiated by writing and intensified by print

and has brought consciousness to a new age of secondary orality. . . . At the same time, with telephone, radio, television and various kinds of sound tape, electronic technology has brought us into the age of "secondary orality." This new orality has striking resemblances to the old . . . but it is essentially a more deliberate and self-conscious orality, based permanently on the use of writing and print. . . . The new medium here reinforces the old, but of course transforms it because it fosters a new, self-consciously informal style, since typographic folk believe that oral exchange should normally be informal (oral folk believe it should be formal). (pp. 135–136)

Ong diverged from his contemporaries, McLuhan and Leavis, who believed that electronic media were a threat to print. Ong believed instead that speech was transformed by print culture, but did not displace it. Similarly, he believed that electronic forms were incorporating, not erasing, print. Ong observed that electronic modes of discourse were actually based on the traditions of print, thus strengthening and reinforcing them. Moreover, the recorded speech heard in electronic media sounded like authentic person-to-person speech, but was merely an echo of the real thing, or as Ong would say, an echo of "primary orality."

Ong determined that the conversation heard in media was "secondary orality," a manufactured speech that is created by using formulaic codes and conventions borrowed from print. Print was used to script dialogue that although constructed, sounded quite natural. According to Ong, the merging of print and oral traditions ushered in a new kind of orality that was a hybrid of both oral and alphabetic conventions. Ong (1982) remarked that in cultures saturated for centuries with print, "orality has come into its own more than ever before" because of the emergence of electronic media (p. 137).

It is the veneer of authenticity that proves most troubling to critics of electronic media. When critics decry the public's ability to distinguish between "reality" and television, they may be criticizing the way that media's apparent "naturalness" disguises the highly constructed nature of media narration. Furthermore, secondary orality, because of its informality, brings private discourse, usually reserved for intimate talks in private settings, into the public arena of mass media. Ong's theory of secondary orality does much to explain the sense of "tastelessness" that critics of media find so difficult to define with any precision.

Although Ong's work predated the proliferation of computer networking, he does mention the computer. In keeping with his deterministic penchant for strong statements about the qualities of each medium, he said:

The sequential processing and spatializing of the word, initiated by writing and raised to a new order of intensity by print, is further intensified by the computer, which maximizes commitment of the word to space and to (electronic) local motion and optimizes analytic sequentiality by making it virtually instantaneous. (p. 136)

Ong recognized the immediacy of computerized communication, as well as its ability to transcend space and time. He also recognized its dependence on the conventions of print media. It is possible however, that if Ong were writing in the age of hypertext, he may have tempered his notions about the "analytic sequentiality" of computers. Nonetheless, a look at the informal discursive style of email—in some cases reminiscent of Victorian letter writing—as well as the emergence of audio and video on the Internet are only two intriguing digital examples of Ong's concept of the informal nature of secondary orality.

CONVERGING LITERACY, COMMUNICATION, AND EDUCATIONAL THEORY

The intertextual nature of the concept of secondary orality has important implications for contemporary teaching and learning. If the secondary orality of media can also be conceived as a unique form of discourse, that is, the discourse of media, Ong's concept of secondary orality offers possibilities for linking the overlapping codes and conventions for oral, print, and electronic modes with theories of literacy. Such a convergence of communication theory and literacy theory also has the added bonus of offering multiple paths of literacy for the learner, who may be predisposed to audial, visual, or textual modes. In addition, the technical convergence of digital literacy tools—allowing text, image, and sound to implode into many forms of digital records—offers a fertile testbed for a corresponding convergence of theory. Nurturing the concept of secondary orality also has the potential to bring a wider range of information form and content into the educational process. Furthermore, when coupled with ideas of literacy as discourse, the potential for a wider range of literacies emerges. While breaking new ground for the use of electronic literacy technologies in the curriculum, new ideas for using oral modes of discourse for teaching and learning breathes new life into the quartet of educational basics familiar to every educator: reading, writing, listening, and speaking.

Perhaps because alphabetic literacy dominates school practices, literacy research already demonstrates a strong research strand that informs the uses of literacy in schooling. Because they explore the way that learners "construct" meaning, theories of constructivist education are compatible with those of reader-response theories. The uses of multiple literacy tools in culturally specific contexts are especially useful for teachers in increasingly multilingual and multicultural classroom environments (Minami & Kennedy, 1991). The vigorous debate about the use of whole language practices and phonics is only one demonstration of the complex marriage of educational theory and literacy theory. Although teachers may disagree, continuous discussion of literacy in action keeps the fields of both literacy and education vital.

In contrast, the field of communication studies is at a significant disadvantage when it attempts to inform contemporary education practices. Because the study of communication does not occupy a place comparable to print in the elementary and secondary curriculum, it has almost no influence on formal educational practices. Although well established at the university level, the research base for communication has proven itself to be neither accessible, nor particularly useful to elementary or secondary teachers. As previously mentioned, aside from the rare elective course in high school, communication study is not recognized as a traditional discipline in K–12 education, and therefore is not as integrated as are the practices of alphabetic reading and writing in schooling.

Furthermore, with its emphasis on the negative effects of television and other forms of popular culture, communication research leaves educators confused about what media effects have to do with classroom practice. Most have responded to the theory base provided by media effects studies by extending their gatekeeping role to include the monitoring of television, the Internet, and other sources of information—or to banning popular culture as much as possible from the classroom.

In the recognition that popular culture is problematic, but here to stay, teachers often take a "fallback" position that attempts to teach children to be discerning about media. Beyond serving as a bellwether for adults about the effects of media on children, communication research offers elementary and secondary teachers little else of practical value.

This still leaves the classroom educator with pressing questions about the uses and purposes of technology for teaching and learning. Because literacy research is not particularly forthcoming on promising uses of electronic forms of literacy in the classroom, either, a hybrid area of study has sprung up to fill the void. The field of Educational Technology is an eclectic collection of research that grew out of the growing awareness that teachers were using more audiovisual and information technologies in the classroom. In addition, there was a growing awareness that technology could resolve some inequities in education, by providing resources at a distance. The use of technology for "distance education" was specifically promoted as a way to offer information and instructional resources to rural, disenfranchised, or other learners who did not have ready access to educational opportunity. Distance education was envisioned as the ultimate "push" technology in a long line of teaching machines which "pushed" highly selective content in front of learners. To put this in some perspective, textbooks are arguably the most dominant of all the mass mediated, push technologies in the classroom. But distance education had the capacity to go beyond print and deliver motion pictures, text, and sound comparable to a virtual teacher. It appealed to those who believed that education should be practical, applied, and results-oriented. Educational technology was promoted as a cost-effective and efficient way to educate. It was positioned in much the same role that literacy occupied in the past: as an economic development issue; as a national priority; and as a panacea to school improvement.

CHAPTER FOUR

Splintering Literacies

New approaches to literacy teaching and learning suggest that instead of approaching literacy as a monolithic concept, for example, a "Good Thing" with sanctioned, printed texts and lofty purposes, it is more useful to break literacy down into any number of multiple literacy modes, each with distinctive characteristics that reveal a variety of social purposes: good, useful, and otherwise. These multiple literacies have been called *technology literacy, information literacy, visual literacy, media literacy*, and so on. The foundations for these literacies are rooted in literacy traditions of oral/aural, visual, and alphabetic/text modalities. As contemporary communication media converge into a sensory soup, the peculiar features of each of these literacies also converge and overlap to combine alphabetic with oral and visual literacy traditions and practices. And because information consumers increasingly use new tools both to receive and transmit messages, it is helpful to get a fix on some competencies and purposes for each of the literacies and then, in jigsaw puzzle fashion, to attempt to put the literacy pieces back together again.

An examination of these literacies in isolation from one another does little to promote either clarity or utility. Such a specialized look at each literacy only serves to reflect the tautology and polemic of its constituents. In practical terms, the various multiliteracies have not been advanced long enough to have a sufficient body of evidence, research, and tradition to make sufficient predictions about the promising practices of literacy that might accompany new and emerging media in educational settings.

The key to understanding the changing landscape of contemporary literacy is to study the areas where the rationale, skill sets, and purposes of various literacies converge and overlap for clues to the common features, competencies, and pedagogies of literacy at this point in time. Only then can a new vision of literacy in its myriad forms begin to take shape.

A NEW LITERACY FOR A NEW AGE

The abundance of information has been called an "information explosion," and it is almost as if the cornucopia of digital and analog technologies shocked literacy scholars into reevaluating popular assumptions about oral and alphabetic literacy practices. The sudden profusion of mass media led researchers into a confusing morass of new and untested theories about the nature of literacy in the electronic age. In a 1946 book on audiovisual teaching, author Edgar Dale defined his vision of this new kind of literacy:

> What do I mean by the term "literacy" and the "new" literacy? I mean by literacy the ability to communicate through the three modes: reading and writing, speaking and listening, visualizing and observing—print, audio, and visual literacy. This literacy, broadly speaking, can be at two levels. First, is at the level of training, initiative reaction. Here we communicate the simple, literal meaning of what is written, said or visualized. . . . Or second, we can have creative interaction, can read between the lines, draw inferences, un- derstand the implications of what was written, said or spoken. We thus learn what the speaker, writer or visualizer "meant to say" which requires a greater degree of literacy. And finally, we learn to read beyond the lines, to evaluate, and apply the material to new situations. We use the message in our own varied ways.
>
> I would also classify responses as uncritical or accepting, or as critical and evaluating. The new literacy involves critical reading, critical listening, and critical observing. It is disciplined thinking about what is read, heard, and visualized. (pp. 92–93)

As technology continues to impinge upon familiar textual/alphabetic lit- eracy practices, literacy researchers and constituents for specific literacy modes are still groping toward workable definitions for the new version of literacy—not that they had any consensus about the definition of alphabetic literacy to begin with.

And definitions are important. Philosophers quibble about the relationship between thought, word, and deed, but there seems to be a consensus that words can be the catalyst for action. In the name of rationalism, great value is placed on naming and classification, specialization, epistemology, and isolation of words. Therefore, the power to name a thing, or better yet, to designate an entire concept or class of things, is a mark of respect in Western intellectual circles, resulting in prominence and wielding influence. Whether the act of defining leads to broad consensus about meaning is another matter entirely.

Naming represents an intellectual process that is as exclusionary as it is inclusive, with the implicit goals of sanctioning some definitions over others, establishing universally accepted classification schemes and then situating oneself within the boundaries of the definition for purposes of identity, resource development, and involvement in spheres of influence. It is by the decidedly circuitous route of definition and classification that words can lead to activity in cultures rooted in classical, western traditions. The hope is that once an entity is named, it becomes manifest. It is also why definitions can cause such *sturm* and *drang* in academic circles.

Librarian Lawrence J. McCrank addressed the problematic process of establishing definitions for emerging concepts in an essay about the historical significance of library competencies defined as *information literacy*:

> What is in a name, then? Everything! . . . The naming of new concepts or coining neologisms is always fraught with problems. Some usage dissolves quickly into jargon, some catches on for short fads, and some is deliberate propaganda, but other words last because they are substantive, are meaningful to more than their inventors, and are sustained by users who give the term life. (McCrank, 1992, p. 485)

Definitions may be sustained, but obviously they don't last forever. This is especially true for "umbrella" terms that shelter a host of related, sprawling ideas. This is apparently the case for the word *literacy*. For some time, it has been of concern to a diverse and growing number of people that traditional notions of alphabetic literacy, that is, the reading and writing of print, do not begin to encompass the wide range of real and perceived literacy needs for contemporary times. To critics and change agents, literacy, as currently practiced in school settings, does not seem to take into account the glut of information available to people, or the amount of electronic information they use, or the new interactive nature of mediated experience, or converged/multiple modalities, or the confluence of digital media forms and content. The all-purpose word *literacy* seems hopelessly anachronistic, tainted with the nostalgic ghost of a fleeting Industrial Age.

> In ancient Rome (literacy) referred to the letters of the alphabet and, by extension, to the epistles of earliest times. With the passage of the years, however, it came to be identified with literature and the increasingly crucial skills required in written communication. Little more than a decade ago, the term "universal literacy" simply meant the hope that all men could have made available to them the skills of reading and writing. But the term continues to change as the means of communication change. Today literacy [consists of]

the skills with which man manipulates the many media of mass communication. (Postman, 1971, p. 26)

Operative definitions for the broad term *literacy* have become so mired in cultural politics and theoretical hairsplitting that a constellation of multiple kinds of literacy has emerged to represent addenda to literacy, or aspects of literacy that are felt to be missing in its common usage. Perhaps this is an inevitable trend at the end of one century marked by the tangible commodities of industry and another century that is synonymous with the more abstract and less tangible concept of information. It is becoming increasingly obvious that there is a disconnect in the old adage, "Knowledge is power." In fact, the relationship between the two gets murkier by the day: Data is certainly not information and information is not, in itself, knowledge and knowledge does not, necessarily, lead to power. And so, what good does it do to live in an age of information? And furthermore, where does literacy fit in? There is a widely held perception that society needs a "new and improved" literacy that is responsive to the times at hand.

> The writers and educators who have used terms like "media literacy" and "visual literacy" do so with that usage in mind. Both terms are, in a sense, analogies; they are used to say that an audiovisual learning experience can be like a reading experience. Clearly, "literacy" has been stretched beyond the definition of reading and writing letters, not necessarily out of irreverence towards print but as a reaction to technological advancements in communication. Perhaps "literacy" is the wrong word to associate with media and visual learning, but lament over the literacy meaning of somewhat oxymoronic terms is too late. Visual literacy and media literacy have become established educational jargon. (Johnson, 1977, p. 7)

A CASE FOR MULTILITERACIES

Literacy theorist David Olson (1977) welcomed the contributions of electronic media to literacy: "To take explicit written prose as the model of a language, knowledge and intelligence has narrowed the conception of all three, downgrading the general functions of ordinary language and common sense knowledge" (p. 75). A more expansive view of literacy has been presented by scholars from a variety of disciplines as "literacies," or "multiple literacies," or "multiliteracies" (The New London Group, 1996, p. 63).

These literacies have been called *computer literacy* (Horton, 1983, p. 14), *information literacy* (Farmer & Mech, 1992; Sutton, 1994), *technology literacy* (Thomas & Knezek, 1993; U.S. Department of Education, 1996), *visual literacy* (Considine, 1986; Considine & Haley, 1993; Messaris, 1994; Moore & Dwyer, 1994), and *media literacy* (Considine, 1990, 1995a, 1995b; Considine

& Haley, 1993; Hobbs, 1994; Lloyd-Kolkin & Tyner, 1991; Silverblatt, 1995; Silverblatt & Eliceiri, 1997). There are others:

> . . . the many literacies in addition to or "beyond" "traditional" alphabetic literacy—from those of science and numeracy, to the spatial literacy that some geographers term "graphicacy," to the loudly touted and seemingly highly vulnerable "cultural literacy," "historical literacy," and "moral literacy." Some among the lengthening lists are long established in presumption but much more novel discursively or semantically: ecological literacy, "teleliteracy" and other media literacies, food literacy, emotional literacy, sexual literacy. (Graff, 1995, p. 321)

As previously mentioned, the current impetus for changing definitions of literacy is a wide perception of roiling institutional change brought about by technology. Attempts to define various literacies represent a complex multiplicity of purposes for literacy that reflect changing social and economic realities: frequent intercultural interaction; rapid use and combinations of a variety of discursive modes; availability of a wide variety of popular texts; converging, multimedia forms; a proliferation of communication channels for both commercial and personal purposes; enhanced opportunities for individual expression outside of commercial media industries; changing ideals and expectations for public schooling; the influence of new media on the political process; and shifts in job roles and opportunities caused by a global, free market economy.

Multiliteracies related to communication and information, notably media literacy, computer literacy, visual literacy, information literacy, network literacy, and technology have stepped forward to define the changing, amorphous shape of communication needs for a society awash in electronic sounds, images, icons, and texts. Indeed, these neologisms have contributed some defining characteristics that might be considered for literacy needs within contemporary contexts.

Little research has been done to link them to the ground breaking concept of multiple intelligences developed by Harvard educational psychologist Howard Gardner (Gardner, 1991, 1993; see also Armstrong, 1994), or the related uses of digital communication to leverage the preferred learning modalities of individuals. The term *multiliteracy* resonates and rides on the name recognition factor of Gardner's theories of multiple intelligences— theories that are increasingly popular with educators.

Multiliteracy practices insinuate a need for a range of modalities that seem to be compatible with Gardner's work in incorporating a wider range of learning modalities in the classroom. In brief, Gardner's theory has been abridged to at least "seven ways of knowing" that include the following intelligences: logical/mathematical; visual/spatial; bodily/kinesthetic; musical/rhythmic; interpersonal; intrapersonal; and linguistic. Later, Gardner added an eighth "way of knowing" he calls "naturalist."

Gardner's compelling theory of multiple intelligence has run into problems of oversimplification when teachers "mis-diagnose" students or when the theory is misused to label, categorize, and pigeonhole students into their preferred modalities. Instead, the theory can be used to structure educational environments that offer students the opportunity to become proficient in all the categories of intelligence. Nonetheless, when encouraged to become proficient in as many "intelligences" as possible, the sensory range provided by multimedia experiences holds the possibility to integrate and expand a learner's preferred approaches to learning to include at least a cursory understanding and some experience with each of the "ways of knowing." This may be especially true of young learners who have not yet mastered alphabetic literacy practices, but who have strong visual and verbal comprehension skills (Robertson Stephens & Company, 1993, p. 9).

Just as oversimplification is a problem found in practical application of the theory of multiple *intelligences*, the tendency to oversimplify the concept of *multiliteracies* can be similarly problematic. Multiliteracies suggest a splintering of literacy into discrete parts that belie the true nature of literacy as a complex and intersecting set of social actions. Multiliteracies also carry the unfortunate connotation that one literacy is as good as the next, when the operant question should instead be, "good for what?" Because their competencies and characteristics overlap, multiliteracies are not necessarily discrete from one another, although there may be discrete facets to each articulation of literacy. This is particularly true in the focus each might have on specialized tools, such as bibliographic search engines for information literacy, video cameras and image-manipulation software for media literacy, computer graphics for visual literacy, statistical software packages and calculating engines for mathematical literacy, and so forth. Furthermore, the goal of the teacher is to expand the number of choices available to students. An understanding of the many literacies and their uses offers opportunities for students to become as proficient in as many literacies and learning styles as possible—not only those with which the student finds an affinity.

The discussion of multiliteracies that center on the use of communication technologies provides some focus to examine the relationship between traditional notions of literacy and multiliteracies. There are more common features to each of the emerging communication multiliteracies than not. It is fair to say that—at least in theory—all of the technology-related multiliteracies strive for some version of critical literacy. Furthermore, multiliteracies are inseparable from and supportive of the many principles associated with the research-base for literacy. For example, no one would suggest that a media literate person would not also be able to critically read novels, or to write letters; or that a person who is numerically literate might not also want to know how to construct a Web page, or to participate in an online chat.

In spite of its potential usefulness, little has been done to highlight the links between various literacies in a cross-disciplinary way. Multiliteracies can be better conceptualized as elements subsumed under the broad and flexible umbrella of literacy. Proponents of new literacies hope to have a positive influence on literacy policies and then get down to the intricate business of literacy teaching and learning by incorporating some effective methodologies. Unfortunately, beyond their respective attempts at definition, even the substance of these hybrid areas of literacy study are still speculative and formative and their methodologies and optimum pedagogies largely untested.

Although their very names—information literacy, visual literacy, computer literacy, media literacy, and especially technology literacy—hint at an important sense of urgency as proponents clamor for inclusion in the circle of literacy, multiliteracies appear more reactionary than responsive to a world in flux. Just as the research base moves from theory building to field-based research and back again as it informs the historical boundaries between oral and print cultures, each multiliteracy must go through a number of rigorous research phases in order to prove its credibility and utility. With the exception of the enthusiastic McLuhanists, who gamely make pronouncements about nearly any communication technology, alphabetic literacy researchers are still as tentative about the nature of multiliteracies as they are about electronic literacy.

> The extent to which the newly proliferating literacies signify little more than a semantic "name game" or a feature of the politics of literacy and education or professional specialization raises hard questions. . . . An enormously important set of critical developments, whose potentially revolutionary consequences for learning and teaching are largely unappreciated, thus far remain prisoner to scholarly, cultural, and pedagogical fragmentation. (Graff, 1995, p. 321)

At present, multiliteracies have proven to be not much more than defensive shields in the face of the rapidly changing societal needs of a technological, information-glutted, increasingly consumerist global village. To be sure, this apparent superficiality does not mean that it is not viable to examine the many facets of literacy, but rather that evidence of their viability is not available. As seen in its broader uses throughout history, literacy can be used to entrench the *status quo* as easily as it can be used to accommodate change. New versions of literacy deliberately set themselves apart from the old monolithic concept of literacy by grafting special tags—qualifying adjectives (media, visual, information, computer)—that attempt to push the boundaries of literacy to address a host of needs and purposes that presumably are not currently represented by operative notions of alphabetic literacy. These hybrids hope to create a synergistic definition from the sum of the parts in a way that one word alone would not. As often happens, the qualifiers themselves are so confusing and jam-packed with purpose that they overreach and obfuscate as much about literacy as they clarify. For example, *media literacy* reacts and sets itself apart from the presumed print bias of literacy in order to nudge a consideration of electronic forms of communication and popular texts into formal educational settings. *Visual literacy* reacts to a relative neglect of design, aesthetics, and graphics in the teaching of literacy. *Network literacy, computer literacy,* and *technology literacy* react to the astonishing proliferation of computerized technology and its influence on education, work, and lifestyles. *Information literacy* is a reaction to the changing nature of libraries and the role of librarians at the turn of the 20th century. *Cultural literacy* reacts—often with anxiety—to the need for cross-cultural understanding in a diverse, global, environment—or conversely, to entrench a dominant cultural perspective. *Numerical literacy* reacts to the perception that ordinary citizens cannot fathom the complex economic, scientific, and technical information that confronts them daily.

Finally, because of the inseparable relationship between literacy and schooling, each new iteration of literacy must also react to the dramatic, cyclical calls to dismantle and overhaul contemporary public schooling. School reform carries with it an urgency that pressures the new ideas for literacy to consolidate quickly in order to define their place in the "schools of tomorrow." Beleaguered teachers are already pressured by special interest groups to insert a mind-boggling array of lessons and units into the existing curriculum. Without a sound rationale about the usefulness of multiliteracies across the curriculum, the call to expand literacy can only add to the classroom teacher's burden.

Because of the paucity of research on the subject, the relationship that multiliteracies have with one another, or even with traditional notions of alphabetic literacy, remains to be seen. Before multiliteracies can demonstrate significant influence on what it means to be literate, a review of the literature on the subject suggests that each needs more time to "cook," that is, interested professionals must have opportunities for discourse around definitions and core competencies and these theories must be field-tested in authentic learning environments in order for the ideas to be credibly served up for general consumption. Teachers must have the room to experiment with literacy in relationship to the needs of their students, and then to reflect on the practice.

This of course takes time, and the public has run short of patience with educational tinkering, no matter how sensible and well-intentioned. It is increasingly difficult to gin up public enthusiasm for educational reform campaigns, especially for literacy, a subject in which most people like to consider themselves expert. Although each of the multiliteracies has its champions, the implementation of new literacy ideas looks less like a traditional literacy campaign and more like an ad hoc revolution already in play, school by school, teacher by teacher, and parent by parent.

Recognition of the multiple meanings and varieties of literacy . . . argues for a diversity of educational approaches, informal and community-based as well as formal and school-based . . . effective literacy programs are those that are responsive to perceived needs, whether for functional skills, social power, or self-improvement. . . . The road to maximal literacy may begin for some through the feeder routes of a wide variety of specific literacies. (Scribner, 1989, p. 81)

People will certainly try to find the literacy they need, and over time it is probable that the boundaries of literacy will eventually collapse to include many of the goals and strategies being promoted by the definers of *multiliteracies*. In spite of alarmist rhetoric that prods educators to keep up with the tumultuous changes in technology with corresponding changes in literacy, a patient and measured approach to the theory and practice of literacy, in all its manifestations, is still in order.

CHAPTER FIVE

Beyond Access

Classroom teachers cannot fail to notice the mismatch between children's use of electronic literacy practices at home and in the community and those they use at school:

> The texture and rhythm of learning when mediated by electronic resources is in sharp contrast to that which occurs in the environment of the printed word. This is the fundamental "two cultures" problem of schools . . . as "literate tradition" teachers try and too often fail to teach "electronic tradition" students. (Fulton, 1996, p. 34)

The field of educational technology grows out of educational theory and strives for practicality. It examines an array of information resources and defines them by their purpose and audience in a euphemistic and arbitrary genre known as "educational" media—educational television, educational software, textbooks, and so on. By separating itself into a narrowly defined category of *educational* resources, the genre of educational media implies that the selection and organizational function traditionally done by the teacher has been prefiltered by the producers of educational products. The production process that renders the information *educational* also has the potential to divorce the products from their original source documents and to skirt the issue of popular culture's place in the classroom. The creation of special educational media saves teacher's time and provides a mechanism for gatekeeping information that adults may deem inappropriate for students. It allows information to be specially designed for instruction. Thus, instead of going to a local theater to see a Shakespearean play, students watch a televised version. Instead of going to a museum to view Impressionistic art, students see a curated show on CD–ROM. Instead of reading a biography of an explorer, students read an abridged version in a textbook. The primary purpose of educational technology research is to address the question of efficacy, that is, "effectiveness": "What educational media, used with what technologies, work with what students, under what conditions?"

Educational technology proponents would find it easier to answer such questions if the field operated from a stronger theory base, grafting ideas from both alphabetic literacy and communication studies onto educational research. Because of the continued link between literacy and schooling, the study of existing literacy practices is a natural testbed for scholars from a number of disciplines to explore and extend literacy research into the digital frontier. Similarly, literacy theory could do much to inform communication scholarship. Literacy researchers could also provide an *entrée* into K–12 education for their colleagues in communication studies. Such collaboration of interested parties in applied settings has the potential to move literacy research into the area of electronic and digital communication modes, multiliteracies, and new literacy practices. At the same time, collaborative research can refresh both educational and communication research with the epistemology, methodologies, and interpretative frameworks of the literacy historian.

The ubiquitous presence of digital tools is an everyday feature of nearly every other contemporary social institution. Youth are wired. They daily use all manner of electronic media at home and in their neighborhoods. Students who do not have computers at home encounter them at friends' houses, in stores, libraries, video parlors, and on kiosks in public spaces. In contrast, digital tools are uncommon and precious in the average classroom. Their special status or relative absence in the classroom is oddly out of step and painfully in the way when students attempt to accomplish classroom tasks. The looming contrast that students perceive between the electronic world of home and neighborhood and the unplugged world of school must seem curious to them. Because there is no straightforward reason for this disjuncture, technology's uneasy role in the classroom goes largely unremarked to students. Students often believe that a lack of money is the explanation for the low-tech nature of their classrooms. But school funding issues are still largely concentrated on the procurement of tools and do very little to address the anachronistic culture of schooling. School's focus on the acquisition of digital tools is understandable, but shortsighted because it detracts from solutions to the processes and organizational structures that stunt their actual use in classrooms. The barriers range all the way from Board of Education policies to curriculum content to the teaching styles of individual teachers. Until the culture of schooling, classroom pedagogy, and curricular issues are addressed in conjunction with technology access, it is not at all certain that high-tech tools would be used to benefit student performance, even if every student had unlimited access to information technologies.

Many more perspectives are needed to shape the debate about the specific uses of new and emerging communication technologies if teaching and learning are to be responsive to students who live in a world awash with information. It is in the best interest of scholars to push past the old bifurcations and dichotomies and extend their support to colleagues who teach in both formal and informal settings, within and outside postsecondary education. In the absence of theory, research about education's place in the digital world continues to be highly speculative, informing the uses of tools instead of the uses of literacy.

EDUCATIONAL TECHNOLOGY:
TOOLS IN SEARCH OF A THEORY

As early as 1983, the National Commission on Excellence in Education saw the need for all students to become "technology literate" as part of a basic high school education. In *A Nation at Risk*, the commission recommended that students: (a) understand the computer as an information computation and communication device; (b) use the computer in the study of the other basics and for personal and work-related purposes; and (c) understand the world of computers, electronics, and related technologies (U.S. Department of Education, 1983, p. 26).

Not since the days of Sputnik has technology been so forceful in capturing the public's imagination. Several surveys have revealed that U.S. citizens have high hopes for computer technologies: 80% believe that teaching computer skills to students is "absolutely essential" (Public Agenda Foundation, 1995); more than 75% have encouraged a child to use a computer (Intelliquest, 1995); and 86% believe that a computer is the most beneficial and effective product they could buy to expand their children's opportunities (U.S. Department of Education, 1996, p. 10).

Responding to the public's desire for more technology in schools, U.S. President Bill Clinton, in his January 1996 State of the Union speech, announced that "every classroom in America must be connected to the information superhighway . . . by the year 2000" at an estimated cost of $47 billion. The election year pronouncement was one of the administration's educational reform strategies, and Clinton's desire to wire schools was echoed by leading politicians from cabinet officers to governors to local officials. It was clear that when politicians said "technology," they meant "computers." And specifically, they envisioned the use of computer networks to deliver "quality," prepackaged information resources to students in a unidirectional way. Although the use of video, videoconferencing, and multimedia "push" technologies are fast-growth areas in both business and education (Michigan Department of Education, 1996), little mention is made in educational technology policy documents of the 1990s about the use of audio and video technologies. Another glaring omission in technology policy documents is pedagogical in nature. Although growing numbers of technology tools are used to support student expression, policy documents about the use of tools by students and teachers to deliver their own noncommercial content is in short supply.

Support for widespread technology use in schools is strong from the business and political sectors, but the rhetoric is unfocused and disconnected from the realities of what must be done to get there. The research is not of much help either. The body of evidence demonstrating technology's use in educational settings is long on testimonials gathered through descriptive case studies of technology in specific educational settings and short on hard evidence of student progress—a case of preaching to the choir. Other types of corroborating evidence are far less available. The little research that does connect technology with student achievement is inconsistent at best. Furthermore, the methodologies that seek to gather evidence of the efficacy of technology for educational purposes tends to be dominated by "heartwarming" stories—descriptive narratives that are overwhelmingly positive and border on the naive. To illustrate this point, Collis and Levin (1993) found that the majority of available research studies followed "a descriptive, single case methodology" and that such research frequently failed to provide justification for the generalizations about computers in education.

Reviews of literature about the uses of technology for learning have been done over the years. In a 1974 report funded by the Council of Europe, Peggy Campeau published an extensive report on the way media are selected for specific learning tasks in adult education. She concluded:

> It was hoped that results of studies on the instructional effectiveness of media under a variety of learner and treatment conditions could be applied to the task of attempting to construct a media taxonomy. The disappointing result of the literature search was that little more than a dozen experimental studies were found. . . . What is most impressive about this formidable body of literature surveyed for this review is that it shows that instructional media are being used extensively, under many diverse conditions, and that enormous amounts of money are being spent for the installation of very expensive equipment. All indications are that decisions as to which audiovisual device to purchase, install and use have been based on administrative and organizational requirements, and on considerations of cost, availability, and user preference, not on evidence of instructional effectiveness—and no wonder. To date, media research in post-school education has not provided decision makers with practical, valid, dependable guidelines for making these choices on the basis of instructional effectiveness. (Campeau, 1974, p. 31)

In 1977, Wilbur Schramm did an exhaustive review of the literature about learning and technology. He compiled experimental studies in a variety of media, including computer-assisted instruction. He compared the literature on mental ability and media and concluded:

> From the experimental studies we have plentiful evidence that people learn from the media, but very little evidence as to which medium, in a given situation, can bring about the *most* learning. We have hints that one medium may be more effective than another for a given learning task or a given kind of learner, but little systematic proof. Thus we can use the media with considerable confidence that students will learn from them, but, if we rely only on the experimental evidence, not with much discrimination. (Schramm, 1977, p. 43)

In his 1965 book, *The Conditions of Learning*, Robert Gagne cautioned that research evidence does not support the generalizations that there are "auditory-minded" and "visual-minded" individuals who work best with like-minded media (pp. 363–364). He said, "While a number of studies have been conducted with the aim of matching media to human ability differences, it is difficult to find any investigations from which one can draw unequivocal conclusions" (cited in Schramm, p. 60). He concluded the obvious: (a) No single medium is likely to have properties that make it best for all purposes, and (b) most instructional functions can be performed by most media (Gagne, p. 364). His point was not that there was no merit in attempting to match learners with media; rather, it was that the research on the subject was of limited usefulness as a guide to classroom practice. Gagne found a need to incorporate experimental evidence with qualitative information about classroom practice and pedagogy.

Little has changed 20 years after these findings were published. There is such a dearth of research about the use of digital technologies in schooling that in 1996, *Model Nets*, a major study of computer networking conducted by a consortium of federal education and energy laboratories, found "*no* large-scale studies of network use in schools that had tested the assumption that computer networking is a powerful tool that can both help students learn better and help teachers teach better" (Los Alamos National Laboratory, 1996, p. 5).

In a 1997 study done by Educational Testing Service, the authors commented:

> More pedagogically complex uses of educational technology generally show more inconclusive results. . . . Evaluations of educational technology are really evaluations of instruction enabled by technology and the outcomes are highly dependent on the implementation of the instructional design. Evaluations of educational technology applications must confront a number of methodological problems, including the need for measures other than standardized tests, differences among students in opportunity to learn, and differences in starting points and program implementation. (Coley, Cradler, & Engel, 1997, pp. 4–5)

Coley et al. (1997) estimated that the cost of technology in 1997 was about $3 billion, or an average of $70 per pupil (p. 5). Even though this accounts for only about 1% of total education spending, it would be comforting to have more research to indicate that the money was well spent. Because of a paucity of evidence that technology actually improves student performance, it is likely that the political call for more digital tools has more to do with issues of social justice and partisan economics than with an expectation in the actual improvement of student gains.

The quest for broad access to information has a particular cultural resonance in the United States that borders on the mythic. "Access" ties into an admirable American cultural preoccupation with fairness and equal opportunity. The equal access concept resonates with the conventional wisdom that information is the cornerstone of a participatory democracy and a healthy economy. Furthermore, multiliteracies that focus on access to electronic tools, in a technological determinist way, are often aligned with familiar modernist beliefs that equate literacy with progress:

> The production, transmission and processing of the most varied information will be at the heart of economic activity and social life . . . through its links with data processing and telecommunications, the electronics complex during the next quarter of a century will be the main pole around which the productive structures of the advanced industrial societies will be reorganised. (Smith, 1982, p. 14)

Policies for what can be done after access is achieved are only beginning to emerge. Confusion about technology's purpose in the classroom is reflected in actual classroom practice. A 1994 study by the Educational Testing Service (Campbell, Voelke, & Donahue, 1996) found that the uses of computers at home and in school were not clearly tied to focused curricular purposes. All students reported that they used the computer mostly to play games (87% of K–8 students and 77% of high school students). They also used the computer to retrieve information, "to learn things" (82% of K–8 students; 71% of high school students) and to write stories or papers (68% of fourth graders; 82% of eighth graders; and 87% of 11th graders). About half of all students surveyed used a computer at home.

What this means to improvements in teaching and learning remains to be seen. Coley, Cradler, and Engel (1997) cautioned: "We need to remember two important things: First, computers in and of themselves do very little to aid learning. . . . Second, no single task or activity has profound and lasting effects on learning by itself" (p. 7).

Because the research base cannot support predictions of educational technologies benefit to the classroom, pragmatic techno-boosters try to steer clear of thorny school reform issues. Instead of converging issues of literacy, technology and school reform, they would prefer to divorce technology from educational reform questions (Loveless, 1996). It is clear that niggling questions about the actual classroom uses of technology are an irritant that threatens to slow their penetration. Technology proponents fear that educational technology can bog down in the mire of school reform:

> Some computer advocates argue that computers will become integrated into our schools only when teachers teach differently than they do now and students study a different curriculum. Others have suggested that we can make headway in getting teachers to use computers in instruction if we stop trying to get teachers to do their jobs differently and begin using technology to help teachers do their jobs as they do them now. Once the use of computers is unhitched from movements to reform teaching and redesign the curriculum, technology stands a better chance of assuming an important educational role. (Coley et al., p. 7)

NETWORKED COMPUTERS AS LITERACY

The term *network literacy* is also thought of as a local economic development issue, although networked computers have important pedagogical implications for content delivery, project-based work, community involvement, peer instruction, and so on.

Students should have access to the communication opportunities, as well as the quality educational resources, offered by networked computers. In the case of mediated online instruction, this might include both informational and human resources. Collaborative software that allows users to interact simultaneously in virtual spaces, such as multiuser domains (MUDDs), multiuser object-oriented environments (MOOSs), multiuser virtual environments (MUVEs), and various "chat" schemes show great promise. As networking tools become more robust, the potential for networks to be used to enhance communication through videoconferencing and teleconferencing is also being explored as a way to enrich the educational experience. The descriptive accounts about classroom practice in the research captures student motivation and engagement with such collaborative networks. Because networking breaks the cloistered atmosphere of the classroom, the question about the power of networked computers in the classroom is: "Which came first, the computer or the audience?"

A case in point is Pueblo, an innovative project funded by the National Science Foundation. Cynthia Olson is a classroom teacher at Longview Elementary in Phoenix, Arizona. Her school partnered with Phoenix College and Xerox Parc, a California think tank, to test the uses of MUDD software for education. MUDD, MOOS, and MUVE are all names for collaborative software that enables users to build virtual spaces, move virtual objects and do other group work to create virtual environments that allow them to log onto the Internet to communicate and to manipulate the digital environment in a way that could be called "hands-on." Longview students call the virtual community that they have created "Pueblo."

Longview is not a wealthy school. It is a K–6 school with a preschool component that serves inner-city children in low-income neighborhoods in Phoenix. Many families in the community are headed by single parents. The majority of the children at Longview speak Spanish as their first language and a significant number of Native American students at the school speak Navajo as their first language. Ms. Olson explained:

The technology group in our school is organized around a specific technology. It's a MOO/MUDD. Basically what that means is that we use a computer programming language that allows us to communicate and do things in a virtual environment. In that environment, there is a whole community of people who you can interact with and who you can talk with. We call that community, Pueblo. All this communication is done with words alone. Right now, there are no pictures involved at all. Kids are very active hands-on learners and most of them are also visual learners—they love visuals. Please keep in mind that I teach an ESL [English as a Second Language] classroom. Because the kids don't have a strong language base, I need a lot of visuals. We just need lots of pictures, anyway, because all my students seem to learn better when I include visuals. Right now we have the computer environment in our classroom and the kids are very excited about it. They like the fact that they can work on a computer, talk with other people. It's a motivating factor for them to use words.

What amazes me is that here I have this group of visual learners, and when we use Pueblo, there aren't any visuals. They have to read and write in words. And some of them are struggling with English, and they love getting on! They love to talk to people, and they love to make it do things. And so they're immersed in language constantly. If I ask them to read or write for 2 hours a day, solid, I'd have a hard time with that. As a teacher, I'd have to really walk around the room, monitor, get people going. But if I say to students, "Stay on the computer for 3 hours. Talk to people: write, communicate, *build* a house, write a story," they would do it. And they would love every minute of it. And they wouldn't go "Oh! I HAVE to do this, I don't wanna. . . ." I mean, there's just something about the computer that motivates them, that excites them.

I do have a couple of computers in the classroom in which kids can get on the Internet and kind of go out and explore. And I have not done any teaching specifically about the Internet—never really explained to them what it is. But there are kids who like to get on and go out there and look around and see what's there. And of course they love playing games on the computer. But even so, they spend most of their time on computers doing Pueblo. I think it is because with the MUDD, there is an audience there to listen to them. It's not just the same old audience in their classroom—same old teacher in the classroom. There are lots of adults out there who aren't teachers that they can learn from, too. We have a whole cadre of mentors. There are lots of other students out there who have similar problems, as well as those who have different lifestyles. There's just a rich audience that they can communicate with, that they can share things with. That just inspires them to keep learning and communicating. (C. Olson, personal communication, March 1997)

Historically, network literacy originated in association with the ability to use the library effectively. The notion expands the concept of library as well as literacy, to include "the larger context of network literacy brought about by the digital revolution and the networking of geographically dispersed digital resources" (Sutton, 1994, p. 13). In spite of its potential, it is questionable whether the concept of "networking literacy" alone has enough substance to qualify as a literacy in the classical sense. Is it the network, the potential for a greater audience, or another element that gives this kind of literacy its depth and dimension? Library scholar and writer Charles McClure seems to be aware of the dilemma of labeling a technology as *literacy* when he cautioned that the knowledge of network literacy is not a simple supplement to traditional literacy, but instead "a reconceptualized notion of literacy in an electronic society" (McClure, 1994, p. 119). McClure framed the concept of network literacy in the following way:

Knowledge: 1. awareness of the range and uses of global networked information resources and services; 2. understanding of the role and uses of networked information in problem solving and in performing basic life activities; and 3. understanding the system by which networked information is generated, managed, and made available.

Skills: 1. the ability to retrieve specific types of information from the network using a range of information discovery tools; 2. the ability to manipulate networked information by combining it with other resources, enhancing it, or otherwise increasing the value of the information for particular situations; and 3. the ability to use networked information to analyze and resolve both work-related and personal decisions and to obtain services that will enhance their overall quality of life. (p. 119)

COMPUTERS AS LITERACY

Behrens (1994) credits the term *computer literacy* to Forest Horton (1982, p. 31), editor of a four-volume analysis of the information infrastructure for the Information Industry Association. Apparently, Horton was moved to coin the neologism after *Time* magazine touted the computer as the 1982 "Man of the Year." Computer literacy, with its dependence on specific tools of production, works from essentially a technological determinist concept of literacy. It is a reactionary term that attempts to respond to the sudden and surprising proliferation of computer technologies in the environment. As computing machines converge and change, becoming less novel and more ubiquitous, it is safe to say that the urgency for computer literacy in the contemporary curriculum will probably recede as a distinct category of competencies. This is not because computer competencies are unimportant, but because the assumption that computer skills are basic to rudimentary education is becoming as engrained and widespread as the assumption that alphabetic literacy is essential. The most likely scenario is that the skill set now associated with computer literacy will be subsumed into other multiliteracy competencies that have to do with hands-on, experiential uses analogous to alphabetic reading and writing and visual illustration. It is interesting that in a millennium of alphabetic print use, "pen literacy" has never vied for its place as a multiliteracy category, perhaps because of its commonplace presence in the classroom. Barbara Kwasnick (1990), a theorist who attempts to marry computers with literacy concepts, does not miss the irony of this:

> As we move into an age where information plays an increasingly central role in our personal, social, and professional lives, reading and writing, long regarded as the cornerstones of literacy, may well come to be seen as instances of the far more generic concept of information-processing competencies. It is likely that, in retrospect, we will conclude that even today's "innovative" concept of computer literacy often refers to only the most superficial and transitory of the skills and competencies that will eventually define information literacy. (p. 127)

Nonetheless, the concept of computer literacy has not yet had its day. Its legitimacy as a multiliteracy may explain why there is still little general agreement about a precise definition of computer literacy, although some competencies have been enumerated. Library science expert Stuart Sutton (1994) breaks computer literacy into two generally agreed-upon components:

> 1. Enabling Technologies. A general understanding of the way computers work, including knowledge about the computer's CPU, operating principles and the principles of networks so that computer users can move around in a computing environment with relative ease. (p. 11)

> 2. Information Productivity Tools. These are software applications that allow computer users to create and manipulate texts and data so as to create new information in a variety of forms and to access existing information. (p. 11)

Computer literacy, as it is currently articulated, is equivalent to the study of how a hot lead press is set, so as to make sense of a printed text; or the study of the components of the VCR as a way to enjoy television programming; or to possess a detailed knowledge of how a billboard is pasted to its mounting, in order to understand the conventions of advertising. Futurist and technologist Stuart Papert thinks that such a technical determinist vision of computer literacy reflects an unimaginative and constricted way of thinking about the uses of computers in education:

> In some cases I think the skeptics might conceive of education and the effect of computers on it too narrowly. Instead of considering general cultural effects, they focus attention on the use of the computer as a device for programmed instruction. Skeptics then conclude that while the computer might produce some improvements in school learning, it is not likely to lead to fundamental change. In a sense, too, I think the skeptical view derives from a failure to appreciate just how much Piagetian learning takes place as a child grows up. If a person conceives of children's intellectual development (or for that matter, moral or social development) as deriving chiefly from deliberate teaching, then such a person would be likely to underestimate the potential effect that a massive presence of computers and other interactive objects might have on children. (Papert, cited in Harper, 1987, p. 53)

THE SUM OF THE PARTS

A number of curricula have been proposed that inform the use of information technologies by integrating cognitive skills with experiential education, critical literacy, and critical pedagogy. Curricula based on these critical processes have important implications for the use of digital technology for dynamic teaching and learning.

One example comes from the international group of scholars who call themselves "The New London Group." The New London Group proposes a "design curriculum" that attempts to integrate literacy theory with the uses of electronic literacy tools in classrooms by merging theories of literacy as discourse with those of constructivist pedagogy. Although specific elements of the design curriculum are "old hat" to both educational and literacy scholars, the concept does attempt to inform uses of emerging communication technologies by grafting it onto the research base of alphabetic literacy. The New London Group's curriculum also attempts to permeate discipline boundaries by providing a sound rationale to incorporate experiential arts education—a much neglected opportunity in U.S. schools—into existing humanities and science curricula.

Critical pedagogy cements the various multiliteracy strands together. The New London Group contends that the traditions of alphabetic literacy are now impossible to separate from pedagogy:

> . . . "mere literacy" remains centered on language only, and usually on a singular national form of language at that, which is conceived as a stable

system based on rules such as mastering sound-letter correspondence. . . .
Such a view of language will characteristically translate into a more or less
authoritarian kind of pedagogy. A pedagogy of multiliteracies, by contrast,
focuses on modes of representation much broader than language alone. These
differ according to culture and context and have specific, cognitive, cultural
and social effects. . . . Multiliteracies also create a different kind of pedagogy,
one in which language and other modes of meaning are dynamic representational resources, constantly being remade by their users as they work to
achieve their various cultural purposes. (p. 64)

The New London Group articulates three domains of discourse that contribute to its concept of multiliteracies, which are the cultural pressure points
for changing literacy needs: changing public lives, that is, the realm of
citizenship; changing working lives in the global context of hyper-capitalism;
and changing private lives, marked by increased media discourse that mimics
public speech and is therefore an inauthentic version of both private and
public discourse. The New London Group's emphasis on the "inauthentic"
speech of media discourse owes much to the secondary orality theory of
Walter Ong, which differentiated "media speak" from authentic, oral literacy
(Ong, 1982).

The key to successful integration of multiliteracies in schooling is to stress
the manipulation of technology tools by students, so that they become
information providers as well as receivers. As is typical of those who have
noted the visual aspects of literacy (Donald, 1977, pp. 80–82; Ferguson,
1977, pp. 827–836; Gauthier, 1976; Ivins, 1969; and Burke, 1972), The New
London Group promotes the integration of a number of literacies through
a curriculum that places an emphasis on design. In this case, The New
London Group calls for literacy teaching that encourages students to become
social change agents who actively design their own futures in each of these
spheres through the manipulation of language, discourse, and literacies. By
emphasizing design elements, The New London Group does not necessarily
suggest creating hands-on experiences that result in end products. Although
tangible products may be part of the learning experience envisioned by The
New London Group, they stress the semiotic nature of design for meaning
making in cognitive work. Figure 1 illustrates some design elements isolated
by The New London Group to inform the pedagogy of their design curriculum concept (p. 83).

As seen in Fig. 1, The New London Group identifies several metalanguages
to describe and interpret some design elements that might be included in
a design for multiliteracies: linguistic, audio, visual, spatial, gestural, and
multimodal. The New London Group has invited scholars and teachers internationally to engage in investigative research about the classroom practice
related to the theory and practice of multiliteracies in the educational experience (p. 89). The New London Group builds on the literacy work of literacy

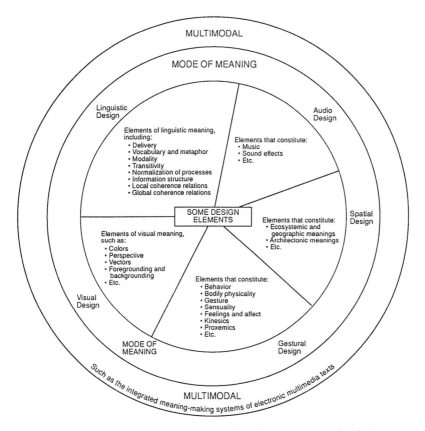

FIG. 1. Multiliteracies: metalanguages to describe and interpret the design elements of different modes of meaning. From The New London Group, "A Pedagogy of Multiliteracies Designing Social Futures," *Harvard Educational Review*, 66(1) (Spring 1996), p. 83. Copyright © 1996 by the President and Fellows of Harvard College. All rights reserved.

scholars who position literacy as discourse. They also incorporate school restructuring ideas from those who place an emphasis on experience in education in the tradition of John Dewey (Dewey, 1938), such as Ted Sizer of the Coalition of Essential Schools, the Breadloaf Network of teachers, and the Foxfire Networks (Foxfire Fund, 1990).

Although many classroom teachers have never heard of The New London Group, the design curriculum idea, in all its permutations, is being played out on an *ad hoc* and idiosyncratic basis in schools all over the world. In the United States, this paradigm of collective teaching and learning strategies might go under the name of *media literacy, information literacy, project-based education, constructivist education,* or even variations of *arts education,* to name a few. Unfortunately, such efforts are not officially tracked in bureaucratic and official databases, so information about programs related to the idea of design curriculum is anecdotal at best. This is partly because such programs require a degree of experimentation that is antithetical to the formal, public schooling bureaucracy. It is no surprise, then, that testbeds for design curriculum ideas have sprung forth in afterschool programs, continuation programs, private schools, magnet schools, and informal school structures that are marginal to the core public school curriculum. A common pattern in informal education structures involves the partnerships of classroom teachers in formal educational settings with artists who work in informal settings, such as afterschool or museum education programs. In some cases, artist-in-residency programs have been employed to include the media arts, as well as the traditional arts disciplines of dance, theater, visual arts, and so forth. Sample programs of this kind include the work of media arts centers such as Appalshop, in Whitesburg, Kentucky; Educational Video Center in New York City; James Coleman (aka HUEY) in Maine; 911 Gallery in Seattle, Washington; Southwest Alternate Media Project in Houston, Texas; the Digital Media Center in San Francisco, California; and Community TV Network in Chicago, Illinois. More of these artist–educator partnerships are springing up all the time around the use of digital media tools for creative expression and experiential learning.

Other efforts that follow precepts of the design curriculum idea have grown from humanities programs with a penchant for hands-on work: the Herald Project in San Francisco; the LA Mobilization Project in Los Angeles; Institute for Research and Learning in Santa Clara, California; and the Media Workshop in New York City are examples. Such programs unite the "making" skills of media artists with the cognitive skills of classroom teachers. Furthermore, the humanities programs have more rationale to go beyond simple student expression to include important social and historical contexts that contribute to a deeper understanding of media texts and audiences. Although the programs are popular and show signs of success in student performance, it is safe to say that their continued survival is precarious, due to the maverick status of media and the arts in the traditional curriculum.

The barriers to programs, projects, and pedagogies related to a design curriculum are made even more formidable because they are not united under a discrete subject area. Instead, because of the centrality of information resources to the curriculum, programs that are organized around the new uses of texts operate more like disciplines—they cut through every discrete subject area and are taught conceptually across the curriculum. Media scholar and documentary producer Eddie Dick, of the Scottish Film Council, made this point when he talked about the related discipline known in Europe as *media studies*:

> There is a linkage of knowledge, understanding and skills which come together to create a discipline, a methodological approach to sets of processes. This

means that it has less to do with content and more to do with the acquisition of analytical and practical skills. . . . Because it is a discipline and not a subject, it is important that Media Studies is not defined in an absolute way. There should be no "exclusion by definition." (Dick, 1987, p. 4)

Eddie Dick's statement about media studies is in reaction to efforts to incorporate it into the existing Scottish school curriculum as a discrete area of study. In contrast, Dick is saying that media education works best as an integral, yet flexible part of every subject area. In fact, the division of the curriculum into discrete areas of study, a prominent feature of education that adheres to the specialization of tasks seen in industrial societies, does not easily accommodate critical thinking strategies that blur the disciplines and work across the curriculum. Attempts to circumvent this reality by introducing design curricula into the existing school schedule as a discrete subject area are a necessary half-measure, but only as a short-term solution.

Although interdisciplinary education brings its own set of pluses and minuses, perhaps strategies for the optimum uses of new literacy are best accommodated by a softening of the boundaries between subject areas. The U.S. Department of Education study *Building Knowledge for a Nation of Learners* (1997) acknowledged the need for educational researchers to think beyond their own discrete subject areas to address three broad methodological challenges. The study recommends:

1. the integration of qualitative and quantitative research;
2. approaches to research that resonate for both national and local policy and practice; and
3. "methodological frameworks—protocols, criteria, strategies, languages—need to be developed that can help us compare, synthesize, and draw lessons from diverse studies even when they chronicle very different kinds of experiences or represent very different categories of data." (p. 6)

Such an approach to research about classroom practice could strengthen overall school improvement efforts, but it is particularly friendly to the strategies that employ the critical analysis and production of information. Because of the need to integrate the theory bases of education, communication, and literacy research in order for new literacy technologies to thrive, any strategy that encourages cross-disciplinary research into the uses of literacy is welcome.

Anecdotal research, opinion surveys, and attitudinal information from teachers hint at the promise of educational technology for school improvement. In a survey of the literature on the effectiveness of educational technology, policy analyst John Cradler (1995) suggested that technology has a significant positive effect on student achievement. He found positive influence for all major subject areas, in preschool through higher education, and for both regular education and special needs students. He stated that "evidence suggests that interactive video is especially effective when the skills and concepts to be learned have a visual component and when the software incorporates a research-based instructional design" (p. 2).

In 1993, technology researchers Margaret Honey and Andrés Henríquez surveyed 550 K–12 teachers who were active users of telecommunications. They found many positive aspects to using telecommunications in the classroom:

- Conducting telecommunications activities with students enables teachers to spend more time with individual students, less time lecturing to the whole class, and allows students to carry out more independent work. (p. 79)
- The most highly rated incentives for using telecommunications with students include expanding students' awareness about the world, accessing information that would otherwise be difficult to obtain, and increasing students' inquiry-based and analytical skills. (p. 20)
- Science, social awareness, and cultural exchange projects are perceived to be the most effective telecommunications activities to do with students. News services and scientific databases are rated as the most useful information retrieval activities for use with students. (p. 20)

Based on their findings, Honey and Henríquez (1993) suggested that in order for telecommunications to become a widely utilized educational resource, administrators and policy makers must implement the following: teacher training and support; school and district planning for use of telecommunications in instruction and administration; time for professional and student learning activities; effective assessment measures; financial support; and phone lines or local area networks (p. 34). The cited key factors that influenced the success of telecommunications include: a shared learning marked by planning, cooperation, and well-defined and relevant project goals (p. 20). In addition, Cradler (1995) found that the use of online telecommunications for collaboration across classrooms in different geographic locations has also been shown to improve academic skills.

Research of this kind makes sense, because it follows a literacy paradigm, that is, it takes a closer look at the pedagogy behind the uses of literacy tools. Educational technology studies are only beginning to focus on uses, or "application." Furthermore, if literacy can be halved into two universes, reading and writing, the literature about technology literacy predominantly supports the uses of technology to deliver instruction—the "reading" half of the literacy equation. This follows a one-way mass media paradigm that is increasingly anachronistic in comparison to the two-way, interactive potential of technology. In the mass media equation, students are primarily receivers of information selected by others.

The concept that users can also be information providers to a wide audience outside the classroom (writers), as well as receivers of information (readers), is only beginning to come into its own as a rationale for technology literacy. The ideal of users as information creators is nurtured by the encroaching presence of networked computers and video cameras in homes and community spaces. Beverly Hunter (1997) of BBN Educational Technologies commented:

> The basic paradigm shift is from an educational emphasis on people as recipients of information and knowledge to an emphasis on people as participants in the creation of information and knowledge. In a knowledge-based society and economy, intellectual capital is the means of production; its distribution is in large part a function of how we are educated. The overarching choice we face nationally and globally is to decide what proportion of people will experience a level and kind of education that will enable them to participate as producers of knowledge as well as its consumers. (p. 103)

Dr. Hunter calls for a technology infrastructure that is designed for "broad *participation*, as opposed to simple *access*" (p. 115). Absent educational "reforms and restructuring necessary to accommodate new literacy tools," she stated:

> It is hard to see how access to the Internet can be more than a distraction or at best a special interest of a few innovative teachers within a school. If the goals and objectives of a school community remain the traditional ones of scores on multiple-choice standardized tests, the cost of acquiring, installing, supporting, and learning to use the technology infrastructure is unlikely to be perceived by the taxpayers as being justified. (p. 119)

Others fear that the focus on machines will defer the dismantling of other more formidable barriers to educational opportunity. Educator W. H. Fraser said, "sometimes [there is] a tendency to search for problems that can be solved by a machine already purchased, rather than analyzing problems and determining what means (possibly including a microcomputer) can be used to solve the problem" (Fraser, cited in Harper, 1987, p. 53). Critics see technology as another "quick fix," a red herring that distracts the public from entrenched problems such as money, time, and community commitment to public education, leaving the original problems unresolved (Oppenheimer, 1997).

There is some evidence that new technologies hold promise to break down the barriers of social inequity. They enhance the curriculum and expand the resource base outside the four walls of the classroom by providing teachers and students with community mentors, information, and tools (Honey & Henríquez, 1996). Networked computers provide access to information that expands the school library of even the wealthiest schools (Berenfield, 1996). By broadening the social context of learning outside the classroom, some researchers have found networking to affect positively students' cognitive skills in reading, writing, and thinking (Powgrow, 1990; Riel, 1990). Beverly Hunter (1997) and others have argued that "in a knowledge-based economy it is the producers of knowledge who are rewarded" (p. 106; Reich, 1991). It is not the acquisition of such tools, but their uses that count. When students are moved toward a process of knowledge creation, then social equity issues can be addressed in positive and productive ways.

> Such systems could . . . be implemented in a manner that is designed to support and scaffold the user's continual learning processes, collaborations, and knowledge construction. The user is assumed to be growing in sophistication and therefore able to take advantage of increased functionality. . . . The choices we make now, at this formative stage in the evolution of cyberspace, will be a major factor in determining the learning opportunities of many people or a few people, which in turn will determine what a knowledge-based society *is.* (Hunter, 1997, pp. 114, 120)

LITERACY TOOLS IN ACTION: CROSSING THE DIVIDE

The conversation about literacy and technology in the United States has been dominated by the access issue, that is, the relationship between social inequities and equal access to information. In the education sector, this plays out in the scramble to wire all schools to wide area networks. Although it is indeed a vital school reform component, the information access issue, as it is currently framed, contains several flaws. Chief among them is the focus on access to information tools, that is, hardware, instead of on the cognitive processes to use the information once it has been downloaded. Often this plays out as a resource allocation issue—deep (and legitimate) resentment that rich schools receive high-tech toys while the children in poor schools are left behind.

The argument that a lack of information creates social injustice, and conversely, that more information technology resources can rectify social equity becomes tautological and obscures some true remedies to social inequity in education. Although access to information resources may be a factor in balancing social equity, evidence of the uses of literacy in the past has shown again and again that no literacy tool, by itself, has that kind of raw power. By focusing reform efforts on the technologies of schools instead of on their uses, creative opportunities to confront and negotiate the issues that may actually lead to social equity—such as critical thinking, knowledge creation, and lifelong learning opportunities—are diverted and postponed. Arguments for a plethora of new hardware stunt the debate about the relationship between information access and equal opportunity in education. The debate results in a kind of intellectual *cul de sac*.

Another such *cul de sac* is inadvertently created in the demand for more information resources, that is, content, for teaching and learning. This argument is especially difficult to tease out, because the need for information resources is genuinely acute. School libraries are closing and resource monies for classroom materials are shrinking. But when the problem is reframed, it becomes clear: More resources do not necessarily equal better educational opportunities. Instead, of more of the same, it would be useful to investigate the nature of classroom resource holdings to look for ways to enrich them with more *diverse* information resources from a wider range of discourses outside the highly managed content found in "educational media" fare.

Quality assurance or quality control schemes that attempt to rate and rank the perceived quality of classroom information resources are fraught with similar problems. The question of quality could be restated as one of purpose. The use of source documents, that is, original texts, as opposed to "canned" curriculum, is one way to get the most learning potential out of information used in the classroom. But the use of source documents, instead of textbook-based resources, creates problems for the average teacher. Teachers are already overloaded with classroom duties and may not have the time to research and organize classroom materials, based on original sources, for their diverse students' needs. Furthermore, most teachers have never had the preservice university training to accommodate the broad use of source documents in the classroom. Source documents create a number of other problems, not the least of which is that they call into question such time-honored structures of schooling as group instruction and the use of standardized tests.

Finally, the professional colleague who may offer the most support for teachers who want to attempt the use of source documents in the classroom is the school librarian or media specialist. Unfortunately, as funding for school library slips, this is the very personnel role that is eliminated at the first sign of budget shortfall.

The overriding problem is that both the quality and quantity of information resources differ so greatly from school to school that some students may never know the full benefits of either access to tools or the more critical processes to use information. Furthermore, those with the greatest need often have the fewest resources. It does no good to envision education without a plan to embrace the poorest, most needy schools. On the other hand, if all schools wait until resource allocation is equitable before they explore new uses for information technologies, all schools could wait forever. Funding schemes that block-grant technology funding to schools based on daily attendance records will always shortchange the rural and small schools—the very schools who have the most expensive start-up costs for technology infrastructures. Clearly, school-funding formulas that are both fair and nonpunitive are essential for information access to be resolved.

A lack of access to technology and information resources continues to reflect and underscore inequities in society and is therefore an entrenched and complex problem. Not surprisingly, evidence about school improvement shows that children from rich communities do better on a variety of school performance measures than children from poor communities. Because expensive technologies are concentrated in wealthier districts, it is difficult to say where technology ranks in relation to all the other educational enrichment interventions at the wealthier schools' disposable. Whether or not access to digital technologies can actually redress social inequity remains to be seen. At the very least, providing more access to technology to poor schools would not only level the playing field, it would help to answer the question of technology's benefit across a wider social strata. Equal distribution of technology tools could provide more sites where digital literacy tools could be studied as a viable intervention in the service of school improvement.

Research about the uses of technology in educational settings continues to be consumed with the information access question. Demographic comparisons are embedded in study after study. A study of nine technology-rich schools concluded that technology resulted in educational gains for all students, regardless of age, race, parental income, or other characteristics (Glenman & Meldmed, 1996, pp. 36–44). Technology-rich schools report higher attendance and lower dropout rates after computers are introduced (Dwyer, 1994, pp. 4–10). Nonetheless, "low-income, disabled and rural children are in danger of being left off the [information] highway" (Lazarus & Lippert, 1994, p. 5). In addition, "girls and children from diverse racial, ethnic and linguistic backgrounds are often marginalized by mass-marketed software and programming" that is created for an audience of boys (Lazarus & Lippert, 1994, p. 5). In 1994, "38% of all households with children [had] a computer, but whereas 48% of households with children whose family income is $50,000 or more have a child using a computer, only 7% of households with family income under $20,000 do" (p. 4). "Poor schools are less likely than rich schools to use networks and . . . schools with high percentages of minority students have less access to LAN technologies than other schools" (Coley et al., 1997, p. 21).

Most of the concern about technology access focuses on computers. In fact, computers are proliferating so rapidly it is almost impossible to pinpoint their growth. Between 1989 and 1992, schools' inventories of computers rose by nearly 50% (U.S. Congress, Office of Technology Assessment, 1995). In 1995, the U.S. Department of Education reported that 75% of public schools had computers with some type of networking, 35% had access to the Internet, and an additional 14% have access to other wide-area networks through commercial services (U.S. Department of Education, Office of Educational Research and Improvement, 1995). According to Quality Education Data, by 1996 the penetration of technology in U.S. public schools had increased significantly to the following percentages: computers, 98%; VCRs, 97%; multimedia computers, 85%; cable TV, 76%; Internet access, 64%; CD-ROM, 54%; networks, 38%; videodisc, 35%; and satellite technologies, 19% (Coley et al., 1997, p. 10). Furthermore, the ratio of students to computers had declined from 125 students per computer in 1984 to 10 students per computer in 1997 (p. 11).

Still, the range of access between states was wide: from a high of 16 students per computer in Louisiana to 5.9 students per computer in Florida (Coley et al., 1997, p. 12). Also, only 4% of U.S. schools had a computer for every four students, a ratio recommended by a California Education Technology Task Force (California Department of Education, 1995) and only 9% of individual classrooms are connected to the Internet. The numbers for schools serving large numbers of low-income students is even lower (U.S. Department of Education, 1996, p. 6). Internet access is provided by 77% of libraries serving populations of more than 1 million, compared to only 13.3% of libraries serving populations under 5,000 (American Library Association, 1994). Although the ratio of computers to users is rapidly shrinking, it is clear that relative income is an important factor in decisions about who has access to information technologies and who does not.

REFRAMING THE ACCESS ISSUE

Without losing sight of the need to equalize educational opportunity, the discussion of technology's place in education must proceed beyond the access issue. As the convergence of digital media promises hundreds of channels, delivering a torrent of digital and broadcast information, questions of who has access to what information become acute. The rush to define policies to ensure equal access to information has obscured other critical facets of both school reform and equal opportunity. In addition to the question of what people will do with more information once they receive it, it also useful to ask: Will citizens have ample opportunity to become skilled information providers as well as information receivers?

Although the focus on access to tools is not antithetical to electronic literacy and learning, it is certainly a narrow approach that makes it more difficult to include the more cognitive and less skill-based analysis of media systems and information texts. Tool-based literacies make it easier to access a range of information resources, but it is becoming increasingly apparent that new tools are delivering the same old content. It is impossible to pretend that digital channels of communication are invisible conduits for information, free of the messy ideological questions about form and content that plague alphabetic literacy. Furthermore, it is questionable that educators are making use of the technologies already available to them, to foster literacy in a critical way.

A broader concept of "technology infrastructure" beyond hardware and software is one step beyond access. Infrastructure can be expanded in an organizational and systems approach to include curriculum, instruction, policy, and the roles of the people involved. Another way out of the "access" cul de sac is to steer the discussion about technology and schooling away from its focus on tools, in order to frame the debate in terms of literacy. Such an approach takes schools where they are, that is, supports the use of their existing information technologies such as books and chalk, yet challenges schools to think of literacy in its most powerful forms. Such an approach rewards critical, investigatory, and creative uses of information, which in turn have the potential to lead to the critical autonomy of students. When cutting-edge information technologies become available to them, the hope is that students will then have the basic cognitive skills and concepts to use them in commanding ways. Such an approach places more emphasis on pedagogy and less on tools and resources.

A 10-year study done by Apple Classrooms of Tomorrow (Dwyer, 1996) found many positive changes after computers were introduced in classrooms. But the computers forced changes in teaching and learning that were not always within the comfort zone of educators. Teachers reported that they were personally working harder and longer hours, but enjoying their work more. They acted more as guides and less as lecturers. They learned new evaluation and assessment techniques. In short, technology moved the teachers away from their roots in traditional instruction techniques. A project research associate reported the staff's ambivalence about the changes:

> Children interacted with one another more frequently while working at computers. And the interactions were different—the students spontaneously helped each other. They were curious about what others were doing. They were excited about their own activities, and they were intently interested.
>
> These behaviors were juxtaposed against a backdrop in which the adults in the environment variously encouraged and discouraged alternative patterns of operating. It was as if they were not really sure whether to promote or inhibit new behaviors. (Phelan, cited in Dwyer, 1994, p. 6)

Although new communication tools show increasing promise for teachers and students, the primary constituents for networked tool literacies are still engineers, technocrats, government bureaucrats, and business interests—not necessarily schools. Furthermore, while calling for equitable access, free market business interests are extending and intensifying the gap between those who have and those who do not have access to information.

> Although we talk about networks' ability to extend literacy to excluded individuals, the reality is that the more technology is brought into our systems, the more chances exist for financial, cultural and social exigencies to limit access. (Wahlstrom, 1989, p. 175)

It remains to be seen if access to literacy resources can be solved without also addressing the larger issue of social inequity and its relationship to schooling. Literacy scholar Carl Kaestle cautioned, "Literacy is discriminatory with regard to both access and content. Problems of discrimination are not resolved just because access is achieved; there is a cultural price tag to literacy. Thus, whether literacy is liberating or constraining depends in part on whether it is used as an instrument of conformity or of creativity" (Kaestle et al., 1991, p. 30).

Further, initial access to technology is only the beginning of the problems created by educational technology in the classroom. More pressing is the question of technology integration into school practice, that is, "Access for what purpose?" Fred Carrigg, Director of Academic Programs in Union City, a model technology site in New Jersey, said, "Technology is a tool, not a philosophy. . . . You can't isolate it; it's meaningless unless it's integrated into the curriculum." His colleague, Rahman Karriem, an employee at Bell Atlantic, a corporate partner in the process, concurred: "You can't throw technology against the wall and expect it to stick. You have to develop internal human infrastructure to make it work" (Drennan, 1996).

In the absence of theory, and largely by default, powerful interests wait in the wings to define the uses of digital media for work, schooling, and recreational purposes. If history is any indication, new literacy tools have the potential to fall on the horns of Plato's Dilemma—either as mechanisms that contribute to personal and political liberation or as powerful tools that are used to maintain social inequity, control, and authoritarianism. In all probability, the uses of electronic literacy modes will vacillate between all possible purposes, sometimes operating at cross-purposes in the tense middle ground.

Literacy scholars are in a good position to inform the way that electronic media can contribute to the general social good by offering plausible theories of literacy in action. In the meantime, educators who try to work from an informed base of research about the optimum uses of literacy and the efficacy of technology in schooling must make do with the anecdotal evidence they extrapolate from educational technology research. Where theory fails teachers, actual practice fills the gap—teacher by teacher. The working relationship between teachers and students transcends the literacy divides, from oral through electronic, every day. The question for teachers at this point is "Which literacy?"

Representing Literacy
in the Age of Information

Three multiliteracies—computer, network, and technology—have implications for the general proliferation of new technology tools in society. For that reason, computer, network, and technology literacies can be discussed as *tool literacies*. Three others—information, visual, and media—are particularly relevant to the uses of technologies within the context of schooling. They stress the need to analyze information and to understand how meaning is created. Because they address the construction of information, as well as tools, information, visual, and media literacies can be characterized *as literacies of representation*. Information, visual, and media literacies have the potential to build on already familiar alphabetic literacy foundations in schooling. Whereas educators may need special training to use new technologies, they are secure in their ability to explicate texts with students. In other words, through the uses of approaches suggested by information, visual, and media literacy advocates, educators can apply familiar principles of alphabetical literacy to further the understanding of new genre and media while their tool skills are getting "up to speed."

Information literacy, visual literacy, and media literacy are closely compatible and provide some foundation for research and practice about the uses of literacy for contemporary schooling, because they contain critical literacy competencies that are familiar in alphabetic literacy. Of these, media literacy has the most established research base, due to its international practice over time in formal educational settings. Research and practice about media education has been ongoing since the 1960s (Aparici, 1996; Masterman & Mariet, 1994; Pungente, 1987, 1993; Quin & McMahon, 1993). Notably, it is embedded in the curriculum in most industrialized countries—except the

United States. It is mandated in the curriculum in Canada, England, Australia, and New Zealand, and offered in a host of non-English-speaking countries, including Austria, Brazil, France, Germany, Mexico, and Spain. Even so, this is not to imply that the research base for media education is particularly robust. Research about its efficacy in particular settings is still in its infancy.

Table 1 uses some popular definitions for several multiliteracies to compare their overlapping missions and skills sets. As Table 1 (p. 94) demonstrates, information literacy, media literacy, and visual literacy are compatible in terms of competencies and overlap with some of the principles of educational technology literacies. Nonetheless, the core constituencies of each multiliteracy differ slightly, and therefore each carries with it slightly different jargon and assumptions. Information literacy has a broad following among librarians and media specialists; visual literacy is often associated with instructional designers, educational technologists, and artists; and media literacy has a following that is embraced by social activists, artists, and educators. Even so, any of these three multiliteracies is appealing to those who wish to approach nonalphabetic literacy in a critical way.

LINKING LITERACIES

Rhetoric that seeks to prove the dominance of one multiliteracy over another raises the specter of yet another set of false dichotomies. Inauthentic continuums of this kind are decidedly beside the point. In the United States, the term *media literacy* is often used interchangeably with *information literacy* and *visual literacy,* and many of their aims are inseparable. In addition, they overlap with those of the tool literacies, that is, computer, network, and technology literacies, and so on. All of these terms are provisional and in flux. Paradoxically, they are neither yet precise enough, nor all-encompassing enough, to convey a broad understanding of the needs for literacy in a digital world, or of the relationship between multiliteracies. Nor is there enough of a consensus among the stakeholders about what can be done to foster "their" brand of literacy. Constituents within each category of literacy are vying for the public recognition of their particular interests and ideologies—sometimes in heated competition with their own allies.

In every problem lies an opportunity. The confusion created by the concept of multiliteracies does not appear to be dissipating anytime soon, and this is probably as it should be in a time of great social and economic upheaval. The encroachment of new communication technologies into every global sphere is serving to push the debate about the nuances of literacy outside academic circles to public forums, creating much confusion, but also enriching the debate through a diversity of perspectives. Literacy historian Harvey J. Graff (1995) commented:

TABLE 1
Comparative Definitions of Multiliteracies

Tool Literacies

Computer Literacy is:

a general understanding of the ways computers work, including knowledge about the computer's CPU, operating principles, and the principles of networks so that computer users can move around in a computing environment with relative ease (Sutton, 1994, p. 11).

Network Literacy is:

Knowledge: 1. awareness of the range and uses of global networked information resources and services; 2. understanding of the role and uses of networked information in problem solving and in performing basic life activities; and 3. understanding the system by which networked information is generated, managed, and made available.

Skills: 1. the ability to retrieve specific types of information from the network using a range of information discovery tools; 2. the ability to manipulate networked information by combining it with other resources, enhancing it, or otherwise increasing the value of the information for particular situations; and 3. the ability to use networked information to analyze and resolve both work-related and personal decisions and to obtain services that will enhance their [users] overall quality of life (McClure, 1994), p. 119).

Technology Literacy is:

a complex, integrated process involving people, procedures, ideas, devices, and organization for analyzing problems and devising, implementing, evaluating, and managing solutions to those problems, involved in all aspects of learning . . . (from the Association for Educational Communications and Technology's definition for educational technology, cited in Silber, 1981, p. 21).

Literacies of Representation

Information Literacy is:

the ability to find, evaluate, and use information effectively in personal and professional lives (American Library Association, 1991, p. 152).

the ability to locate, analyze, evaluate, synthesize, and use information from a variety of sources (Cleveland State University, 1990, p. 1).

Media Literacy is:

concerned with helping students develop an informed and critical understanding of the nature of the mass media, the techniques used by them, and the impact of these techniques. More specifically, it is education that aims to increase students' understanding and enjoyment of how media work, how they [media] produce meaning, how they are organized, and how they construct reality. Media literacy also aims to provide students with the ability to create media products (Ontario Ministry of Education, 1989, pp. 6-7).

the ability to access, analyze, and produce communication in a variety of forms (Aufderheide & Firestone, 1993, p. v).

(Continued)

TABLE 1
(Continued)

Visual Literacy is:

---

the ability to comprehend and create images in a variety of media in order to communicate effectively. It is important to note that this is broader in scope than are critical-viewing skills—the ability to analyze, understand, and appreciate visual messages . . . visual literacy contains the competencies of reading and writing. Visually literate students should be able to produce and interpret visual messages (Considine, 1986, p. 38).

the ability to understand and use images and to think and learn in terms of images, that is, to think visually (Horton, 1982).

the ability to understand (read) and use (write) images and to think and learn in terms of images (Johnson, 1977; Moore & Dwyer, 1994, p. 25).

That alphabetic literacy is one, albeit exceptionally valuable, set of abilities and competencies, among others, slowly influences thinking about schooling and learning . . . we find contradictions in literacy's and education's history in part from overvaluing alphabetic literacy *by itself* and slighting (or worse) other "literacies." Enormous implications for teaching and learning . . . follow from placing "traditional alphabetic" literacy within its appropriate communicative context along with, say numeracy and scientific literacy, oral and aural abilities, spatial literacy or graphicacy, visual and aesthetic literacy, etc. . . . How little we know about these "many literacies" sadly corresponds to poor instruction in a limited range of literacy and ignorance of the extent of common elements among different literacies that might support a potentially revolutionary remaking of schooling. . . . For such study, history provides a rich laboratory. The challenges of precise comparison across space as well as time, while absolutely mandated, loom large. Any useful notion of literacy or literacies must confront them. (Graff, p. 326)

What is at the center of the debate about multiliteracies is a host of questions about literacy in action: the uses of information in homes, communities, workplaces, and classrooms and the most promising pedagogies for optimum learning with information. By far, the most important and vexing question at the center of literacy inquiry is also the most deceptively simple: Why is it important for people to be literate at all?

Just as educational researchers can benefit from collaborative literacy studies, proponents of various multiliteracies could take advantage of compatible ideas, themes, and research. There are many points of mutual interest between the two. The dearth of collaborative research in multiliteracy study appears to be an ironic blind spot for those who call for an expansion of literacy in order to broaden the horizons of human communication. In spite of the potentials of a far-flung global telecommunications system for connecting people through computer networking, new theories about how the frontiers of literacy can be breached seem to be developing simultaneously among isolated interests. Given the specialized nature of work and study at the turn of the 20th century, perhaps it is simply too early to expect the cross-pollination of literacies. At the least, this lack of coordination between compatible interests indicates a missed opportunity for synergistic international work among those who are investigating the potential for an expanded kind of literacy. Projects that go beyond definition into a vision of curriculum and school change hold the promise for cross-disciplinary work.

> For a nation and a world in accelerating flux and change, the ability of people to mobilize their intellectual resources and renew their lives through flexible educational opportunities would seem to place a compelling burden on the new narrowcasting technologies, and on a new era of collaboration between educators and communicators. (Bonham, 1980, p. 35)

Where there is awareness of compatible ideas, there is also contention between and among the various literacy "camps," as they struggle for prominence. This tension goes well beyond academic myopia or philosophical disagreement and hints at the ideological bias inherent in various approaches to literacy. The most common of these biases demonstrates the chauvinism of alphabetic literacy in reaction to the perceived threat that other literacy modalities pose to its dominance:

> No mode or means of learning is neutral. Not only does all "knowledge" however elementary, incorporate the assumptions and expectations, the biases of emphases of its production, association, prior use, maintenance, and preservation. So too do the so-called tools or skills. With them, there are biases with respect to their transmission—the circumstances of learning and practice . . . the newly appreciated textual biases of formal schooling—"school" literacy—and most reading and writing shaped by such formative encounters, tutelage, and generally restricted or regulated practice at relatively early ages. Studies of the "media" of literacy, from script to print and beyond, only begin to suggest the intricately interacting relationships; contemporary confusion about the "future of print" compared to the visuality and aurality of electronic media have an impressively lengthy set of precedents. (Graff, 1995, p. 326)

On another level, the competitiveness between and among champions of various multiliteracies takes on the characteristics of job insecurity, most probably professional insecurity growing out of a context of changing social institutions and resulting opportunities for work roles within them. As criticism mounts and schools struggle to respond, the function of schools and libraries, as well as the roles and professional identities of educators, is increasingly speculative. Under this barrage of criticism and uncertainty, it is no wonder that educators try to depersonalize and deflect the blame for school "failure" to social shifts in the uses of literacy. This is done by either pointing out the shortcomings of alphabetic literacy in a technological age, or conversely, by decrying its demise in a futile attempt to shore up the fading dominance of print.

Instead of exploring fresh combinations of multiliteracies as a response to new media, the research literature represents an unfortunate tendency to promote one multiliteracy over another. It is as if proponents hope to define and position the most promising version of literacy in order to deflect educational criticism and maybe to even shore up some sagging professional status in the process. It is likely that proponents for each different kind of literacy will attempt to jockey "their" definition into existence through a range of methods that involve academic marketing, public relations, and other ways to appease the disgruntled public. In the context of such personal and professional confusion, framing the debate about "reforms" in education by reforming literacy begins to look like a solution in search of a problem.

There is certainly much work to do to harness the passion of multiliteracy proponents in order to foster a collaborative atmosphere for research and practice, for without some longitudinal evidence that new concepts of literacy are beneficial, these literacies will not prevail. The Appendix lists some of the groups who are attempting such collaboration. Through more collective, cross-disciplinary efforts to understand contemporary literacy needs and practices, a climate of both theory building and reflective practice can take root and grow. This is the first step toward their implementation in classrooms. Because multiliteracy efforts are coming at the issue from diverse perspectives, a coherent theory base is vital for its incorporation into formal schooling, but has yet to emerge. Until it does, organizing the independent ideas of the various multiliteracies into a vision for literacy at the turn of the century is like trying to herd cats.

THE LITERACY OF LIBRARIES

Information literacy is an abstract concept. As a metaphor, it is a neatly packaged, imaginative, and descriptive phrase that is not literally applicable or easily interpretable, employing something more qualitative and diffuse than is evident in the historical meanings of both *literacy* and *information*. Symbolically, information literacy appears to represent the ability to use information, or possibly the possession of a knowledge of information (Behrens, 1994, p. 309).

> *Information literacy* is difficult to define but easier to describe because it is an abstraction, an ideal, and an interlocking set of skills and knowledge that

is characterized by an ability or behavior rather than a specific subject domain. Standards for these criteria are lacking everywhere. (McCrank, 1992, pp. 485–486)

Following a failed attempt by library science advocates to require library skills courses across the core college curricula in the late 1960s, the term *information literacy* began to be used in library science circles interchangeably with *library-based research* in the mid-1970s (Osborne, 1989; McCrank, 1992, p. 487). In 1974, Paul Zurkowski, then president of the private sector's Information Industry Association (IIA), proposed an information literacy campaign to the National Commission on Libraries and Information Science (NCLIS) in response to businesses' need for skilled workers in an information service economy.

> People trained in the application of information resources to their work can be called information literates. They have learned techniques and skills for utilizing the wide range of information tools as well as primary sources in molding information-solutions to their problems. (Zurkowski, 1974, p. 6)

In an article that traces the history of information literacy, Shirley J. Behrens (1994) noted that various definitions of the term included the uses of information for problem solving, as well as the need to use new and existing tools to locate and manipulate information. "In analyzing the definitions of the 1970s, one can infer that information was seen as essential to society, and that information handling was becoming more complicated, owing to the perceived exponential growth in the amount of information available" (p. 31). As Behrens pointed out, in addition to the needs of information literacy for work-related problem solving, the term has been used to suggest a prerequisite for active citizenship (p. 310).

> Beyond information literacy for greater work effectiveness and efficiency, information literacy is needed to guarantee the survival of democratic institutions. All men are created equal but voters with information resources are in a position to make more intelligent decisions than citizens who are information illiterates. The application of information resources to the process of decision-making to fulfill civic responsibilities is a vital necessity. (Owens, 1976, p. 27)

In order to move information literacy away from a technical, skill-based approach into one that recognized the critical and cultural elements of literacy, it was necessary to go beyond information literacy's association with computer literacy. In an article for librarians, Forest Horton (1983) linked computer literacy to information literacy:

Computer literacy has to do with increasing our understanding of what the machine can and cannot do. There are two major components of computer literacy: hardware and software . . . information literacy then, as opposed to computer literacy, means raising the level of awareness of individuals and enterprises to the knowledge explosion and how machine-aided handling systems can help to identify, access and obtain data, documents and literature needed for problem-solving and decision-making. (pp. 14, 16)

Lawrence McCrank, Dean of Library and Instructional Services at Ferris State University in Michigan, cautioned that computer literacy is not an educational goal: "One does not communicate with a computer through literacy . . . one uses a computer as an electronic means of communication" (1992, p. 489). During the 1980s, the computer was nearly synonymous with information handling, and as a result, computer literacy became entwined with the information handling aspects of information literacy. At the same time, library scientists were beginning to modify computer literacy strategies with existing criteria for library user education. The emerging tenets of information literacy were starting to take shape with some actual skill and knowledge foundations.

In 1985, the Aurora Library at the Denver campus of the University of Colorado made a conscious attempt to update its library user education to embrace information literacy. A definition, attributed by Behrens to Martin Tessmer (Breivik, 1985, p. 312) emerged: "Information literacy is the ability to effectively access and evaluate information for a given need" (p. 723). Moreover, the University proposed some characteristics of information literacy that went beyond the narrow bibliographic location of information to include the understanding and evaluation of information in contexts both inside and outside the library (Behrens, 1994, p. 312).

By the 1990s, a nod toward the uses of information was incorporated into the concept. Librarians rallied around information literacy, spurred by a 1989 report of the American Library Association Presidential Committee on Information Literacy that provided a new definition:

To be information literate, a person must be able to recognize when information is needed and have the ability to locate, evaluate, and use effectively the needed information . . . information literate people are those who have learned how to learn. They know how to learn because they know how information is organized, how to find information and how to use information in such a way that others can learn from them. They are people prepared for lifelong learning, because they can always find the information needed for any task or decision at hand. (ALA, 1990, p. 1)

At a 1990 Midwinter Meeting, the ALA refined the definition of information literacy as "the ability to find, evaluate, and use information effectively in personal and professional lives (ALA, 1991, p. 152). Although useful as a starting point for library education programs, the content of such programs is still left up to the individual institutions of learning.

The evolution of information literacy occurred simultaneously with the release of *A Nation at Risk* (U.S. Department of Education, 1983), a scathing criticism of American education from the National Commission on Excellence in Education. Librarians were outraged that the report completely ignored the role of libraries and librarians in its recommendations for educational reform. It is impossible to know how this sense of exclusion played into the tenor of the discourse about information literacy. Certainly, librarians felt the need to market their role to the educational community. Information literacy was a reasonable concept that could demonstrate the responsiveness of library science to the needs of an information society. There was a heartfelt need to reiterate the central role of the library in school reform:

> Libraries are where the knowledge of all disciplines is related within a meaningful framework. Libraries provide a model for the information environment in which graduates will need to work and live. Libraries are a natural environment for problem solving within the unlimited universe of information. Libraries provide the framework for synthesizing specialized knowledge into broader societal contexts. And finally, libraries and librarians can help students master critical information-literacy skills. (Breivik & Gee, 1989, p. x)

McCrank (1992) is circumspect about the effort to use information literacy as a public relations ploy to promote the relevance of libraries.

> In the case of public relations *qua* public instruction, effective marketing would seem to depend upon a differentiation between library promotion *per se* and the library's promotion of information literacy. . . . The irony is that by creating independent and autonomous "amateur" librarians, information literacy has the potential to make the traditional library even less relevant to users. The aim of information literacy is to convert every man and woman into his or her own librarian—at least as well-intentioned and educated amateurs . . . . the aim of information literacy is to eliminate the mediation of librarians! (pp. 488–489)

Furthermore, with broad public acceptance of the credibility of information from a variety of nonlibrary sources, especially the Internet, the library can no longer be defined by its architectural space in time.

> If information literacy is meant to be ecumenical, embracing all forms of information, then librarians must also recognize that libraries have never had a monopoly on information as institutions or by virtue of their holdings. The scope of information literacy campaigns should include an array of information agencies and media in whatever formats . . . [while] libraries must show that

using collections is much more than reading a book, the thrust of information literacy programs must aim at more than using libraries. (p. 488)

The use of information literacy is still growing among librarians, but "its use is still largely confined to the delimited idea of finding, evaluating and using information in libraries" (McCrank, p. 487). Nonetheless, there are some attempts to try to broaden the constituency for information literacy by relating it to other literacy efforts.

In the mid-1990s, in response to what library scholar and author Charles R. McClure (1993) has called an "educational disconnect" between literacy needs in the late 20th century and the fare offered by universities, the Office of the Chancellor of the California State University (CSU) system began an initiative to integrate information literacy into the course requirements for every campus in California. The recognition that networked computers represented the future of educational computing was reflected in policy documents.

> There is an educational disconnect between the rapidly developing communications technologies and the public's ability to use these resources. An elite few, typically academics, researchers, technology enthusiasts, and "network junkies," are network literate. While the gulf between these network-literate "cybernauts" and the nonliterate continues to widen, the educational system remains largely oblivious. Individuals in this emerging electronic society primarily learn on their own to be productive in and empowered by this new environment, or they are left behind. (McClure, 1994, p. 115)

Working with the system's library science professionals, a taskforce was formed to create model standards and requirements for the California State University system. The effort sparked interest and activity on each campus to refine and customize information literacy requirements. After years of pondering their contribution to reform, information literacy was a catalyst for librarians in the field. Interest and activity rapidly spread among professionals and administrators to a number of community colleges and universities not affiliated with the California system.

In 1994, San Jose State University, a campus in the California State University system, outlined a proposal for a campus-wide program called *The Information Literacy Initiative (ILI)*. Stuart Sutton (1994) began the report by addressing the need for a new kind of literacy:

> The unfolding information age demands that we broaden our concept of traditional literacy to embrace a more generic notion of information-processing competencies. This broader notion consists of an array of competencies embodied in four "sub-literacies"—traditional literacy (reading and writing), computer literacy, media literacy and network literacy. (p. 1)

Sutton interjected a pedagogy of "problem-solving" as the purpose for this new kind of literacy and recommends that the competencies of the "sub-literacies" be combined. He defines *information literacy* as the confluence of all the "sub-literacies."

> It is not possible to be information literate in the absence of some level of skills and competencies in any of the sub-literacies. So framed, the information literate individual is empowered through the ability to speak and write fluently in the traditional sense of literacy; however, in addition, the information literate is empowered through knowledge and skills to: (1) use the computer effectively as an instrument in the creation, storage and management of information-bearing products of the intellect; (2) use the powerful post-print media as effective tools of expression through their integration into information-bearing products; and (3) use the emerging National Information Infrastructure as an effective means of accessing, acquiring, managing and manipulating information regardless of its geographic location of medium. (p. 14)

Although there are efforts at the elementary and secondary education levels (Wisconsin Educational Media Association, 1993), the majority constituency for information literacy is comprised of librarians from higher education institutions across the United States. The National Forum on Information Literacy is an umbrella group that represents over 65 national organizations concerned with information literacy issues. The Association of College and Research Libraries surveyed 830 institutes of higher education nationwide to investigate their information literacy efforts. Of the 85% that responded, ACRL found that 22% (19 institutions) reported that their campus had a "functional" information literacy program. Some of them, notably the New York and California state systems, recommended information literacy as a requirement for all incoming freshmen (State University of New York, 1992; California State University, 1995).

The working definitions of information literacy for these programs cluster around some themes: information access, evaluation, analysis, and use. Cleveland State University has promoted information literacy since at least 1990 and defines it as "a set of skills and concepts essential for students to function well in today's information-based society . . . the ability to locate, analyze, evaluate, synthesize and use information from a variety of sources, including books, periodicals, computer databases and government agencies" (Cleveland State University, 1990, p. 1). The State University of New York issued similar goals, objectives and guidelines for instituting information literacy in their system (State University of New York, 1992). Arizona State University West calls it "the ability to access, evaluate and synthesize information" (Arizona State University, 1990). Cornell University (Olsen & Coons, 1987), Wayne State University and a host of community colleges have instituted information literacy programs.

Indicative of the trend, the Commission on Learning and Resources and Instructional Technology (CLRIT) of the California State University system launched a task force in 1993 to explore information literacy requirements for library science across the entire CSU system. They found defining *information competency* to be a significant hurdle, "one of the most difficult tasks":

> On one hand, it is used to denote "library literacy" or "bibliographic instruction." Another definition equates "information competence" with "computer literacy." At the other extreme, it is almost synonymous with "critical thinking" . . . information competence, at heart, is the ability to find, evaluate, use, and communicate information in all of its various formats . . . a [recommended] definition . . . is that information competence is the fusing or the integration of library literacy, computer literacy, media literacy, technological literacy, ethics, critical thinking, and communication skills. (California State University Commission on Learning Resources and Instructional Technology, 1995, p. 5)

In an attempt to recognize and fuse some of the multiliteracy categories, McClure proposes a Venn diagram (Fig. 2) to show the commonalities between various multiliteracies. The diagram puts information literacy at the center: The Venn diagram is a sincere and well-intentioned attempt to integrate the overlapping competencies of the various literacies and to further a much-needed interdisciplinary discourse about the many goals and competencies that literacies have in common. It is problematic to adherents of the "other" multiliteracies because it positions "their" literacy in the service of information literacy.

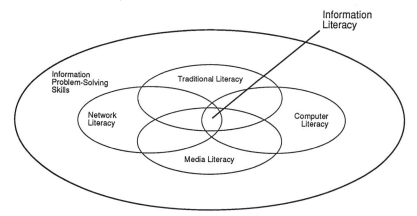

FIG. 2.   Information literacy typology. Reprinted with permission of Charles R. McClure (1994). Network literacy: A role for libraries? *Information Technology and Libraries, 13*(2), 118.

The similarities between the stated competencies of information literacy, visual literacy, and media literacy are so close that separating them seems unnecessarily artificial. In a 1993 article on information literacy, English professor Dan Jones, and Patricia Breivik, the chair of the National Forum on Information Literacy, called for information literacy skills that are nearly identical to those found in documents promoting media literacy and other multiliteracy modes. The authors echo the age-old tension between correct and incorrect interpretation of texts:

> We now believe that the teaching necessary to achieve . . . a liberal education must include models for exploring the uses and potential abuses of all information resources and technologies . . . [students] must become sophisticated users of these resources and technologies as they: (1) gather needed information from all sources; (2) test the validity of information as it remains constant and as it changes from discipline to discipline; (3) place information into various contexts that ultimately will yield its pertinent meaning; and (4) remain skeptical about information and discriminate *fact* from *truth*. (Breivik & Jones, 1993, p. 26)

The need to set one literacy apart from another can only be explained by a need to use the concepts for other reasons, that is, to strengthen the professional status of its constituencies, or to take issue with the approaches used by proponents. In fact, there is fertile ground for cross-collaborative comparisons between information literacy and other literacies if librarians are willing to take the long view. Much to the chagrin of librarians who hope to collaborate with literacy colleagues, position papers promoting media literacy, visual literacy, and the various tool literacies are equally short-sighted—they rarely mention *information literacy*, either.

A CLOSER LOOK AT VISUAL LITERACY

The overlap between the competencies and purposes of various multiliteracies is so close, that their differences have more to do with constituencies than anything else. Still, there are some subtle differences in emphasis. Information literacy places an emphasis on bibliographical referencing and using indexing schemes for finding information. Although it certainly delves into the uses and contexts for texts that include the symbol systems of image, sound, and text, these aspects of information construction are more heavily stressed in visual literacy and media literacy approaches. Visual literacy and media literacy analyze the representation of various media and, similar to information literacy, use literacy tools to access texts and for self-expression. As such, visual and media literacies are often associated with the use of popular culture. They are based on linguistic and critical literacy theory and have been embraced by diverse ideological concerns—from the promoters of liberation theories of literacy (Freire, 1970, 1973, 1985) to those who hope to use them defensively, to preserve a sanctioned canon of mono-culturalism (Hirsch, 1987).

Visual literacy was pioneered and conceptualized in the 1960s by John (Jack) Debes, an executive with the Kodak Corporation in Rochester, New York. Debes, with Clarence Williams and Colin Turbayne (Turbayne, 1970) and backing from Kodak were instrumental in organizing an international forum for the emerging field and invited researchers, instructional designers, educators and artists to form the International Visual Literacy Conference. The visual literacy pioneers are sometimes referred to as the "Rochester School."

At the First National Conference on Visual Literacy in the 1960s, Debes outlined four major principles for promoting visual literacy: (a) a visual language exists; (b) people can and do think visually; (c) people can and do learn visually; and (d) people can and should express ideas visually (Debes, 1968; Homan, 1992). General definitions for visual literacy can be construed to include audio, moving images, and still graphics:

> Visual literacy refers to the ability to comprehend and create images in a variety of media in order to communicate effectively. It is important to note that this is broader in scope than are critical-viewing skills—the ability to analyze, understand, and appreciate visual messages . . . visual literacy contains the competencies of reading and writing. Visually literate students should be able to produce and interpret visual messages. (Considine, 1986, p. 38)

In their 1994 book, *Visual Literacy*, Moore and Dwyer conduct a cogent analysis of the theory strands used to justify visual literacy theory. They found strong evidence in linguistics, art, psychology and philosophy. A summation of their findings includes:

Linguistics: Fries (1952) contended that meaning was made possible through the study of verbal structures and elements. Visual literacy theorists extrapolated that theory to include the study of visual elements. The linguistic theories of Noam Chomsky's (1957, 1964, 1968, 1975), in particular the idea that there is a universal or innate grammar, was used to argue that there are also certain universal elements in visual language.

Art: Arnheim (1967, 1969) promoted a theory of visual thinking. Visual literacy proponents contend that visual literacy is the first step on the road to visual thinking.

Psychology: The perceptionists had a strong influence on visual literacy theory. Amey (1976) believed that perception itself was a form of learning (p. 14) and Gibson (1954) argued for the experiential nature of visual perception. The importance of "mind" in perception also led to forays into research about brain chemistry, psychobiology, and brain hemisphere. These and other mind–body connections were attempted by visual literacy theorists.

Philosophy: The philosopher Turbayne, in *The Myth of Metaphor* (1970) was a strong influence on visual literacy. Although the book is really about the use of metaphor, visual literacy theorists have seized upon Turbayne's defense of visual language to justify a link between visual language and verbal language (pp. 21–24).

Other theory strands that Moore and Dwyer credited (Moore & Dwyer, pp. 301–303) with building the concept of visual literacy include: *semiotics*, the study of signs (Wollen, 1969); and *intertextuality*, that is, the relationships between various texts and their historical ideologies (Ellsworth & Whatley, 1990). In addition, *poststructuralism* is the postmodern form of interpretation that expands the contexts of semiotics to include the complete discourse around visual representation. Goffman (1974) has said that meaning constructed from signs represents a community's "belief system, its cosmology" (p. 27). Postructuralism accommodates multiple meanings and positions the reader of a text as an active partner in meaning (Fish, 1980; Freund, 1987).

In keeping with the need for more cohesive articulation of theory, Moore and Dwyer commented, "As the visual literacy movement stands today, more cooperation among the perceptionists, instructional technologists, philosophers, brain specialists, linguists, artists is need before the theoretical foundations can be fully established" (p. 24).

Although important forays have been made into interpretation of the moving image from an aesthetic and visual literacy perspective (Zettl, 1990), studies about visual literacy are dominated by examination of still images, graphics, and iconography. Furthermore, because it favors semiotic approaches for interpreting visuals "within the frame," visual literacy has been criticized for not going far enough into the ideological territory "outside the frame," that is, into the contexts and complexities involved with how people make use of image, sound, and text.

There is also a general perception that because the creation of meaning is so arbitrary and idiocyncratic, varying from individual to individual, it is impossible to come up a taxonomy that could be applied to teach about visuals. According to visual literacy scholar Paul Messaris (1994), the work of arts scholar E. H. Gombrich and philosopher Nelson Goodman contributed to the perception that viewers made sense of media due to their own idiosyncratic cultural conditioning (p. 5). In *Art and Illusion* (1960), Gombrich studied pictorial representations across cultures and postulated that "different visual cultures may have quite different standards as to what constitutes a realistic rendition of the world in an image." Gombrich also explicitly assumed that "someone who had never before encountered a particular pictorial style . . . might initially not be able to make sense of it" (Messaris, 1994, p. 5). Goodman (1976) reinforced this view. He argued that "because

it was impossible . . . to specify any necessary and sufficient rules of correspondence between pictures and their referents, it follows that pictures are
just as arbitrary in their connection to what they represent as language
is—and that, in consequence—almost anything can serve as a picture of
almost anything else if a culture so wills it" (Messaris, p. 5).

Messaris counters this "contemporary received wisdom" by citing the
contrary tradition of those who study the psychology of perception (Cassidy
& Knowlton, 1983; Gibson, 1982; Hochberg, 1983, 1984; Kennedy, 1984;
Kipper, 1990). He notes that even Gombrich contradicted himself when he
remarked that first-time viewers could adjust to pictorial styles "with surprising
speed" (Gombrich, 1960, p. 53; Messaris, p. 6). In *Visual Literacy: Image, Mind
& Reality*, Messaris (1994) argued that prior experience with the codes and
conventions of media is not a necessary prerequisite to understanding visuals.

> Although I do think it is true that viewers get better at the interpretation of
> visual media as they acquire more experience with them, I also think that to
> a substantial degree the formal conventions typically encountered in still or
> motion pictures should make a good deal of sense even to a first-time viewer.
> (p. 7)

Messaris supports his assertion that prior knowledge of visual codes and
conventions is not necessary to construct meaning from visuals, by commenting on the conventions used by early filmmakers. He relates that when
early filmmakers experimented with the replacement of the intertitles of the
old talkies with transitions, such as cuts, dissolves, fades, and so on, they
assumed that the audience had some familiarity with transitional devices
due to their readings of the novels of Charles Dickens and others (see also
Williams, 1980, p. 35; Eisenstein, 1944, pp. 213–216. Messaris (1994) comments that the idea that a contemporary filmmaker would construct a movie
based on any assumption of today's familiarity with print literacy conventions
seems rather quaint (p. 18).

> Although it may sometimes appear that interpreting communication is simply
> a matter of applying the appropriate codes, the fact . . . is that human com-
> munication always entails an interaction between code and context. This
> interaction makes it possible for intended meanings to be inferred despite
> ambiguities in the code, misuses of the code, or external sources of "noise."
> [The] fact that interpretation can be based on context is, as I see it, the reason
> that both verbal and visual narratives have been able to dispense with explicit
> explanatory devices for certain kinds of transitions . . . the notion that viewers'
> ability to make sense of space/time transitions in contemporary films and TV
> programs requires prior familiarity with a visual language or grammar, i.e.,
> with a set of medium-specific codes—seems self-evidently untenable . . . there
> are hardly any transitional codes left for viewers to be familiar with . . . we
> might want to speak [instead] of narrative literacy. (pp. 18–19)

Scholar Joshua Meyrowitz (1985) explained the apparent mismatches between the codes and conventions of alphabetic, language, and visual literacy by stating bluntly: "Understanding visual symbols has nothing to do with literacy" (p. 77). Messaris (1994) took a more tentative stance on the relationship between images and literacy, but still questioned whether the principles of language literacy can be directly used to promote visual literacy.

> To argue that there should be more of a balance between linguistic and pictorial education doesn't mean such a balance would enable us to do with images all the kinds of things we now do with words . . . even if images do have a potential role to play as cognitive tools, it does not necessarily follow that this function is dependent on prior visual education. (pp. 21–22)

He makes an important distinction between two functions of language: the descriptive function and the analytic function. He believes that the way people use descriptive language, "an account of a particular series of events or of the features of a particular object or situation," is highly compatible with the way they use images (p. 22). But Messaris questioned whether the interpretation of images can lead to a sophisticated degree of analysis:

> Conveying information about the features of particular objects or the details of particular events is so central a part of what we do with images that even raising the question in this connection may seem peculiar. However, when it comes to analysis, we face a very different situation. Analysis . . . often deals with general categories rather than individual items, and it is characterized by a focus on causality, contingent relationships, hypotheticals, estimates of likelihood. . . . For all these aspects of meaning, verbal language contains conventions (individual terms or syntactic devices) that indicate explicitly what kind of statement is being made. In the case of images, however, such conventions are almost totally lacking. (p. 22)

Messaris concedes that generic icons, such as "no smoking" signs and other pictures limited to the world of concrete objects or events are a minor exception. But, he contends, they are too general to actually imply cause or other characteristics of analysis that can be used in sophisticated ways through language. Icons and images are, he says, "poor substitutes for genuine analytic discourse" (p. 23).

Nonetheless, Messaris' study of visual literacy has led him to believe that there are general cognitive consequences to the interpretation of images and that visual literacy should be included in formal education. He suggests that the study of visual subject matter would enhance the curriculum because:

(1) there is a need for critical literacy that includes an examination of visual aesthetics and ideologies, in order to "sharpen a viewer's appreciation of skill and awareness of the manipulative intent of visuals;

(2) certain images, primarily photographs, have been so intimately and significantly intertwined with the social developments from which they emerged that the teaching of history, among other things, seems also most inconceivable without some reference to these images; and

(3) certain images about which one might want to instruct younger generations because of the role they have played as a reference point in the public life of older generations [such as the work of] Norman Rockwell and Jackson Pollock" provide a vital way to pass on social values and cultural understanding from one generation to the next. (pp. 176–177)

VISUAL LITERACY IN PRACTICE: CODES AND CONTEXTS

Because many of the codes and conventions of visuals are aesthetic, visual literacy has been criticized for concentrating on deconstructions, devoid of the necessary social, cultural, historical and economic contexts that contribute to the deeper, critical reading of a text. Visual literacy exercises that re-contextualize or "inter-textualize" images have shown the most promise when critical literacy is the goal.

A good example of this kind of "contextualized" activity that also follows Messaris' vision for visual literacy in classroom activities can be seen in *Photographic Discourse: Guide to Understanding Photographs* (Nolker & Tyner, 1991, pp. 4–6). The *Guide* uses Dorothea Lange's famous photograph from the 1930s, *White Angel Breadline*, to teach some codes and conventions of photography so that the viewer can appreciate the artful way in which they are used. The Guide also asks the viewer to begin to deconstruct how he or she makes sense of media. It begs the question: How do I know what I know?

The *Photographic Discourse Guide* includes aesthetic elements such as punctum, framing, composition, etc. In a nod to theory about the psychology of perception, it also includes an "emotional appeal" factor. More importantly, it encourages students to analyze the image within the broader context of history, ownership, intent, and genre. If students are subsequently encouraged to construct images using the codes and conventions they have learned in deconstruction exercises, both aesthetic appreciation and critical literacy tasks can be accomplished simultaneously. As Gombrich pointed out, strict deconstruction of meaning can be quite subjective. Commenting on the significance of color and composition is an interesting parlor game, but its usefulness for literacy and language learning is questionable. When formal classroom exercises are used to analyze images in the context of

1. Aesthetic Elements. Aesthetics include contrasts of light and dark, color, composition, shapes and figures, stasis, etc.

2. Punctum. This is a term sometimes used to refer to the focal points in a photograph. Often the focal point is the subject and appears in the center of the frame. But there can be more than one focal point to provide eye-catching details elsewhere in the photograph. These details generally offer the most telling clues. They may support the narrative title of the photo, or they may raise problems and disjunctions in its continuity.

3. Title. A title supplements the photo with additional clues and functions to direct and inform the viewer's interpretation.

4. Photographer. Research about a photographer's life can tell us much about the intent and meaning behind photographs. A citation for a photographer's work often includes the dates of birth and death to provide important historical clues to the meaning of the photograph.

5. Ownership. The photographer and owner of a photograph are not necessarily the same. Photographs are almost always copyrighted and it is necessary to find the owner and seek their permission to reproduce them.

6. Intent. A photographer's intent is often revealed through their choice of title, the composition of aesthetic qualities, the emotion evoked and the focal points. Ownership of the photograph may also imply that the photograph was taken for hire.

7. Historical Context. Historical context is essential to understanding a photographic message. A photograph's date is generally included in the title, sometimes along with the location of the photograph.

8. Genre. Categorizing photographs is only useful with the understanding that the different kinds of photography overlap and that few great photographs fall under a single category. Different kinds of photography include photo-journalism, fine art, advertising, portraits, commercial, documentary, tabloid, etc.

9. Emotion. Our visceral response to a photograph and its impact are important clues to its meaning, but highly subjective. We want to look at both the emotion represented in the photograph and the emotion it evokes in the viewer. We also might want to consider whether the viewer's emotional response might be different today than it would have been in the past.

10. Framing. Framing is a tool for raising questions about the photographer's choices, the creative process of selectivity, and to speculate about what remains outside the borders and why.

WHITE ANGEL BREADLINE

Photograph copyright the Dorothea Lange Collection, The Oakland Museum of California, The City of Oakland. Gift of Paul S. Taylor.

Photographic Discourse: Contextual Analysis of *White Angel Breadline*

1. Aesthetic Elements. An important aesthetic element in the black and white photograph, *White Angel Breadline,* is seen in the contrast in the man's hat. In a sea of dark coats, the hat draws our eye and points to the face, the cup, and the hands.

2. Punctum. In this photograph, a man's hands, his cup, and another man's face are turned from the crowd. These are the most instantly arresting details. The cup supports the "breadline" in the title. The hands tell us about destitution and despair. The "turned" face in the photograph offers a disjunction, or jarring element. It looks more distinguished than the other faces in the crowd and out of place. We do not know why the man is turned around, out of step, going against the crowd.

3. Title. It is useful to know that a wealthy San Francisco woman was a benefactor for poor people during the Depression. They called her "The White Angel." If the viewer does not know this, the full meaning of the title will not be revealed. From the title, the viewer also learns that men are waiting for food handouts.

4. Photographer. Dorothea Lange (1895-1996) moved from New York to San Francisco in 1918 and established a career as a commercial photographer. She became best known for her work as a photojournalist for the Farm Security Administration where she photographed scenes from the Great Depression.

5. Ownership. *White Angel Breadline* is owned by the Dorothea Lange Collection, the City of Oakland (CA) and the Oakland Museum who have allowed it to be reproduced here. Fair use copyright laws allow educators to use the copy for face-to-face communication within the confines of a classroom. This usually is not interpreted to mean that teachers may make a copy for every student or that a copyrighted work can be reproduced in digital form and disseminated over the Internet without permission of the owners.

6. Intent. The stock market crash on Wall Street in 1929 changed Dorothea Lange's life and photography. It also forced her to change her way of working. *White Angel Breadline* has become one of the most famous photographs from the Depression. Legend has it that it was taken on the day she decided to begin to experiment with other subjects and to work just to please herself.

7. Historical Context. *White Angel Breadline* provides its own clue to its setting in San Francisco. The date of the photograph, 1933, was the worst year of the Depression. Over 14 million people were out of work. That alone is enough information to allow the viewer to make essential inferences about the photograph's meaning and to speculate about the story behind the photograph.

Photographic Discourse: Contextual Analysis of
White Angel Breadline
(Continued)

Relating historical information to present-day subjects enables a fuller range of understanding about events. Even so, there are essential differences between contemporary breadlines and those of the Great Depression. Care must be taken to contrast, as well as to compare, historical factors when making links between similar situations in different time periods.

8. Genre. Dorothea Lange began making studio portraits, but became famous as a photojournalist. She thought of herself as a photojournalist, but was aware of the fine arts potential of her photographs, and she made no attempt to compartmentalize her work by type. Nonetheless, her work can sometimes be classified with her contemporaries such as Imogene Cunningham and Walker Evans, as well as with other artists who documented the Depression era, including the author John Steinbeck.

9. Emotion. The single man at the rear of the crowd faces the viewer. He appears to signal an alienation and a resolve to work against his fate. He does not belong here. He is not like the others. The man with the empty cup and worn hat has his hands clenched. In resolve? With anxiety? In defeat? In prayer? *White Angel Breadline* raises a storm of conflicting emotions in the viewer.

10. Framing. Is the man in the left-hand corner looking at the photographer or at something/someone behind her? What are the men facing away from the photographer looking at? What was the photographer trying to convey to cropping the photograph this way? What are the limitations of the frame?

---

their own times, visual literacy demonstrates the potential to contribute to the critical literacy of students.

(WHAT IN THE WORLD IS) MEDIA LITERACY?

Media literacy attempts to consolidate strands from the communication multiliteracies that correspond with the convergence of text, sound and image, including the moving image. It has been associated with the ability to make sense of all media and genre, from the more classic educational fare to popular culture. Its stated definitions and competencies are compatible with both information literacy and visual literacy. Whether it can manage to front other literacies under its broad banner remains to be seen. Its all-encompassing nature is both a strength and a weakness that is reflected in attempts at consensus about its definitions and purposes.

The first media literacy curriculum was proposed by Marshall McLuhan in the fall of 1959 for eleventh graders in Toronto, Ontario, for the Canadian National Association of Educational Broadcasters (Marchand, 1989, pp. 136–138). Because of its early beginnings there, it is probably no accident that leadership for media literacy education in North America continues to emanate from Ontario, Canada. Canadian media educators are in turn, influenced by influential media education in England, Scotland, and Australia. These international media education efforts provide the most longitudinal evidence of media education in practice.

MEDIA EDUCATION IN EUROPE

English media researcher Len Masterman, in *Media Education in 1990s Europe* (Masterman & Mariet, 1994), found that the major paradigms used as rationales for the teaching of media in Europe over the last 50 years include views of media as: agents of cultural decline; popular arts; and representational or symbolic systems. Developments in the fields of semiotics, theories of ideology and the social contexts of media production contributed to a view of media as representational systems. Course content, student performance, and assessments based on this view followed (p. 32). For example, in England, operant aspects of media that are open to critical study include: media content, contexts, organizations, technologies, and the ways that various audiences respond to and use media (Buckingham, 1991, p. 18). Masterman's findings have important parallels in the evolution of media education in the United States. Each of the three paradigms, proposed by Masterman, are discussed below.

Media as Agents of Cultural Decline

Masterman tracks European media education between the early 1930s and the early 1960s. In particular, this paradigm was influenced by British cultural critic F. R. Leavis who, as previously noted, also influenced McLuhan:

> This view of the media . . . as corrupting influences, or virulent diseases—rather like diphtheria or polio—which threatened the cultural and moral health of us all, particularly children, is perhaps best understood as part of an even longer tradition of respectable middle-class fears of the cheap and debased amusements of working people. . . . The media as creeping diseases . . . produced one of two responses from teachers . . . media could be legitimately ignored as irrelevant . . . [or] the increasing popularity and persuasiveness of the media led to a call for schools to adopt a more active role of cultural resistance to the shallow emotional responses which they were believed to encourage. (p. 21)

He states that "although it would be very unusual at a meeting of media teachers anywhere in Europe today to find adherents of the view that the media are agents of cultural decline, it is an opinion which remains common enough amongst educators generally . . . a reminder that 'inoculative' media education has not yet had its day" (p. 22).

Media as Popular Arts

Masterman tracks this period from developments in film theory, particularly *auteur* theory, in the late 1950s through the 1960s. *Auteur* theory elevated the creative talents of the director and met with reception from teachers who actually liked media, especially cinema. It was akin to explicating a literary work. When media education was taught from a popular arts perspective, it implied that some—but not all—media was worthy of study. For example, film was privileged over television and the press. Some media, usually teacher-selected media, was distinguished as good and other media—often student favorites—as bad.

Masterman stated that although the "Popular Arts Movement . . . did constitute a distinct step forward from inoculative media education, it did not break entirely with older attitudes. The 'value' question, i.e., good vs. bad media, remained central. Discrimination (*within* not *against* the media) remained a primary objective. Media education continued to be 'protectionist' . . . the assumption still held that students' media tastes needed to be improved . . . an essentially defensive and somewhat negative enterprise . . . it ultimately failed to mobilise the energies and enthusiasms of large numbers of teachers and students" (p. 27).

Media as Representational or Symbolic Systems

By the 1970s, media education in Europe was beginning to investigate new approaches to the study of media. Masterman credits three areas of theory development in this paradigm for media teaching: semiotics, ideology, and audience response to media texts. Masterman (1994) notes that although the Swiss linguist Ferdinand de Saussure (1974) gave the field of semiotics its shape, it was Roland Barthes, in *Mythologies* (1973), who first applied semiotics to media texts. According to Masterman, semiotics established "the first principle of media education: the principle of non-transparency" (p. 33). In other words, media are not invisible conduits for information, but shape content in specific, representational ways; they are not "windows of the world," but carefully manufactured products. This concept gave rise to "a kind of professional pun: the media do not present reality, they *re-present* it" (p. 33). Semiotics allowed a wider range of cultural products to be viewed and read as texts, opening them up to critical analysis (p. 35). Media education now had a rationale to break from inoculation traditions once and for all. Barthes' "very choice of subjects—striptease, wrestling, toys, tourists guides, a plate of steak and chips—involved the sharpest possible rejection of established tastes" (p. 35).

Theories based in ideologies—from neo-capitalism to Marxism—also provided paradigms for the study of media as representation. During the 1970s and 1980s in Europe, the concept of *cultural hegemony* advanced by cultural theorists such as Althusser (1971), Williams (1976), Hall (1977) and Gramsci (1971) saw teachers as "cultural workers" in a constant struggle between the dominant class structure and subordinate groups (p. 36). Similarly, the media are sites for struggle. As Masterman noted, intellectual debates about the ideological nature of media as hegemonic instruments have never been particularly salient to the practical concerns of teachers. Marxist ideology, in particular, has arguably less credibility now than at any other time in its history. Correspondingly, the view of media as "consciousness industries" that spread "false consciousness" has lost favor in most European media education circles (Bazalgette, 1992; Bazalgette & Buckingham, 1995). Not only do critics see blatant ideological perspectives as heavy-handed in their vision of media industries as propaganda machines (Buckingham, 1991, p. 16), they also charge that this perspective seeks to blunt or discount the authentic enjoyment that audiences derive from media, that is, "the pleasure principle":

> Pleasure is regarded as the sugar for the ideological pill, as a distraction which enables television to exert its unpleasant effects on children's minds. Pleasure is something to be deeply suspected, and which we must encourage children to "own up" to if we are to free them from it. (Buckingham, 1991, p. 17)

Masterman believes that ideological debates around cultural materialism and economic determinism did move the deconstruction of texts toward a more contextual approach and beyond arbitrary issues of taste. As a result, for better or worse, political "rather than aesthetic value" was included as a "key function of contemporary media" (Masterman & Mariet, 1994, p. 39).

> [Teachers] were attempting to challenge the media's common-sense representations by asking whose interests they served, how they were constructed and what alternative representations were repressed. What the debates on ideology did was to bring a sharper political focus to these concerns. They established the importance of politics of representation. . . . And they provided a demystifying strategy for dealing with topical media material in classrooms. (p. 38)

Theory development in the sociology of mass media became interlocked with similar developments in semiology and ideology to suggest the need to move beyond the simple sender–message–receiver mass communication models of the 1950s. The investigation of context—the audiences' uses of texts and the creation of meaning from the representations within texts, have proven to be fruitful. Masterman breaks the contexts into two universes: the industrial process of production/encoding; and the audience processes of reading/decoding. The complex individual and cultural interpretations by media consumers, who create a wide range of meaning for media texts, point to the concept of active engagement with media. This is in sharp contrast to the concept of passive receivership, implied by inoculationist/protectionist paradigms. An emphasis on contextual issues offers teachers a way to move away from strict textual analysis "within the frame," that is, viewing the actual media artifact, to a consideration of more ephemeral and complex issues of economic, social, cultural, and historical importance "outside the frame" (Masterman & Mariet, 1994).

Masterman sums up the theoretical basis for media education that have emerged for European media teachers since the 1970s by suggesting eight principles for their application in the classroom:

1. The central and unifying concept of media education is that of representation;
2. A central purpose of media education is to "denaturalise" the media;
3. Media education is primarily investigative. It does not seek to impose specific cultural values;
4. Media education is organised around key concepts, which are analytical tools rather than an alternative content;
5. Media education is a lifelong process;
6. Media education aims to foster not simply critical understanding, but critical autonomy;
7. The effectiveness of media education may be evaluated by two principal criteria: (a) the ability of students to apply what they know (their critical ideas and principles) to new situations; and (b) the amount of commitment, interest and motivation displayed by students;
8. Media education is topical and opportunistic. (Masterman & Mariet, 1994, pp. 53–57)

Finally, Masterman aligns these principles with experiential, democratic pedagogy. He comments on the relationship between media analysis and practical student media work, which he calls "practical criticism and critical practice," saying that "practical work was not an end in itself, but a necessary means to develop a critical understanding of the media" (Masterman & Mariet, 1994, p. 59). The marriage of theory, analysis, and practice is evidenced in European media education efforts. Media educator Roberto

Aparici, from Spain, has recorded such an approach in anthologies from researchers throughout Europe and other parts of the world (Aparici, 1996; Aparici & García-Matilla; 1989). Groundbreaking classroom research about critical analysis with hands-on media making has been conducted by British educational researchers such as Cary Bazalgette (1989), David Buckingham, and Andrew Hart (Buckingham, 1990/1992, 1994; Buckingham & Sefton-Green, 1996; Hart, 1998), who similarly emphasize the role of pedagogy and experiential education as an increasingly important paradigm for their work in media education in England and other parts of Europe. Buckingham and Bazalgette are part of a generation of British researchers who begin with an emphasis on the pleasure that people receive from media, thus turning the debate away from the "harmful effects" paradigm. Although cross-cultural comparisons must be made with caution, it is not difficult to find many of the same underlying assumptions in operation in the paradigms and approaches to media study seen in the United States.

DEFINING MEDIA LITERACY

In 1992, the Aspen Institute, a nonprofit "think tank," assembled leaders from the United States and Canada who were working in the media literacy field at their conference center in Maryland to discuss some strategies and directions for nurturing the emerging field of media literacy. The Aspen Institute regularly conducts intensive retreats for a number of new and emerging ideas and this gathering was a major milestone in media literacy, reuniting critical viewing scholars from the 1970s with new leaders in the field and reviving interest in the subject. It soon became apparent that the leaders in "the field" were proponents of a number of eclectic approaches, based on a wide range of underlying theoretical foundations and ideological assumptions—all operating under the all-purpose multiliteracy term, *media literacy.* The assumed purposes for media literacy ranged from promoting artistic self-expression, to enhancing school improvement, to protecting children from the harmful effects of media, to fighting the consolidation of media industries, to strengthening citizenship, to all of the above and beyond.

Because the various approaches were so diverse, the most difficult task and ultimately the most lasting outcome of the Aspen Institute's National Leadership Conference on Media Literacy Education was a working definition that could unify the various approaches. A background paper circulated before the conference was streamlined by the collective group. The early version of the paper advanced a definition of media literacy as "the ability to analyze, augment and influence active reading (i.e., viewing) of media in order to be a more effective citizen" (Davis, 1992, p. 13). This definition was rejected by the Aspen leaders as too confusing and jargon-laden.

The assembled group of North Americans turned to their more experienced Canadian colleagues for assistance in formulating a workable definition. In Ontario, where media literacy has been mandated in the language arts curriculum since the 1980s, media literacy is defined as that which is:

> concerned with helping students develop an informed and critical understanding of the nature of the mass media, the techniques used by them, and the impact of these techniques. More specifically, it is education that aims to increase students' understanding and enjoyment of how media work, how they produce meaning, how they are organized, and how they construct reality. Media literacy also aims to provide students with the ability to create media products. (Ontario Ministry of Education, 1989, pp. 6–7)

In keeping with the long standing American tendency to truncate complexity, the definition was shortened to:

> Media literacy is the ability to decode, analyze, evaluate and produce communication in a variety of forms.

The Canadians at the gathering assented to the definition with caution, because they were not only moving away from their original definition, but were even questioning the term *media literacy* itself. During much of the 1980s, the British and Australians have debated the use of the terms *media studies, media education,* and *media literacy*. Reflecting their roots in the British and Australian versions of media education, as well as the need to center the practice of media criticism firmly in the educational sphere, the Canadians announced that for the most part, they were calling the practice of teaching about media, *media education.*

> The study of the media must be seen now to be both a domain (or subject in its own right) and a dimension (or aspect of all other subjects). Media Studies, the domain, exists as a discrete element on timetables, has its own object of study, its own set of concepts and pedagogy. . . . Media education, the dimension, may be viewed and taught as an aspect of all subjects . . . there have been other such initiatives, most notable language across the curriculum and more recently information technology across the curriculum. (Robson, Simmons, & Sohn-Rethel, 1990, p. 172)

The experiences of international media educators have shown that the debate about terminology for media education represents a failure to fully reconcile the analysis of classroom media and popular culture with the hands-on, experiential production of media by students. In spite of attempts to broaden its analytical focus, *media studies* most often involves the "making" of media, usually in arts-based or vocational course work. *Media education* reflects the cognitive analysis of media, that is, "teaching about media." There is broad consensus that the ideal curriculum integrates the two practices.

International leaders in the field of media education outside North America consider *media literacy* to be a hopelessly vague term, mired in the complexities of literacy and commandeered by those outside the field of education. Furthermore, the term has been coopted by cultural critics from each end of the political spectrum, from the British cultural elitist Leavis (Leavis & Thompson, 1933) to culture jammers such as the Media Foundation Canada, a liberal activist organization that decries the commercialization and effects of media. Those who take issues with the term *media literacy* say that it subtly implies that children are passive users of media and denies the knowledge, pleasure, and autonomy that children seek in mass media and popular culture (Buckingham, 1990/1992; Davis, 1996; Masterman & Mariet, 1994). Critical pedagogists prefer the use of *media education,* because it eschews literacy as a finite, consumable commodity and positions it as a complex, lifelong process.

North Americans have used *television literacy, critical receivership skills,* and *critical viewing* simultaneously. Like *media literacy,* these terms imply a narrow and defensive posture toward the watching of television. The shift toward the use of *media education* to describe teaching about media, indicates a nod toward educational process over product. A value is placed on the cognitive process of media analysis, as well as on the end product, or record, of skill-based literacy. In this case, the literacy record could be a student produced multimedia piece, an illustrated story, or a radio play. The marriage of media analysis with practice places media education in line with mainstream literacy theories that emphasize the social acts of literacy. *Media literacy* is still an operable term in North America, with a broad following.

At the Aspen Institute Media Literacy Leadership Conference, after much contentious debate between various constituencies who advanced one definition after another, the group decided to retain the term *media literacy* and to adopt the simplified Canadian definition with one change—the verb "decode" was changed to "access," reflecting the U.S. leaders concern about equity of access to information. The definition that finally emerged from the Aspen Institute Leadership Forum on Media Literacy Education became:

> Media Literacy is the ability of a citizen to access, analyze, and produce information for specific outcomes. (Aufderheide & Firestone, 1993, p. v)

At the conference, Deirdre Downs, a media producer, announced the formation of a foundation to promote a statewide media literacy initiative in the state of New Mexico. Her goal was to build standards and activities around the four parts of the Aspen definition: "access, analyze, evaluate and produce" and to initiate statewide training and implementation for media literacy skills and processes in schools throughout New Mexico. The Aspen working definition provided the subsequent foundation for the effort (Tyner, 1993, p. 1).

Reflecting dissent about the purposes of media literacy work in the United States, the written report that was widely disseminated to the public following the Aspen conference included no less than two other definitions. Although both definitions had been discussed and dismissed by the assembled group of media educators at Aspen, they were prominently featured in the document. The report gratuitously incorporated complex ideas about the purposes of media literacy that certainly would have found vehement disagreement among media literacy's various proponents. These competing definitions, although subtle and innocuous to outsiders, exacerbated emerging divisions in the ranks of core constituencies:

> Media literacy, the movement to expand notions of literacy to include the powerful post-print media that dominate our informational landscape, helps people understand, produce and negotiate meanings in a culture made up of powerful images, words, and sounds. A media literate person—everyone should have the opportunity to become one—can decode, evaluate, analyze and produce both print and electronic media. (Aufderheide & Firestone, 1993, p. 1)

> Media literacy is the ability to analyze, augment and influence active reading (i.e., viewing) of media in order to be a more effective citizen. (p. 26)

Furthermore, under the subheading "Definitions," the purposes for media literacy were listed as: "citizenship, aesthetic appreciation and expression, social advocacy, self-esteem, and consumer competence" (p. 1). The range of constituencies listed were equally broad: "young people, parents, teachers, librarians, administrators, citizens" (p. 1). In the interest of inclusiveness, the Aspen Institute document blurred a simple and focused definition of media literacy, resulting in understandable public confusion about its overall aims and purposes. By assuming the sweeping power of both media and literacy to effect "citizenship," the document's various definitions drove the principles of media literacy further away from reconciliation with alphabetic literacy research.

In the face of such confusion, *media literacy* became a catchall term for a wide range of social purposes and was co-opted by constituencies with dissimilar aims. For example, in his position paper on information literacy, library science expert Stuart Sutton chooses one of the many Aspen Institute definitions for media literacy found in the Leadership Conference report. Sutton (1994) cites media literacy as "the ability to decode, evaluate, analyze and produce both print and electronic media." He enumerates the purview of media literacy as: (a) an expansion of knowledge and use of productivity tools beyond those of basic computer literacy to include new and emerging media; (b) knowledge and ability to create information that integrates more than one digital medium in complex, new information structures; and (c) an expansion of aesthetic and critical sensibilities to encompass those new information structures (p. 12). Sutton conveys the need for both analysis and production, but he also frames media literacy in ways that ignore some key features, such as the call for equitable access to information. He also marginalizes its grounding in traditional alphabetic literacy by downplaying media literacy's relationship to print, while playing up its association with the tools of digital convergence. Given such an amorphous range of goals and purposes, it is no wonder that even those who are friendly to media literacy are confused.

CONSTITUENCIES FOR MEDIA LITERACY EDUCATION

In countries outside the United States, media education is teacher driven, characterized by a grassroots teacher movement and rooted in the research-base of educational theory and practice. For example, teachers formed a powerful constituency for the inclusion of media education in the curriculum in Ontario, Canada. Media education standards, lesson plans, resources, assessments, and research followed. Established educational bureaucracies work with teacher networks and preservice university programs to create standards and resources in England. The Australian Teachers of Media (ATOM) is an entirely teacher-run professional association of media teachers.

In the United States, demands for media education have come as much from high-profile social activists and politicians as from educators, creating many more purposes for media literacy, some of them conflicting. In contrast to international grass-roots teacher efforts to integrate media education into the curriculum, the constituency for media education in the United States represents many more "top-down" efforts to encourage its inclusion in schooling. These come from government agencies, social activists, religious organizations, and from media industries. These groups envision a variety of purposes for media education, but most do not represent a strong constituency of classroom educators. These include: The Church of Christ, parishes of the Catholic Church, and the efforts of many other religious denominations; groups that lobby for regulation of children's television, such as the Center for Media Education in Washington DC; media access groups such as the National Alliance of Television Access Producers; medical practitioners, such as the American Psychological Association and the American Academy of Pediatrics; and government agencies, such as the Office of National Drug Control Policy and the Center for Substance Abuse Prevention. Each hope to use media education as a strategy to advance their primary causes of social morality, television regulation, media access, public health, and health risk prevention.

There are some fledgling efforts by educators to address media education. The subject of media literacy has been mentioned in passing, in public policy speeches by U.S. Department of Education officials—usually positioned as a response to controversial content in media and popular culture

(Riley, 1995). Also, the National Council of Teachers of English and the Speech Communication Association are two teacher-based advocates for media literacy education. These two professional educational associations established special interest focus groups to investigate media literacy education's integration into the existing school curriculum. Although professional education organizations have begun to take notice of the need for media literacy, with a host of competing interests to consume their time and resources, the integration of media literacy education across the curriculum has not emerged as the top priority for grassroots teacher groups.

Instead of offering either credible models or the necessary funding for implementation, top-down campaigns appeared informal, superficial, confusing and vague to classroom teachers. Top-down calls for media education from those outside the educational bureaucracy had the adverse effect of slowing down the consensus necessary to deeply integrate media literacy education across the curriculum and then, to investigate its efficacy in small, incremental ways. Teachers have to field competing demands on classroom time from educational movements whose rationale and motives can be clearly reconciled with their existing scope of work. In contrast, support for media literacy in the curriculum comes from sectors in society with a confusing array of motives.

MEDIA TEACHING ABOUT MEDIA

Some of media literacy education's strongest support comes from media industries. Based on a business perspective, media industries offer information resources to schools that serve several purposes as: (a) public relations vehicles in response to negative perceptions about the media industries; (b) new cost centers to re-purpose news and entertainment media for educational purposes; (c) community philanthropy to enhance the image of media as good corporate citizens; and (d) audience development to educate young people about media industries and to develop sophisticated appreciation of media content.

Media education under industry auspices usually manifests itself in the form of free or low-cost information resources provided to schools. This idea is in keeping with a long tradition industry involvement in the curriculum of U.S. schools ranging from industries as diverse as coal, cookies, milk, toothpaste, and nuclear energy. Reporter Sheila Harty did historical research into the use of industry-created classroom resources in her books, *Hucksters in the Classroom* (1979) and *The Corporate Pied Piper* (1985).

> Business involvement in education is mostly in the form of propaganda that furthers the goals of a commercial culture. Under business' tutelage, knowl-

edge becomes the means to an end—quantitative, pragmatic and marketable. The result is an anti-intellectual emphasis which creates a trade school mentality to secure jobs and a consumptionist drive to purchase status goods. (Harty, 1979, p. 5)

On the more positive side, many of the information resources created by media industries are valuable to media educators, because they offer original source materials that are accessible and copyright free. If a student wants to learn about media industries "straight from the horse's mouth," these materials can prove productive for media education, because they can be read "between the lines" for both their explicit information and the ideological subtexts they reveal. At their best, media education materials produced by media industries are rich databases of source material.

Still, the controversy about media education materials produced by media industries vs. noncommercial or independently produced teacher materials raises questions about the ability for media industries to promote active criticism of their own industry practices. Media industries seem to be most interested in producing critical viewing kits and other materials during times of the highest public outrage over media content and the resultant veiled threats from politicians about regulation and control. In some cases, the media education resources generated by media industry sources serve as a panacea to vocal critics of commercialism, sex, and violence in media. They are an intelligent marketing response to criticism about media content—one that offers a comfortable middle ground and positions the industry as a responsible corporate citizen. In addition, the media education materials demonstrate responsiveness by media industries while skirting troublesome First Amendment, regulatory, and censorship issues. Such an example was seen when critical viewing materials proliferated in the 1970s after a Surgeon General's report on media violence (Surgeon General's Scientific Advisory Committee on Television and Social Behavior, 1972).

Television critical viewing programs in schools took a decided upturn in school districts that had instituted the controversial Channel One television program in the early 1990s. Channel One presented news programming over satellite and cable for school children. In order to pay for its programming, Channel One included television commericals and other interstitials modeled on broadcast television. Parents were incensed that their children were exposed to commercials in schools. The public outcry was ferocious and a new round of debates about the excessive commercialism of children's media and schooling ensued. Such debates touched all media industries—not just Whittle Communications, the company that originally produced Channel One. It is possible that the Channel One controversy is the reason that a new wave of critical viewing materials were produced by media industries for schools. Media education was featured on evening news programs. And documentary specials were produced (Continental Cablevision, 1994; The Family & Community Critical Viewing Project, 1997; The Learning Channel, 1995; NBC Today, 1992; McGee, 1996).

About the same time, the cable industry partnered with community-based groups such as the National Parent Teacher Association and professional organizations, such as the American Medical Association, to produce books, magazines, guides, and videos about critical viewing. Partnerships between the Public Broadcasting System and professional media groups such as the National Academy of Television Arts and Sciences provide other examples (Pacific Mountain Network, 1993; Mertes, 1996). These industry-related efforts are similar to international efforts to create media education support materials by the British Film Institute, the Scottish Film Council, the National Film Board of Canada; TVOntario in Canada; United Artists and Warner Brothers in Australia and Canada; newspaper-in-education efforts in almost every industrialized country; and a host of smaller industry-related partnerships. Again, media education offers media conglomerates an opportunity to kill two birds with one stone—it opens a new cost center that allows them to re-purpose video for the educational market, while simultaneously enhancing public relations and audience development.

Many of the critical viewing resources created by media industries are very useful to teachers. Moreover, they spawn the creation of diverse classroom media education resources from a variety of sectors. Industry involvement creates heightened interest in media literacy education. But to say that the materials created by U.S. television industries were teacher-driven is an overstatement. It is doubtful that teachers expressed a need for them or, upon close examination, that the needs of teachers were central to their instructional design. Furthermore, the high-tech educational materials "pushed" to schools over the Internet are of similar mixed value to the classroom. Although they combine digital video, chat rooms, and Web pages in impressive ways, many of these information resources have yet to transcend the didactic model of the worst textbooks.

The rationale that media industries have inherent self-interest in audience development remains the most plausible explanation for media industries' involvement in education. The audience development argument goes as follows: Sophisticated and discerning audiences will demand higher quality media and media producers will have more opportunities to meet that demand with more satisfying, quality assignments. Of course, this argument teeters on the collective definition of "quality." The disjuncture between media's commitment to discerning media consumers and media industries' pandering to less-refined public tastes remains jarring. Raising the quality of media fare through media education curricula is at best an untested idea in the global media marketplace, where audience demand and good taste often clash.

MEDIA EDUCATION IN PRINT

Inasmuch as alphabetic literacy is still at the center of schooling, the task of creating teacher resources is somewhat easier for media industries that deliver classroom resources via print. This includes both print and computer industries, because both can promote general, familiar, and relatively un-problematic literacy goals within the context of schools.

It could be argued that contemporary media education in the United States has its roots in the acceptance of the popular novel as text for study alongside anthologies and readers in the classroom of the early 1900s, but as early as the 18th century, the study of popular media was thought to be a good idea. An editorial from the Portland (Maine) *Eastern Herald* on June 8, 1795, stated:

> Much has been said and written on the utility of newspapers; but one principal advantage which might be derived from these publications has been neglected; we mean that of reading them in schools, and by the children in families. Try it for once—Do you wish your child to improve in reading solely, give him a newspaper—it furnishes a variety, some parts of which must infallibly touch his fancy . . . newspapers are plenty and cheap—the cheapest book that can be bought, and the more you buy, the better for your children, because every part furnishes some new and valuable information. (Newspaper Association of America Foundation, 1993, p. 1)

As each new medium and genre came of age in the 20th century, the study of media and popular culture was applied to rhetoric, speech, drama, newspapers, cinema, radio, and television. The Newspapers-in-Education (NIE) programs, funded in the United States in part by the Newspaper Association of America Foundation, offered instruction using newspapers as early as the 1930s (p. 1).

The NIE programs were the first of a host of media literacy education materials produced by media industries. Newspaper-in-education programs offer resources and training to K–12 educators that present an opportunity for media criticism, but in the past, they have not constituted a media edu-cation program per se. Instead they are known primarily as a vehicle for promoting alphabetic literacy in reading, literature, current events, civics, and spelling. Only occasionally does the program stress critical thinking *about* media. However, new guidelines for NIE programs indicate that the primary objectives are changing toward more critical literacy goals such as:

> (1) a continuing desire and ability to read a newspaper critically and reflec-tively; (2) a concern for public issues and a motivation to involve themselves in our self-governing process; and (3) an understanding of the role of a free press in our society. (Newspaper Association of America, 1993, p. 2)

Although a step in the direction of critical literacy, the goals reflect their industry origins. The first goal addresses the need to critically question information, but is vague about applying criticism to the information provided by media gatekeepers, as well as to those quoted as sources in the newspaper. The second ("our self-governing process") is parochial, if not hopelessly confusing and the third ("a free press") is self-congratulatory and assumes that freedom of the press is an unproblematic notion, when it is instead fraught with tension between the freedom and responsibility of the press. Savvy media teachers will take the materials one step farther than the media industry public relations staff is likely to promote.

The NAA educational materials pass muster as a viable media education effort, *depending on how they are used.* Deciding what "counts" as media education can roughly be boiled down to a litmus test. Media literacy insiders call this the "through-or-about" test. As advanced by Barry Duncan (Duncan, D'Ippolito, Mcpherson, & Wilson, 1996), Canadian author, educator and past-president of the Association for Media Literacy, media literacy education depends on whether or not it is "education *about* media," as opposed to "education *through* media." Every educator uses media to teach—information resources ranging from the physical presence of a teacher to print to electronic media. But the "about–through" argument stresses that to simply use new and emerging technologies is not necessarily the same thing as questioning media in a metacognitive way—the form, content, and contexts of the information. In other words, a rigorous media education program demands critical literacy competencies that are applied to information, on some level, every time it appears in the environment.

The term *media literacy* has turned up in government policy documents, professional documents for educational standards, speeches by educational leaders and politicians, and as a subject of television and radio programming (*National Teleconference on Media Literacy,* 1996). A number of political officials ranging from the White House to social service agencies such as the U.S. Department of Health and Human Services (Baruch et al., 1996; U.S. Department of Health and Human Services, 1996), the U.S. Department of Education (Riley, 1995), and the Office of National Drug Control Policy (McCaffrey, 1996), have called for an increased focus on media literacy. Because of the push and pull of politics, embedding the term in documents and speeches raises the profile of media literacy without necessarily clarifying its aims and purposes, or without a coherent strategy to unify and support its core constituencies. The vision for media literacy that emanates from official channels reflects a cramped and protectionist view that some media are "good" and some "bad."

In a stump speech that kicked off the 1996 election season, a presidential campaign year marked by political pressure to control depictions of sex, violence, and a vague kind of "tastelessness" in television, the Internet, and popular music, Richard W. Riley, the U.S. Secretary of Education under President Clinton addressed a middle school audience in Maryland with these remarks:

> Young people need to stretch their minds and avoid being passive consumers. This is where media literacy can play a positive role. These courses can help young people make sense of the many media messages that bombard them daily. Media literacy courses can give young people the power to recognize the difference between entertainment, television that is just bad, and the information they need to make good decisions about their lives. . . . Our young people need to be educated to the highest standard in this new information age, and surely this includes a clear awareness of how the media influence, shape and define their lives . . . these young people today will hopefully prepare them to raise the quality of the media in the future. (Riley, 1995)

Before media education could be tried and tested in educational settings in the United States, it was taken into the public arena, embedded into policy documents as "media literacy," and touted as a problem-solving strategy for a wide range of social and educational ills, without regard to its potential efficacy for teaching and learning and with no time for field-based work to amass a research base. Because the concept was vague in the United States, and thus did not carry undue political baggage, expectations were raised for its ability to address social problems for a broad range of constituents, without either political fallout or accountability. The end result was more hollow rhetoric about the virtues of media literacy—pronouncements that echoed past uses of alphabetic literacy to rouse the body politic. For proponents of other multiliteracies who might hope to widely disseminate a broader recognition of their key terms, there is a lesson learned from attempts to raise the issue of media literacy in the public consciousness. It is: "Don't wish for something—you might get it."

Treading Water:
Media Education in the United States

The history of media literacy education in the United States is a cautionary tale for proponents of other literacies who are attempting to insinuate their approaches into formal educational practices. By further delving into the nuances, constituencies, and schisms in the emerging practice of media education, it is possible to shed some light on a whole host of communication-related multiliteracies and their relation to one another. The idea that students can be taught to "access, analyze, evaluate and produce" media in a variety of forms is central to the concept of media literacy. Whether its constituents can agree upon some common purposes for the concept remains to be seen. After several impressive attempts to form a critical mass of advocates, media literacy has yet to muster compelling and coherent arguments for its inclusion in formal schooling practices. Nonetheless, a heightened interest in media education by a host of special interest groups indicates that media literacy is an idea whose time has come.

Media are so commonplace and transparent in U.S. culture that it is entirely possible that it never occurs to people to study it. When Marshall McLuhan was asked why he thought that people needed to study media, when they were already inundated with pop culture, he quipped, "We don't know who discovered water, but we're pretty sure it wasn't a fish" (Marchand, 1989, p. 184). Needless to say, popular culture is big business and people spend a great deal of time using media daily. The United States exports more cultural products than any other nation on earth. Media are the third largest contributors to the U.S. economy, running slightly behind weapons and aircraft in gross national product revenues generated (Valenti, 1992). By the mid-1990s, sales of U.S. movie, TV, and home video products abroad totaled over $18 billion (Sandalow & Lochhead, 1993) and continues to climb. Records, publications, advertising, and software generated billions more in international markets, and the numbers continue to mount. Different cultures vary in the amount of U.S.-produced media that they buy, but all add up to position cultural products with a U.S. spin as leaders in worldwide media sales—a thorny issue in international trade agreements. Canadian television is made up of 75% U.S.-produced programming, and 95% of the movie business in Canada comes from U.S. films (Crary, 1995, p. B-1). In Europe, U.S. cultural product sales are at least $8 billion, dwarfing home-grown, European-produced products' gross receipts of $4 billion. Media markets on every continent have shown a voracious appetite for U.S.-produced media that reflect Western cultural sensibilities and compete with their own, locally produced media products (Sandalow & Lochhead, 1993).

Media are national obsessions and circulate additional billions within North American economies. In the mid-1990s, U.S. consumers spent nearly $56 billion on media products: $5.4 billion for movies; $23 billion on cable television; and $12 billion to buy music products. Over $15.3 billion was spent to produce music videos (Federman, 1996, p. 23). One in every four U.S. consumers owns a computer in their home, a ratio that is leaping exponentially, and purchase billions more in software (Escobar & Swardson, 1995, p. 17). U.S. telephone service is nearly universal, as is television ownership. An additional $160 billion in advertising media is pitched to potential consumers, 20% of which is for broadcast television (Federman, p. 23).

Clearly, the United States is an economic leader in the manufacturing and distribution of media. Job opportunities in media industries abound. This is apparently news to public schools. Contrary to their usual responsiveness to market-driven economies, media education is rarely mentioned as a priority for curriculum reform. Unlike Australia, Britain, Canada, and other developed countries, where attempts have been made to address the information glut by mandating media education in public elementary and secondary education, the United States comes in dead last in the integration of media education across the curriculum.

In fact, the dominance of U.S. cultural products on the international market may help to explain the relative strength of media education as a required competency in public school curricula in England, Canada, Australia, and other English-speaking countries. In these countries, the tidal wave of U.S. media provokes a vivid affront to the local cultures that receive them and has served as a stimuli for the teaching of media since at least the 1960s. Because they conflict with local values and swamp local media economies, U.S. movies, software, and related pop culture artifacts as far a field as theme parks, do not need to be problematized by teachers in these countries. Although international audiences enjoy U.S. media products, the values embedded in them already comes across as strange.

By examining the cultural messages and contexts of media from outside their cultures, teachers internationally have applied the same media analysis techniques to locally produced media. The framework for critical critique, learned through the study of popular culture, can also be applied to other genre, such as information resources used in more traditional, fine arts, and educational media fare. International proponents of media education have remarked that cultural criticism of U.S. media is a valuable strategy to steer students back, in a metacognitive way, to a better understanding of media discourses emanating from their own home cultures.

In typical technological determinist fashion, U.S. media education has focused on the *media* of media education. In this way, the media component is assumed to be more problematic than the educational component. In contrast the emphasis of international educators is on the *education* component of media education. It is also significant that outside the U.S., the mass communication theory base is only incidental to media education practices. Instead international media education efforts derive from a rich foundation of critical theory that demands a sophisticated and contextual analysis of culture. These teachers draw from eclectic and sometimes conflicting traditions based in constructivist education, formal structuralism, deconstructionism, semiotics, Marxist theory, technical determinism, and conservative versions of New Literary Criticism, to name a few. These critical theories become a weak echo in the United States and contrast significantly from the decontextualized mass communications models such as content analysis, or from the single-case, descriptive, qualitative methodologies used in the study of educational technology.

This is not to say that the theory base for media education in international circles is not problematic—by all accounts it is. However, there are many more pockets of consensus and a more thorough understanding about schisms within the field, than is often seen within U.S. media education circles. This may be due to the fact that because it is mandated, media education is formalized and studied in preservice teacher training and other areas of the university curriculum, thus offering more of a foundation for common understanding. In the United States, where the study of media has been *ad hoc* and autodidactic, there are relatively few opportunities for discourse among adherents.

Media literacy education has had its moments in the United States. As seen in other offshoots from literacy, it initially positions itself as a panacea to cultural and economic change. Emerging in fits and starts throughout the 20th century, it seems to run 10-year cycles. Conceptualized in ways similar to other multiliteracies, media literacy has been the operant term for a wide range of competencies and approaches practiced by an eclectic band of adherents. Media literacy's purposes have been so varied as to pique factional internecine disagreements among constituencies who rally in the United States under its broad banner. As seen in the emergence of other multiliteracies, definitions, goals, and purposes for media literacy depend on who is telling its story.

Even when media education programs can be said to teach about media vs. through media, distinctive differences in the assumed purposes for media education emerge. Roger Desmond of the University of Hartford, offered an explanation for the lukewarm response of academia to media literacy:

> The major difference between the path to implementation in the U.S. and other countries is that in the U.S., there is far less consensus among the scholarly community for a need for media literacy intervention, and paradoxically, there is a greater reliance on the academic community for approval of such programs. The result is that grant proposal approvals and endorsements for the activists from the research community have not been forthcoming. One important reason for this tension is that media educational activists have focused on the deficit model, promoting their programs as prophylactics for a host of diseases that have not been supported by existing media research. . . . What is clear from the interactions of researchers and activists at [international media literacy meetings] is that the goals of the groups have been so different, and their educations have differed so much, that necessary dialogue among them will be a long time coming. One issue that has the potential to unite them is the temporary abandonment of the deficit model, and shift toward an acquisition model. (Desmond, 1997, p. 338)

Desmond based his concept of the deficit vs. acquisition model of media literacy on an analysis of the definitions put forth for early media literacy efforts that looked at the critical viewing of television. He gleaned five purposes, or dimensions of media literacy from the research that include:

1. awareness of one's own relationship with media;
2. knowledge of how media organizations shape their fare, and the conventions of production for each;
3. a critical-ideological awareness;
4. the role of effortfulness [including critical effort, mindfulness to the task of creating meaning, etc.]; and
5. relationships among prior knowledge, media comprehension and the "real" world. (p. 327)

According to Desmond, "since they grew out of a fear of television-related child deficiencies," these dimensions were based on deeper rationale and assumptions about media, as seen in the research of James Brown (1991), who conducted an extensive review of critical viewing programs of the 1970s and 1980s. Rationale for the critical viewing programs include:

- Television erodes academically related skills including reading ability, concentration, and attention.

- Television watching causes aggression.
- Entertainment television is the source of sexual and ethnic stereotypes.
- Advertising elicits poor consumer habits in children, including the adoption of "junk foods" and renders them extremely susceptible to advertising claims. (Desmond, 1997, pp. 327–328)

Desmond sees hope for media education if it moves away from a deficit model of media education to one that he calls an "acquisition" model. In short, instead of focusing on all that is potentially wrong with media, the acquisition model would focus on the positive aspects of information acquisition for teaching and learning:

> An acquisition model would provide a framework for questions regarding issues such as (a) transfer of information to new contexts—how lessons from home entertainment and in-school viewing are or could be applied to other domains of learning; (b) mental effort—how can viewers, listeners, or users of CD-ROM, electronic games, etc., be stimulated to allocate more efforts and attention to important content? (c) can visual media production synthesize knowledge from other forms, e.g., scriptwriting elicits the author's research for script detail which in turn may lead to reading skill and practice? These and other issues related to skill and information acquisition have the potential to unite the concerns of researchers, educators and activists in ways that may prove fruitful. (pp. 338–339)

In spite of efforts to turn media literacy education from a deficit to an asset, the deficit model of media literacy education in the United States remains a primary rationale for media literacy. Desmond comments, "One problem inherent in such a shift is that the deficit model gets good press; media literacy activists are the first to admit that public fear of negative media effects is a politically correct entry into program acceptance by school administrators and parents" (p. 338). In order to fully understand the entrenched roots and development of the deficit model of media education in the 1990s, it is useful to look carefully at the critical viewing movement of the 1970s—perhaps the heyday of media literacy implementation in the United States.

DISSECTING THE CRITICAL VIEWING
MOVEMENT OF THE 1970s

Media education efforts proliferated in the United States in the 1970s, driven by the report of the Surgeon General's Advisory Committee on Television and Social Behavior (Surgeon General, 1972) and fueled by a subsequent report from leading social psychologists and mass communication scholars, published by the National Institute of Mental Health (Pearl et al., 1982). Four projects were funded by the U.S. government and several others by private sector funders at the cost of hundreds of thousands of U.S. dollars. Buoyed by ample funding and a sense of optimism, media education in the 1970s was at its peak. By 1981 the ambitious programs were gone.

The 1970s marked the first concerted and significant effort to involve elementary and secondary students in media studies by focusing on the medium of television, that is, "critical viewing skills curricula (CVS)." The rise and demise of the critical viewing skills curricula in the late 1970s is a cautionary tale of missed opportunity that informs contemporary thinking about media education. If media teachers heed the lessons of the 1970s there is a chance that they can learn from the experience of their international colleagues and witness a successful rebirth of media education in the United States, as the 20th century comes to a close. If not, the media literacy education will likely end in the same way—marked by factional infighting and increasing alienation from the realities of contemporary educational reform.

Individual researchers began work in media education as early as 1969 when Professors James A. Anderson and Milton Ploghoft from the University of Utah worked with the Broadcast Research Center and Cooperative Center for Social Studies at Ohio University to develop a series of critical viewing curricular packages for U.S. school districts in Eugene, Oregon; Syracuse, New York; Las Vegas, Nevada; and Jacksonville, Florida (Anderson, 1992, p. 11; Anderson & Ploghoft, 1981).

In 1973, the Ford Foundation called for a new day in American education with more instruction about mass media in public schools (Ford Foundation, 1975). The Foundation's proclamation represented a belated acknowledgment of a 1964 UNESCO report from Norway on the need for critical viewing skills education (Hodgkinson, 1964, p. 78). The Ford Foundation report on television and children challenged education institutions: The literacy of young persons in regard to mass media is the proper concern for educational institutions analogous to their concern about language literacy (Ford Foundation, p. 31).

Three years later, Ford, Markle, and the National Science foundations translated rhetoric into action by funding an invitational Television and Children Conference and its subsequent report that called for a curriculum to address many of the issues that are still considered important for media education:

> . . . such subjects as production conventions, analysis of media appeals, the character and role of non-verbal cues, overview of the history and structure of the broadcasting industry, the economic basis for television, analysis of typical formats for entertainment programming, analysis of the values portrayed in television content, standards for criticism of television content, and

if possible, some direct experience with television equipment. (Lloyd-Kolkin, Wheeler, & Strand, 1980, p. 120)

By 1978, fueled by the Surgeon General's report and a subsequent call for research on children and television violence the U.S. Library of Congress and the U.S. Office of Education hosted a national conference on "Television, the Book and the Classroom" (Pearl et al., 1982). That conference resulted in a request for proposals to develop four major critical viewing projects in the United States aimed at elementary, secondary, and adult education.

In 1979, the United States Office of Education funded four of the CVS proposals: Far West Laboratory for Educational Research/Development, secondary education; Southwest Educational Development Laboratories, upper elementary education;[1] WNET/Channel 13, New York, middle school education; and Boston University, a critical viewing package for adults. Other critical viewing projects were funded by private sources such as General Mills, ABC Television, The Learning Seed Company, The National Congress of Parents & Teachers, and others.

The Educational Testing Service (ETS) in the United States was charged with designing and conducting formative research and evaluation of the secondary critical viewing curriculum created by Far West Laboratory for Educational Research and Development in San Francisco in the early 1980s. The team of curriculum developers from Far West Lab, reported on the ETS evaluation in 1979. ETS selected 25 reviewers, all teachers or public school administrators. The reviewers found the curriculum to be of high interest to students, relevant to teaching critical viewing skills, and a good addition to courses already offered. The primary criticism of the curriculum was that it was too difficult for low-achieving students.

In spite of their positive rating, 46% of the reviewers did not think that teachers would be enthusiastic about using the curriculum and 41% thought that administrators would not consider it for their schools. An administrator on the panel said, "I believe this curriculum is not only important but necessary. . . . I'm not sure my colleagues would agree" (Wheeler, Lloyd-Kolkin, & Strand, 1981).

Donna Lloyd-Kolkin, lead researcher on the Far West project, notes that even though the project might have been better with more follow-up research and teacher training, the secondary critical viewing materials were state-of-the-art at the time. She said that in spite of plentiful funding, high praise from reviewers, some community support and extensive efforts to train teachers, little implementation was ever achieved, a common experience for all the materials developed between 1978 and 1983 (Lloyd-Kolkin et al., 1980).

---

[1]Far West Laboratory and Southwest Educational Development Laboratories changed their name to WestEd in 1996.

The need to protect children from television, as though it represented an electronic form of toxic waste, was the clear impetus behind the critical viewing skills programs in the 1970s. With a perceived increase in violence in society, researchers began to look to its cause. The study of television viewing's link to violence was isolated and effectively divorced from other aspects of the peculiarly American culture of violence, such as easy access to firearms, historical incidences of sanctioned violence, institutional racism and sexism, and so forth.

The U.S. Office of Education (USOE) framed the issue of critical viewing in a way that excluded the historical, economic, and additional cultural contexts of media representation. The USOE issued the following guidelines in its request for proposals for critical viewing projects:

- to understand the psychological implications of commercials;
- to distinguish fact from fiction;
- to recognize and appreciate differing and/or opposing points of view;
- to develop an understanding of the style and content of dramatic presentations, documentaries, public affairs, news and other television programming;
- to understand the relation between television programming and the printed word. (cited in Brown, 1991, p. 73)

With the USOE (Brown, 1991) guidelines, media education was narrowly confined to a television universe devoid of troublesome cultural context. The guidelines presumed that commercials *have* psychological implications, that there *is* a clear difference between fact and fiction in media; that it is *important* to know the difference between print and television; and that balance and objectivity *is achieved* by selecting some opposing points of view. Whereas all of these assumptions represent important concepts for exploration, the USOE (Brown, 1991) guidelines offered vague and arbitrary instructions to curriculum developers about why these concepts were vital to their projects. That television should be isolated as a medium of study, because of its "power," was simply assumed.

Television was such a prominent form of media study that the term "critical viewing" is still associated exclusively with television and widely identified as the sole purpose of media education in the United States. In hindsight, the focus on television was one of the major pitfalls of the period. The exclusion of other media forms was understandable for research purpose, because the subject of media must be delimited for purposes of implementation and measurement. Nonetheless, it was difficult for teachers at that time to take television watching seriously as a worthy curriculum task. Long considered an informal and recreational form of entertainment, the public, as well as many teachers, had difficulty understanding the relationship between television watching and learning.

Then as now, the public's response to television is one of ambivalence. Although concern is voiced for its effect on children, the majority of individual viewers enjoy television and rely on it for information. By creating the blanket "problem" of television, the Office of Education offered a "solution"—critical viewing skills curricula. For the public, the problem of "television" covers a host of social ills—many only tangentially related to television.

Teachers are accustomed to short-lived educational trends and curriculum imposed on them by nonteachers. When the critical viewing skills curriculum was tacked on to their busy day, many of them saw it as simply another educational fad—this time with a TV twist. James Anderson expressed the frustration of trying to give the amorphous competencies of media education some structure and definition:

> I began to think, "What if our problem is that media education is trapped inside the attitude that it is a television show, that it is a movie, that it is a radio or a record . . . instead of a way of conceptualizing the world?" (Anderson, 1992, p. 11).

Anderson has done extensive analysis of media education as a curriculum developer, researcher, and theorist (Anderson, 1980). Others have echoed his recommendations for successful implementation strategies in the field:

> The prognosis for curriculum development is tied to three forces: commitment by state school officials in terms of time, space, and money; the production and marketing by major textbook publishers of instructional materials; and the initiation of pre-service and in-service instructional support in teacher education institutions. School officials are in the pinch of inflation and the "back to the basics" movement. No major textbook company has yet announced the publication of regular classroom materials. . . . Teacher education institutions, historically conservative, have been slow to consider the new media. (Anderson, 1992, p. 19)

Political pressure contributed to the rise of the critical viewing movement in the 1970s, but no one factor contributed to its demise. The most likely culprits are its:

- focus on television instead of on a wider range of media forms common in classroom practice;
- failure to come to terms with the pleasure and attachment that people feel about the television medium as weighed against their relatively mild concerns about television content;
- failure to articulate a unified consensus of purpose for educational achievement;
- failure to include classroom teachers and students at the beginning and to ask if they wanted critical viewing curricula;

- lack of integration into daily teaching and learning practices;
- emphasis on media analysis over student media production skills;
- general *naïveté* about introducing new approaches and subject matter into the formal educational bureaucracy.

The media literacy projects of the 1970s were amply funded, the materials were professional and creative, and the curricula received high evaluations from teachers who used them. In spite of this, as soon as funding ran out for these projects, around 1981, media education activities ground to a halt in the United States. Although a few teachers still use the outdated critical viewing skills materials, new media education efforts, and the funding that sustained them, slowed to a trickle. As the 1980s ensued, public attention and federal funding was geared to new problems—an uneven economy, drug use and crime, and a strong "back-to-the-basics" movement in public schools. As federal monies and working coalitions dried up in the early 1980s, so did media literacy efforts. The critical viewing efforts in the 1970s did reinforce the "problem" of television in the public mind, but it missed the opportunity to establish a wider interest level beyond its stated concern about television content. Critical viewing lost its rationale when the obsession with television violence ebbed and the federal monies stopped. In the end, critical viewing curricula had demonstrated only limited usefulness to classroom teachers, who had not asked for it in the first place.

Media education was out of the limelight, but it did not die away. By the 1990s, media education programs sprouted anew, many of them beginning from scratch in community-based organizations. As new technologies and new audiences abounded, critical viewing became one of a host of issues for media education to investigate. For example, those who emphasized critical literacy suggested that users explore, analyze, and produce media in a variety of forms, including but not privileging television. And information management is increasingly a contemporary survival skill that begs for corresponding curricular support.

British researcher Andrew Hart (1998) commented on the need to extend media education into the digital frontier:

> The Media teacher of the future who recognizes the need to be in touch with the vernacular cultures of young people will need to incorporate information technology, in all its forms, in a curriculum that goes beyond embracing the traditional "mass media" and that is not distracted by the inherent fascination of new technologies without reference to their ownership and sociopolitical functions. This will mean going beyond both the existing English/Media curriculum and the currently instrumental role of digital technologies in education as expressive tools. It will mean including critical examination of software developments and information exchange and even employment patterns on a global scale. (p. 190)

Even so, media education in the United States still struggles to reinvent itself as a response to the critical uses of media beyond television. In the 1990s, new media literacy adherents picked up the debate about media effects as if it were yesterday (Brown, 1991, pp. 58–61, 69–72). Desmond (1994) commented:

> In the harsher light of the current global economy, poorly designed and administered programs of media literacy will go the way of marching bands and instruction in the arts—"extras" quickly and easily sliced from school budgets. Those who survive will require hard data on effectiveness from the research community, a difficult requirement in light of the schisms between researchers and educator-advocates. (p. 11)

CONFLICTING PURPOSES OF LITERACY

Disagreements about the uses of literacy continue to plague all the literacies, but because of its focus on the analysis of media representations, media literacy often gets caught up in debates about appropriate content, as well. It is likely that debates between media education advocates about the uses of media literacy from a deficit vs. an acquisition model will rage for some time. Most adherents agree that media literacy teaches students to be critical about media, but disagree about what "critical" means, as well as the purposes for such criticism. At least two approaches to media education in the United States are familiar to international educators in the field: media as agents of cultural decline; and media as popular arts. Two others also emerge: media production as an arts-based approach; and media education as a strategy for participatory democratic citizenship. These approaches are rooted in general assumptions and beliefs about the overall purposes for education and parallel approaches can be found in alphabetic literacy. Although not all constituencies are comprised of teachers and students, every approach positions media education as a way to address improvement in U.S. education, as well as an overall strategy to use media to improve the lives of children.

Vague goals for improving the social good through media education have broad consensus, but specific underlying assumptions about the nature and purposes of a broader concept of "education" can be very different. The problem arises when ideological differences and conflicting assumptions about the purposes of education remain submerged. When different assumptions about the purposes of education remain hidden, they become formidable obstacles that stymie understanding about the aims or purposes of *media* education.

Conflicts between present-day approaches to media literacy are in line with historical tension between the purposes for schooling as a mechanism to maintain the social status quo and those of critical literacy, which demand that the social status quo be questioned and challenged. To say that critical literacy has not always been welcomed in public education in the United States is something of an understatement. Schooling was established by the first colonists in Massachusetts in 1642 as a means to teach children to read the Bible, certainly a text whose status quo was not to be questioned at the time. In contrast, the presence of *belles lettres*, that is, literature as fine art, is notably absent from the Colonial Period. This is no surprise given the decidedly taciturn nature of Puritanism, but even the public press was constrained by puritanical ethics until the press became useful and powerful in the fight against England. "I thank God," Governor William Berkeley of Virginia said in 1671, "there are no free schools nor printing, and I hope we shall not have these [for one] hundred years; for learning has brought disobedience, and heresy, and sects into the world, and printing has divulged them, and libels against the best governments." Cotton Mather, one of the most famous clergymen and authors of the time, owned over 4,000 books—one of the largest private libraries in the world. He stated that he wanted children to read "handsomely," but cautioned that they could "stumble on the Devil's Library, and poison themselves with foolish Romances, or Novels, or Playes, or songs, or Jests" (Wiley, 1996, p. 65).

As previously noted, international media educators in Australia, Canada, and Europe report similar origins in the research and development stages for integration of media education in mandated programs. The difference is that since the 1950s, broad consensus about the purposes for media education has moved away from protectionist approaches to media education. Although international media educators may still choose to work from a protectionist model of media education, they are at least highly aware of the other approaches as the debate ensues. In contrast, media literacy movements in the United States appear to be cyclical, never venturing far from top-down, protectionist rhetoric. There are many reasons for this, not the least of which is the penchant for U.S. researchers to skirt the theories of cultural materialism that gave impetus to many of the initial media education efforts in Europe and South America. Until such conflicting and long-standing ideologies are understood and negotiated through compromise, as they have been in some international circles, the consensus-building necessary for implementation of media education remains elusive in the United States. Much of the tension can be reconciled, but the split between those who advocate a deficit model of media education and those who wish to work from an acquisition model is wide.

PROTECTING OTHER PEOPLE'S CHILDREN

The deficit model for media education that posits media as agents of cultural decline may be on the wane in international media education circles, but is alive and well in the United States. Media seem to be the lightning rod for a general frustration with the values inherent in the pervasive, hyper-capitalistic consumer culture of the West. Conspicuous consumption, the supremacy of the individual over societal concerns, environmental destruction as a cost of progress, competition vs. cooperation, and the blurring of the public and private spheres are only a few of the concerns that drive campaigns against media. Attacks against consumer culture are in line with old-time populist philosophies that balance the rights of individuals against the broader social good. It is much easier to denounce media, the perfect delivery systems for consumer culture, than it is to resolve the inherent conflict of values raised by America's attempt to graft aggressive capitalism to democratic principles and the doctrine of equal opportunity.

As researchers attempt to define the digital frontiers of literacy, stubborn assumptions about media literacy fuel the same false dichotomies and over-blown, totalizing pronouncements that plagued the early theory base for alphabetic literacy crop up again with media literacy. The approach that has been called "inoculation" or "protectionist" falls into this category and provides a compelling rationale for the institution of media literacy education. Hart (1998) commented:

> One of the keys to the absence of developed forms of Media Education in the United States is the existence of a powerful tradition of "prophetic" denunciation of the media. Such writers as Wilson Key, Jerry Mander, Neil Postman, and Marie Winn are well known within the United States (and beyond, as frequent mention by Ontario teachers show) but nowhere else have they managed virtually to monopolize the Media Education agenda and determine its most dominant discourse . . . it is almost as if the United States is determined to experience its own Leavisite tradition. Whatever the truth of this, it is clear that the major institutional frameworks in operation in the United States have not hitherto been supportive of Media Education and may, in fact, have functioned as negative constraints on its growth. (p. 179)

The age-old literacy question about the appropriate gatekeeping and interpretation of media that James Gee calls "Plato's Dilemma" again rears its head. The protectionist stance toward media is a logical extension of a perfectly appropriate parental gatekeeping responsibility—that of providing moral instruction and guidance in children's exposure to the adult world. The educator's surrogate role *in loco parentis*, as gatekeeper to the curriculum and arbitrator of taste, is even trickier. Educators must be attuned to the values of the whole community, and reconcile the expectations of individual parents for values inculcation with their own conscience.

Protectionist activists have been known to take the traditional gatekeeper role of the parent and extend it beyond the nucleus of the family or school and into the public sphere. In effect, they wish to define the appropriateness of media and information for other people's children, the wards of strangers, as well as for the children under their care and guidance. Thus, books are removed from libraries, television turn-offs are organized, movies are denounced, and viewing guidelines and ratings are hotly contested. The most aggressive protectionist rhetoric seeks to involve government in the legal regulation of content, for every medium, including speech.

Television still draws the most fire, but increasingly the Internet is the source of concern about the effects of media on young minds. As the number of corporate Internet gateways narrows in economic shakeouts and mergers, content is more easily scrutinzed and censored as a business decision. These economic decisions are often made under the guise of community concern. Proponents of information regulation pick and choose supporting arguments for their beliefs about the harmful effects of media from a spate of well-funded media effects studies in the 1970s through the 1990s. Because a distaste for certain media is based on complex personal values systems, it is not quantitative data, but popular opinion, sometimes called "common sense," that drives it. The fuzzy line that separates truly odious media, such as pornography, from media that is merely in bad taste, only fuels the impulse to curb and control a wider range of media—just in case harmful content may inadvertently be made available to minors. Effects studies are used to provide a veneer of scientific research to the already entrenched conventional wisdom that television, popular culture, and the Internet harbor ideas, images, and realities that are potentially harmful to children.

In fact, evidence about the harmful effects of media is mixed. Television has been particularly singled out as a medium of social decline. It has been blamed for everything from childhood obesity, to impaired comprehension and creativity, to hyperactivity. The favorite lament of the public and of some educators is that low reading scores on standardized tests are a result of excessive media use outside the classroom, especially the use of television. All of these characterizations may be true—or not. Much depends on a host of external conditions beyond the user and the media. Although there is a preponderance of evidence that points to a possible link between media and social ills, comparative studies, including international reviews of the literature have also concluded that after nearly 40 years of research on television's effects, the data is still inconclusive or contradictory: "Television leads to hyperactivity in children; television makes children passive. Television causes viewer isolation; television comforts the lonely. Television brings families together; television drives families apart" (Cooke, 1992, p. 42).

The issue of TV viewing and academic performance is a case in point. There is ample evidence that academic skill has a negative correlation to television viewing (Beentjes & Van Der Voort, 1988; **Gadbury**, 1980; Singer, Singer, Desmond, Hirsch, & Nichol, 1988; Singer, Singer, & Rapazynski, 1984). In an exhaustive review of the literature about the correlation of television viewing and academic performance, Comstock and Paik (1991) concluded, "There is no question that the amount of time spent viewing television by American children and teenagers is negatively associated with their academic performance" (Desmond, 1994, p. 4).

Other scholars are not as sold on the connection between television viewing and poor academic achievement. A 1988 U.S. Department of Education review of the literature on the effects of television indicates that there is no conclusive evidence that television use has any correlation to reading scores. The study found that the documentation claiming that television was harmful to children's academic achievement was simply not very reliable. The report also found that too many of the researchers were biased by prevailing social attitudes about the dangers of television, or sloppy in their research methodology. The report stated that researchers were quick to announce a trend in television viewing effects on children when in fact, the research did not justify any such sweeping statement (Anderson & Collins, 1988).

Problems with the research include the use of terms such as "concentration deprivation" which "connotes a general mindlessness resulting from prolonged viewing for which there is scant evidence" (Desmond, 1997, p. 329). The same could be said of "passive viewing." Even the definition of "heavy viewing" is by no means standard from study to study. Analysis of information about the uses of television by children as young as age 6 is questionable, due to the fact that their overall literacy and academic skills are not developmentally sophisticated by that time and therefore, are difficult to compare with viewing skills. Behavior that goes against the grain of the culture of schooling, such as "not sitting quietly," or "impulsiveness," is often attributed to the effects of television watching and thus are weighted as negative behaviors in the comparison of viewing and academic achievement.

The link between media violence and aggression in children has been made in countless studies. But as early as 1961, researchers questioned the correlation between media violence and real violence (Schramm, Lyle, & Parker, 1961):

> Although the studies that find the most-dramatic correlations between television and violence get the most publicity, there are other respectable studies whose conclusions are more restrained. "Television in the Lives of Our Children," for instance, one of the first major undertakings in the field, was published in 1961 after people became concerned about violent new shows like *The Rifleman* and *The Untouchables*. Researchers examined ten North American communities from 1958 to 1960, scrutinizing in great detail any aspects of television's effects. Their conclusion was a model of common sense: "For some children, under some conditions, some television is harmful. For other children, under the same conditions, or for the same children under other conditions, it may be beneficial. For most children, under most conditions, most television is probably neither harmful nor particularly beneficial." (Schramm, Lyle, & Parker, 1961, p. 1; in Sossel, 1997, p. 104)

Daniel Anderson, a psychologist at the University of Massachusetts and coauthor of the Department of Education report commented:

> Beliefs about the negative influences of TV on kids seem to satisfy some kind of need among educated people. It's almost part of an American mythology. Those beliefs are easy to reinforce by simply repeating the same things over and over. What we tried to do in this paper was to challenge people with what the actual evidence shows and doesn't show. (Anderson & Collins, 1988, pp. 18–19)

As access to media tools and information proliferates, the debate about the effects of media intensifies. On the one side is a demand for the free flow of information and freedom of expression made possible by digital media. On the other side is the legitimate need for parents to protect children from media content that violates his or her own family's values or, in the case of schools, the collective values entrusted to them by the community. The line between freedom of expression and media regulation seems to get fuzzier every day. The two sides can strive for balance, but the history of literacy has shown the debate to be inherently unresolvable.

Some see the attack on media as an elaborate ruse that diverts the conversation away from weightier matters of social inequity and sacrifice. Cultural critic Todd Gitlin concedes that contemporary media content is sometimes odious, but questions the wisdom of crusades against it. Of campaigns against television violence, he said:

> The campaign against the devil's images threads through the history of middle-class reform movements. For a nation that styles itself practical, at least in technical pursuits, we have always been a playground of moral prohibitions and symbolic crusades. . . . That media violence contributes to a climate in which violence is legitimate—and there can be no doubt of this—does not make it an urgent social problem. Violence on the screens, however loathsome, does not make a significant contribution to violence on the streets. Images don't spill blood. Rage, equipped with guns, does. (Gitlin, 1994, pp. 42–45)

As Gitlin noted, the demonizing of media has been a staple of middle class moral panics about media throughout history. Pop culture scholar Paul Gorman reminds readers that such panics occurred prior to the popularity of television (Gorman, 1996, p. 2). Such campaigns resulted in curbs on media in the real world. For example, condemnation of movies in the 1930s resulted in a long period of cinema censorship by the Hayes Commission, an industry censor. McCarthyism contributed to curbs in liberal political sentiments in media, as well as in matters of taste. Psychiatrist Fredric Wertham wrote *The Seduction of the Innocent*, a book that fed into a prevailing concern about juvenile delinquency in the early 1950s, by linking juvenile crime to the influence of comic books. In 1954, Wertham's crusade ignited two years of hearings by the Senate Subcommittee to Investigate Juvenile Delinquency. They attributed the primary cause of juvenile delinquency to mass-media entertainment (Gilbert, 1986, pp. 91–108, 143–161).

The objections of political conservatives to mass culture are predictable:

> The popular arts were repugnant to conservatives because they found them dangerously sensational and irrational, and therefore threatening to middle-class virtues. The popular forms also interfered with the vessels of elite culture that helped give society its grounding. Finally, they catered to the debased [tastes of the] working classes, whose interests deserved attention only in the name of maintaining their passivity. (Gorman, 1966, pp. 32–33)

Gorman noted that moral panics originate from both ends of the political spectrum. Liberal reformists present a far more complex, though equally suspect, rationale for their attacks on mass culture. According to Gorman:

> Beginning with the progressives, the attack on entertainments allowed individuals to be concerned for the state of the lower classes and to defend them actively while still maintaining the superiority and universality of their own standards for the arts. The mass culture concerns thus encouraged the intellectuals' paternalism and hastened the formation of what might be called a "democratic clerisy," an intelligentsia that justified its superior standing by its devotion to protecting democracy. (p. 10)

From both the political left and right, "Critics presented patrons from all groups as similarly harmed. . . . The critics ignored the desires of the groups that differed from their own, and they did not confront their own social prejudices. Intellectuals could [then] legitimately speak for the people . . . because the critique artificially recast the people as being all of one interest" without regard to the different uses and pleasure that people derive from mass culture based on class and other ascribed characteristics, such as gender, age, and ethnicity (Gorman, p. 11).

It is curious to some that activists on opposite ends of the political spectrum share an urge to regulate media that violates standards so arbitrary that at most they can be described as "tastes." Upon closer examination, this alliance is not so strange after all. Diverse viewpoints can be forged around the vilification of media because they have similar underlying beliefs about literacy:

1. that literacy (media/technology), especially advertising, has powerful effects;

2. that some types of media are better for society than others ... and the superiority of print over television and computers and the superiority of [fine arts over popular culture;] and

3. that literacy tools can effectively be used in sweeping campaigns—to either foster or destroy civilized societies.

The problem with either the lauding or the demonizing of media is one of degree—it boils down to literacy theory, which is characteristically temperate in its hypotheses and reticent to make sweeping judgments about literacy's uses. The common thread that unites the two ends of the political spectrum—the belief that new literacy technologies are either extremely good or bad for society, is the belief that literacy, in its many forms, has a totalizing and predictable effect upon individuals and societies. Literacy theorists such as Graff (1995), Gee (1996), Clanchy (1993) and a host of others have devoted their professional careers to tempering such simplistic views of literacy. Nonetheless, sweeping claims for new versions of technical determinism are tenacious, partly because they contain enough truth about the legitimate power of literacy to remain compelling.

Literacy is indeed problematic and its mis-use can do harm, but literacy scholars would take exception to hyperbole about the degree and kind of problem that media present. Most lay people hold a more tempered view of both literacy and communications technologies: artfully balancing their loathing of Big Science and megaconsumerism with their enjoyment of new and emerging modes of communication technologies, weighing their distaste for some forms of popular culture against a desire for a free flow of information and comparatively liberal freedom of expression.

Issues of content, such as the degree and kind of violence in media, sidetrack teaching about media and muddy the debate about the purposes of media education. The presumed value of media education, from a protectionist perspective, is its ability to neutralize the harmful effects of media. If media are forms of toxic waste, the argument goes, then media education is a prophylactic to protect citizens, especially children, from it. James Anderson (1980), in an article entitled, "The Theoretical Lineage of Critical Viewing Curricula," reflects on the conventional wisdom that education can protect children from the presumed negative effects of media. He calls such a strategy the "intervention construct":

Curricula which are based on the intervention construct are designed to teach students to recognize certain types of negative portrayals of social behavior and to provide them with alternative ways of interpreting these portrayals. ... Thus, the goal of curricula derived from this construct is essentially therapeutic; the influence of television is managed and redirected toward selected goals. ... The two configuring elements of this construct are ... first, that television does things to the viewer and second, that intervention can change the consequences. (pp. 65–66)

Two decades before the critical viewing movement was in full swing, Schramm, Lyle, and Parker (1961) cautioned against the notion that media is unidirectional and viewers passive:

> The connotation is that television is the actor; children are acted upon. Children are thus made to seem relatively inert; television, relatively active. Children are sitting victims; television bites them. Nothing can be further from the fact. It is the children who are most active in the relationship. It is they who use television, rather than television that uses them. (Schramm et al., p. 1)

The rationale for such uses of media literacy goes something like this: If only children could be given the skills and awareness to uncover the manipulative strategies of media, they would be able to discern the good media from the bad media and recognize the bad media for the unmitigated trash that it really is and summarily reject it. Because the field is too new and amorphous to provide longitudinal research data, there is scant indication that media education will work in this way to protect children from the presumed effects of media. Certainly not enough field-based evidence has been compiled to make this claim.

Protectionism is already practiced to varying degrees in homes and classrooms—as a legitimate and appropriate adult gatekeeping and parenting function. This is a task that parents and teachers consider appropriate to their role and one that they have a great deal of experience negotiating, based on age-appropriateness, community standards and intimate knowledge of their own children.

Desmond (1997) notes this in his suggestion that critical viewing curricula be extended to the home, as well as the school:

> The role of the family in mediating television comprehension and enjoyment has long been investigated in the traditions of effects research, phenomenological and cultural studies, but is seldom discussed with respect to media literacy. Since the viewing done at home is the major concern of the deficit arguments, the role of the family context in reinforcing and originating media education is crucial. (p. 340)

A protectionist paradigm demands an increased sense of vigilance for teachers and herein lies the seeds of resistance for its inclusion in formal schooling. Media education, when practiced in such a way, asks teachers to directly address—and provide redress for—media content that is potentially harmful. Although teachers inevitably are confronted with the ramifications of sex and violence in media, they do not wish to bring content with a sexual or violent bent into classrooms knowingly. To ask them to try to counter sex and violence in media in the world outside the classroom, means that they have to somehow bring it into the curriculum in the first place. Teachers have enough to worry about in the normal course of the day, without adding content that carries a high degree of risk. Resistance to such an idea can be expected.

In addition, the critical teacher, that is, one who wants to work from a student-centered, inquiry-based approach, has an inherent dilemma when confronted with the protectionist approach to media education. The problem with the protectionist approach for critical educators can be summarized as twofold: (a) If media literacy is to be student-centered, then is it fair or even productive for teachers to deride student taste in popular culture? and (b) if a goal of media education is to ask students to investigate critically and to question all forms of media in a way that leads to independent thinking, then doesn't it behoove educators to give them the abilities to reflect upon and defend their own taste in media? This inherent conflict is especially difficult to resolve for teachers of older students, or when teacher taste in media differs with student taste. Shifting the goal of media education to that of elevating student taste so that they will begin to dismiss "offensive" popular culture is a compromise between the approaches. This is a strategy that Masterman assigned to the "media as popular arts" viewpoint. Upon closer examination, the goal to use media education to elevate student taste is a not-so-subtle way of telling students what is appropriate to like or dislike from the perspective of an authority figure. Although the introduction of popular culture into the classroom may be of interest to students, this is a teacher-directed, not a student-centered approach.

If the primary goal of media education is to promote what Masterman calls "critical autonomy," that is, the ability to think for oneself, then to tell students what to think about media, no matter how subtly, would be inherently counterproductive. The fact remains that even though students might learn to deconstruct and question "bad" media, they may still choose to take pleasure from it. For example, it cannot be ensured that sophisticated, detailed deconstruction of action and adventure video games will curb little boys' desire—in the least—to enjoy them. Or that teenagers can be persuaded to dislike popular music, or that media literacy education will turn college students against soap operas. Not only may it be impossible to use media education to ruin *bad* media for children, given a child's psychological need to establish independence from parental influence, adult interference in a child's cultural taste may even serve to make children embrace the demonized media all the more. Although teachers must be true to themselves and maintain their responsibility to be positive role models, they can only be asked to go so far. Students will try very hard to tell their teachers what they think adults want to hear. Whether this constitutes authentic teaching and learning is another question entirely.

JAMMIN' FOR A BETTER TOMORROW

Some of the objection to media has to do with form, as well as content. Although obsessed with television, protectionism can extend to a general distaste for everything technological, that is, not books. Technology can symbolize a cluster of cultural paradigms, including the decline of individualism, consumerism, and erosion of the ecosphere. Upon closer examination, the split between technophobes and technophiles could also be described as another in a long line of false dichotomies in the history of literacy.

There have been innovations in technology throughout history, notably in China, that did not engender resistance, because they spread organically, if at all, and did not necessarily build on one another. By the turn of the 19th century, the ideology of progress dictated that one technological innovation built on the next in a very deliberate way. The assumption that progress means ramping up to "bigger, better, faster," continues to this day in the rhetoric about the link between digital technologies and progress. Since the Industrial Revolution, resistance to the juggernaut of progress occurs sporadically.

Those who actively resist technology are called *Luddites*, a derogatory term coined for English weavers of the early 1800s who smashed machinery as a symbolic protest against the mechanization of labor while the juggernaut of the Industrial Revolution swept through Europe. Actually, it could be argued that the Luddites are unfairly represented in history. The Luddites did not initially set out to counter the Industrial Revolution, nor were they necessarily ideologues. Instead, they were far more practical—skilled weavers who smashed the automated textile looms that threatened to automate the workplace and take away their jobs. Although their sabotage seemed effective, the Luddites actually were more likely to smash equipment that was already broken. They did, however, especially target those machines that were customized for operation by children. Contrary to their image as backward thinkers, early Luddites were not against the idea of technology per se. This fine point was lost as their cause became more effective. The Luddites' threat to the status quo made them the targets of powerful enemies. In 1812, the British sent 24,000 troops and local militia to put down the Luddites—more than had gone abroad to fight Napoleon (Boal, 1995).

The Luddite label has transmutated into an all-purpose generalization for those disgruntled by and resistant to the prospects of a high-tech, virtual world. The moral outrage that drove the original Luddites provides the core metaphor for a new pack of contemporary rabble-rousers. This time around, the target is not the "monkeywrenching" of the machinery of industrial production, but the subversion of cultural production. The Luddites have reached out over the centuries to influence contemporary kindred spirits, this time known as "culture jammers."

Culture jammers answer to that name. "Jamming" is CB radio slang for the illegal practice of interrupting broadcasts or conversations between fellow hams. . . . Culture jamming, by contrast, is directed against an ever more intrusive, instrumental technoculture whose operant mode is the manufacture of consent through the manipulation of symbols. . . . Part artistic terrorists, part vernacular critics, culture jammers . . . introduce noise into the signal as it passes from transmitter to receiver, encouraging idiosyncratic, unintended interpretations. Intruding on the intruders, they invest ads, newscasts and other media artifacts with subversive meanings. Simultaneously, they decrypt them, rendering their seductions impotent. (Dery, 1993, p. 57)

Culture jammers subvert the intended purposes of existing media produced by mainstream corporations (subvertising), but also produce content and forms that are an alternative to the discourse of mainstream media (antiads, or countermedia). This content ranges from altering ads and billboards, to creating messages that reflect everything from liberal social causes to fundamentalist Christian ideology—by using the tools and techniques of mainstream mass media in subversive ways.

Culture jammers have turned their most withering scorn on those who control the technologies of communication—multinational media conglomerates. The belief is that access to diverse, quality information sources is increasingly rare, as information becomes commodified and privatized. In addition, existing media is believed to promote the empty values of a consumerist society. Trevor Barr touched on this subject in a keynote for an Australian Teachers of Media Conference in 1988:

Whilst we pour money into the technological infrastructure to deliver more and more information, rarely have we investigated the issues of user needs, carriage to whom, and why? All the plethora of distribution systems—who are they designed for? Who is going to make the programs? Who will have access? It doesn't necessarily follow that greater abundance of information leads to better informed users. There is not a causal relationship there at all. . . . The majority of our high-tech information systems are predictably run as commercial enterprises. Little information, generally speaking, is designed for the needs of ordinary citizens. . . . The short answer to the questions: "Information revolution: whose revolution?" is a revolution for the world's biggest brand names; it's their revolution. (Barr, 1988)

Culture jammers are a voice for widespread frustration with the formulaic and stereotyped range of representation in media and want to present a wider range of alternative representations. Most of all, culture jammers consider themselves a bulwark against the values of consumerism:

By far the most dangerous disinformation in our system is consumerism: the slogans, jingles and lifestyles that two generations of mass media merchandizing have seared into our brains. These information viruses are deadly, for even as they weigh our future down with an unconscionable debt load, even as they systematically zap the ecosystems that sustain us, they demand that we consume MORE. . . . To survive . . . we've got to scramble the message of mindless consumerism, discredit the dysfunctional paradigms that are driving us to ruin and install a new mass media software package in our collective psyche. In short, we've got to culture jam. (Lasn & Schmaltz, 1993, p. 2)

Jamming has proven useful as a way to further a wider range of viewpoints. Public access producers, independent media producers, computer hackers, community activists, and social service agencies have learned the techniques of media production to subvert the uses of media to promote values they believe are for the social good. Public health activists are a case in point. Although generally more genteel than some other types of culture jammers, public health advocates have also been successful in the use of a culture jamming approach to the prevention and promotion of healthy behaviors. Advertising has proven particularly useful to their efforts—tobacco and alcohol advertising have been perennial targets of media advocacy.

Just as the Luddites sabotaged technology, culture jammers subvert mass media's intended messages—especially those targeted to children. Culture jamming activities range from defacing alcohol and tobacco billboards to producing health-friendly public service announcements in mainstream media. Media advocates view media as both dissemination channels and as political tools for social justice.

> On the surface, the dialogue centers on access to health care and disease risk factors such as alcohol, tobacco and nutrition, but the core reveals the tension among competing values to determine how benefits should be distributed in society—the issue of justice. A progressive perspective regards social justice as the foundation of public health. . . . The larger society, however, resonates more closely with the principles of market justice . . . [which] suggests that benefits such as health care, adequate housing, nutrition, and sustainable employment are rewards for individual effort (on a level playing field), rather than goods and services that society has an obligation to provide. (Wallach, Dorfman, Jernigan, & Themba, 1993, pp. 6–7)

Many health professionals have advocated the use of media to a form of social marketing. When public health advocates borrow from the codes and conventions of advertising they hope to produce powerful results:

> Using the media as a political tool is not the typical way public health professionals have approached the media. . . . Social marketing has become a key concept in addressing some of the shortcomings of previous public communication campaigns . . . [it] provides a framework to integrate marketing principles with sociopsychological theories to develop programs better able to accomplish behavior change goals . . . it takes the planning variables from marketing—product, price, promotion, and place—and reinterprets them for health issues. Ideally, social marketing also involves the mobilization of local organizations and interpersonal networks as vital forces in behavior change

process. A key principle of social marketing is that it seeks to reduce the psychological, social, economic, and practical distance between the consumer and the behavior. (Wallach et al., 1993, p. 21)

But does such media advocacy yield results? The implication is that media offer surrogate role modeling so powerful they can be employed in a positive way to make the environment healthier, to change risky behaviors, and to make children resilient to unhealthy influences in media. It is a seductive argument and the belief in the power of advertising has yielded high-profile results—notably the 1997 withdrawal of ads that appeared to target children by tobacco companies. Other evidence is hopeful. For example, University of California researchers in San Diego found a 17% reduction in smoking over 3 years, after a California antismoking media campaign was instituted (Williams, 1996, p. A-13). Nonetheless, the jury is still out on the ability of media advocacy to effect changes in public health. This is especially true of those campaigns that produce healthy message ads without a companion component of face-to-face activism at the community level. Occasionally, well-intentioned campaigns may inadvertently lend themselves to a counterproductive result:

> Most evidence has shown that public service announcements [are] a very limited application of social marketing, have limited effects and may [only] serve to reinforce an individualistic understanding of health and social problems. . . . These campaigns may reinforce a politically safe, but practically ineffective approach to using media. (Wallach et al., p. 22)

Wallach is not against the use of PSAs, per se, but instead argues for a more holistic community approach to public health education, one that does not position a single intervention, such as a PSA, as "a silver bullet" of prevention. As powerful multinational media corporations tighten the noose on media ownership, culture jammers fear that the window of opportunity for widespread dissemination of alternative messages is rapidly closing. When analog channels dry up, computer hackers await on the digital fringe. Ironically, computer hackers and media jammers who see themselves on the radical fringe are rapidly becoming part of the digital mainstream. They are increasingly in evidence as employees of media companies, where their technical skills, ideas, and style are in much demand.

Driven by a sense of moral outrage and righteousness, culture jammers are protectionists at heart. They have contributed to the media literacy movement by broadening the dialogue about media to include corporate ownership of media; by calling for more diversity in the form and content of media messages; and by insisting that every citizen have the opportunity to be a media provider as well as a media receiver. Died-in-the-wool protectionists, armed with TV Turn-offs, would argue that society has too much of the wrong kind of media. Culture jammers would counter that we don't have enough of the right kind.

CHAPTER EIGHT

Moving Toward an Acquisition Model of Media Education

Individual teachers still practice media education in the United States, but their efforts have yet to add up to a coherent critical mass that can be called a media literacy "movement." Media education efforts remain isolated, sporadic, and disjointed. There are teacher-driven efforts in every state, notably California, Hawaii, Minnesota, New Mexico, Indiana, Illinois, Kentucky, Massachusetts, New York, North Carolina, Texas, and Washington, but they are *ad hoc*—driven by the initiative of small groups of educators, and undercut by a lack of support from formal educational bureaucratic structures and related funding streams.

Furthermore, higher education is tepid in its support for media literacy education. Media education programs that teach *about* media in the elementary and secondary curriculum are a 20th-century phenomenon. After World War II, a major purpose of mass communication at the university level was to train workers for the upstart radio and television industries. The focus on job training is a form of educational pragmatism that has always figured prominently in any change in U.S. education and media study is no exception. When mass media and new technologies are introduced into preservice teacher education, it is usually through a "teaching through" audiovisual or computer class that familiarizes teachers with teaching machines. Major exceptions can be found as departments within education programs at Appalachian State University (North Carolina), Clark University (Massachusetts), New York University, and Webster University (St. Louis), to name a few.

In the 1990s, as U.S. media literacy advocates regrouped, progress in North American media education was going forward in Canada. Taking the lead from educators in England and Australia, a grassroots coalition of teachers from the Association for Media Literacy and the Jesuit Communication Project in Toronto pushed through a mandated media literacy strand in the Language Arts curriculum for all secondary students in Ontario. Their work was influenced by Birmingham cultural critics Stuart Hall and Raymond Williams, but also by the emphasis on form provided by Toronto native Marshall McLuhan, as well as by the principles of critical democratic pedagogy promoted by Paolo Freire of Brazil. The aims of the Canadian curriculum were to unite media analysis skills with hands-on practice; to explore the contexts as well as the content for media messages; and to recognize that students take great pleasure in the use of media and popular culture. The Canadian media education movement placed its emphasis on education, specifically on the social construction of knowledge:

> It is education that aims to increase students' understanding and enjoyment of how the media work, how they produce meaning, how they are organized, and how they construct reality. Media literacy also aims to provide students with the ability to create media products. (Ontario Ministry of Education, 1989, p. 7)

In the resource guide created for all secondary language arts teachers in the province of Ontario, key concepts, classroom activities, and teaching strategies were outlined. Media industries coordinated their educational offerings with the curriculum to produce supporting materials. Resources were created from the National Film Board of Canada, TVOntario, and a host of local teacher organizations. According to the Media Literacy Resource Guide, the key concepts are not necessarily taught. They work instead from underlying principles for those "teachable" moments in the classroom. Key concepts are:

1. All media are constructions
2. The media construct reality
3. Audiences negotiate meaning in media
4. Media have commercial implications
5. Media contain ideological and value messages
6. Media have social and political implications
7. Form and content are closely related in the media
8. Each medium has unique aesthetic form. (Ontario Ministry of Education, 1989, pp. 8–10)

A growing group of new media educators in the United States, looking for succor and resources, began to drift north to attend conferences at

Guelph, Ontario and the University of Toronto and to correspond with Canadian media educators at the Association for Media Literacy, the Canadian Association of Media Education Organizations (CAMEO), and the Jesuit Communication Project. By the time the Aspen Institute convened the National Leadership Conference in 1992 (Aufderheide & Firestone, 1993) to discuss the state of media literacy in the United States, the Canadians had already organized and implemented their media literacy curriculum with tangible success.

The Canadian curriculum created something of a dilemma for U.S. media literacy advocates. It presented an opportunity for international collaboration and testbeds for collecting evidence about the efficacy of media education in action. It provided formative evaluation of teaching strategies and resource development for scaling up and customizing emergent U.S. media education efforts. The Canadians were doing groundbreaking work on media education standards and assessment strategies. But the Canadian media literacy curriculum also challenged the prevailing rationale for media literacy in the United States, that is, as a protection against the negative effects of media. Although the Canadian educators insisted that media are meant to be "made problematic" for the K–12 classroom, they questioned the need to demonize media and popular culture. Remnants of protectionism were still in evidence, but popular culture was celebrated as an asset to teachers and learners, because it opened opportunities for teaching and learning through the questioning of a wider range of social artifacts. Such a vision of media literacy education goes far beyond the protectionist "television effects" paradigm and hinted at the kind of acquisition model suggested by communications scholar Roger Desmond (1997). Such a model turns the "problem" of media into increased opportunities for teaching and learning.

The Canadian model provoked discourse about the assumed goals and purposes of media education and forced the U.S. media literacy movement to try to understand and resolve the competing ideologies in its ranks. In the process, fissures in the loose coalition of media literacy advocates in the United States began to vex consensus-building efforts. Many of the problems that led to the decline of critical viewing in the 1970s were returning in force to sabotage media literacy efforts at the end of the century.

Media education has yet to prove its efficacy in either formal or informal settings. There is no clear evidence that media education is broadly practiced in the home. It still does not occupy a formal place in the elementary and secondary classroom. Beset by special-interest curricula and concerned about student performance, many classroom teachers are left to wonder why they should take up the cause for movements that seemed tangential to their busy classrooms. In fact, teachers deal with multiliteracies in the classroom on a daily basis. The dilemma that teachers face is one of providing a clear rationale to the question: Why should media education be privileged in the curriculum? Until some consensus is reached in response to educators' sincere need for justification, media education still risks becoming a solution in search of a problem. Nonetheless, there are some hopeful signs that media education can move past the protectionist rationale toward strategies that offer more choices to educators and are less limiting. Two approaches to media education in the United States show promise in moving media education from a deficit model to an acquisition model. They are: media production as an arts-based approach and media education as a strategy for participatory democratic citizenship. Both position media literacy as an opportunity to increase and enhance the life chances of students.

AN ARTS-BASED APPROACH TO MEDIA EDUCATION

Industrialized cultures maintain a longstanding love affair with technology. Just as spirituality was the prevailing metaphor of the Medieval world, technology provides the defining force for the Industrial and Information Ages. An arts-based approach to media education builds on this passion for gadgets and the cultural ramifications of an increasingly electrified, mediated, and virtual world. The best media arts programs attempt to use experiential education to unite media analysis with practice.

> An aim of media education is to close the gap between analysis and practice, between criticism and doing. Only those who have engaged in practice are in the "correct" position to criticize; practice without critical awareness is blind, "commonsensical" and sterile. The media are best understood as sets of processes (e.g., technical, professional, aesthetic, ideological, economic, political) whose purposes include the social generation of meanings. In the context of that view, production work and the simulation of professional production are of vital importance. However, Media Studies is not in the business of training technicians or of merely informing armchair critics but, in a developed post-Leavis sense, encouraging practical criticisms and critical practices. (Dick, 1987, p. 5)

One danger of a media arts approach is that in the process of "learning by doing," students can inadvertently fall into a technicist trap by marginalizing the analysis component in the quest for production. Practice devoid of analysis is an unnecessarily narrow perspective—overly specialized, sterile, and prefunctory. More often than not, the technicist approach places an emphasis on skill-based manipulation of media tools, ignoring the critical component and creating an artificial fissure between the analysis and production components of media education. Such a use of information tools becomes a teaching through, not a *teaching about* use of media. Technicist approaches to media education, masquerading as media arts programs can be recognized by at least three criteria: (a) the analysis of media and information is not emphasized in a formal and structured way; (b) mainstream, commercial media formats are replicated in the classroom; and (c) media and technology are presented as unproblematic channels of information.

In contrast to their protectionist colleagues, who dramatize the problems of media, technicists assume that communication technologies are unproblematic "windows on the world." Such a viewpoint violates a key concept of media education: All media are constructions. As systems of representation, media are not mirrors of society, or windows on the world. Instead, they are carefully constructed and manufactured products with a wide range of commercial, ideological, social, and political implications.

Because one prevailing purpose of education in the United States is to secure gainful employment, technology education feeds into the need for job readiness in a global, information economy. Technology education also plays off a Western cultural fetishism about technology and machines. While linking *this* cable to *that* computer in a teacher-centered classroom, technology education defines communication in terms of machines, and skirts more complex questions that can lead to reflection about technology, society, and culture.

In one of the relatively few books to advocate teaching about computers, as well as teaching with them, Wessels (1990) observed that "The power of computers as information tools is well appreciated by now. . . . What is less apparent is that computers are instruments of social change." He advocates teaching about the social, political, economic, cultural and ethical contexts of a computerized society (pp. xi–xii).

In contrast, an arts-based approach to media education may evolve from a creative, artistic/aesthetic skill set. While the purpose for technology education may be job readiness, the purpose for arts teachers who use media tools with students is to foster self-expression, creativity, and to find their own "voice." Many of these programs are centered in after-school, nonprofit, or museum settings. Artists also come in to formal school settings through artist-in-residency programs.

Access to media information and hardware is an important and logical adjunct to a complete media education program. It is cynical indeed to encourage students to question media and then not to supply them with access to quality sources of information that can help to inform their decisions. Students need access to diverse media resources, the skill to make sense of information, and opportunities for hands-on practice that inform their analysis of media and includes elements of creative self-expression. Students and teachers also need the hardware and software to produce their own media messages in a diverse variety of media. Although digital hardware is proliferating, the major hardware used in U.S. classrooms is still chalk.

School residencies bring visual and media artists, writers, independent film and videomakers, and multimedia wizards into the classroom. Hands-on

video and multimedia production are especially popular with students and
the classes are most often student-centered and engaging to students. Many
of these programs were instituted to increase student *self-esteem*—especially
for students who have not been successful in school. Aside from the fact
that self-esteem is a controversial educational goal, these programs can be
soft on structure, thus shortchanging those students who may be in most
need of educational opportunity.

The emphasis by artists on vague goals and objectives such as self-esteem
is an example of the gulf between lay teachers and professional teachers.
Artists and teachers have been apprenticed under two widely different professional systems. Artists who come for short residencies are outsiders to
school culture and as a result, the media arts programs and the artists who
institute them, are in danger of being marginalized within the institutions.
Furthermore, artists are not usually trained in the fine points of assessment
and do not always understand the rigors of standards-tasks-assessment that
teachers must continually monitor to ensure that learning is taking place.
"Learning by doing" does not take place by accident, but involves a good
deal of attention to structured events—a tedium that seems overwrought
and unnecessary to informal, lay educators.

Upon observation, it is often clear that the artists-in-residence are aware
of learning events, but it can be difficult to get them to articulate what these
events are in a way that responds to the arcane vocabulary and discourse
of the school. And it is not even that artists do not fuse analysis with practice.
It is simply that it is sometimes difficult for them to make these learning
opportunities explicit to colleagues, because it is couched in the discourse
outside official educational "bureaucratese." As a result, artists often look as
if they are "doing their own thing" to teachers. Teachers look unnecessarily
school-marmish and fussy to artists.

One of the most important things that an artist can bring to the classroom
is a sense of the wide range of aesthetic expression. Without this openness,
hands-on production too often replicates commercial formulas for media-
making: news shows, game shows, talking heads, trendy music, and textbook
publishing that are the mark of an amateur producer, or at least one who
has only experienced a narrow range of media forms and genre. Artists can
provide models for a much wider range of independent, non-narrative,
experimental, and alternative media—formats that are not available in commercial media channels and therefore media that teachers and students may
never before have seen.

The problem for practioners is to include analysis and practice—cognitive
with skill-based learning—and gracefully unite it in a formal and structured
way. The best way to do this is to create a partnership between reflective,
critical teachers and skill-based technicists that exploits the strengths of both
for dynamic teaching.

Teachers do not have the same opportunities—in either preservice or in-service training—both to learn to manipulate tools and to see the wide range of expression available to artists. Artists and some "techies" do not usually have the opportunity to study learning theories and strategies, and are sometimes insecure about addressing the cognitive side of learning. Trained together in principles of media education, artists, teachers, and technical enthusiasts can create a force that takes a structured and formal approach to media teaching, based on sound pedagogical principles and high levels of skill and understanding. The artist–teacher team approach to media education has been used successfully in several U.S. programs, as media arts centers team up with public schools. A list of programs that stress arts and critical literacy education can be found in the Appendix.

Another way to bridge the vocational use of technology with a deeper emphasis on the analysis of information takes advantage of the way that technology education is disseminated in a school. School librarians have expanded their roles to become "information resource specialists," and are most often the technology gatekeepers for local school sites. Because of their grounding in information literacy, information resource specialists have expertise and interest in the free access to information and the ability for information users to organize, analyze, and evaluate information. Although they have traditionally focused more on the dissemination of information, they are beginning to also explore ways to facilitate the creation of information by students. Librarians are teachers first. Like their colleagues in the classroom, they understand that the power of information cannot be fully tapped without a human interface.

The synthesis of analysis and practice is the key to media education. Articulating the relationship and designing tasks that balance analysis and production is tricky for media teachers. For one thing, there is a normal and predictable mismatch of cognitive and physical skills. Students who have strong production skills may find it difficult to talk about their work and that of others. Students with strong discursive skills may be all thumbs on the computer or video camera. It is one thing for a student to recognize that media have commercial implications, and quite another for a teacher to structure learning events that enable them to point this out in mass media products, or break down a hands-on project so that students can understand the concept of commercialism in a sophisticated way. An approach that goes back and forth to build the analysis and production sides of the equation takes a combination of skilled teaching experience and creative talent. A team-teaching approach ensures that the wide range of skills needed to do so are available. Team-teaching also is beneficial because it allows for reciprocal feedback about pedagogy, curriculum, and assessment of student learning. When teachers have the opportunity to critique one another's practice, it provides a valuable growth opportunity not available to the solitary teacher.

THE SAN FRANCISCO DIGITAL MEDIA CENTER:
AN ARTS-BASED APPROACH IN ACTION

Throughout history, as new literacy forms emerge and overlap, the need for literacy instruction has been filled by agencies outside formal educational bureaucracies. The home has had a traditional role in literacy instruction at least equal to that of the formal schooling environment and contemporary scholars have suggested the home as a promising setting for new concepts of literacy (Desmond, 1997). Labor unions, trade guilds, religious movements, and other special interests have provided literacy instruction as part of their service to constituencies.

The San Francisco Digital Media Center carries on the tradition of literacy instruction outside formal educational bureaucracies. Although the group works with high-tech tools, the purposes and approaches of the Digital Media Center is not centered on digital technology skill-building. Instead, the work of the Center explores age-old oral and written traditions of storytelling for the purpose of community-building. Their key to success is that they combine old practices of literacy with new.

The Center was created by a group of artists to explore the way that their skills and knowledge about theatre could be used with new and emerging media forms. It grew out of a theatrical arts organization know as Life on the Water, which was involved in multigenerational, community arts projects in both formal and informal educational settings. In 1994, Life on the Water collaborated with a number of San Francisco Bay Area artists to move their existing community-based work into storytelling through digital media. The storytelling program was developed in collaboration with a number of artists, including Dana Atchley, Joe Lambert, Ron Light, Nina Mullen, and Ellen Sebastian. Lambert and Atchley had previously collaborated on a theater piece called *Exit*, which was based in autobiographical and family images about Achtley's life. From this, the artists designed a program that was initially called *Home Movies* and has evolved into *Movies for Digital Storytelling*, a training program that works with people's family pictures, home movies, and material they've created to produce short, 3–5 minute pieces in digital video environments. Many of their workshops are complete in one day or one weekend.

The artists had worked in video for many years. Once they had mastered digital editing tools, their production work was streamlined and there was no going back to analog. Joe Lambert, artist and founder commented on the impetus for San Francisco Media Center:

> For us, the development of the idea of digital storytelling comes from our own experiences with digital media. We've witnessed the initial years of the multimedia explosion. It was exciting to be in the San Francisco Bay Area,

because it felt like one of the epicenters of the creative, productive industry of multimedia. We also saw that the design and production of computer-based media was led by technical-type development. It was not being led much by—the word in the industry is "content," but we would just say "story," or even "meaning." It was definitely not led by a very broad definition of "point of view."

People were making work that would show off what the machines could do, but their reason for making the work was not clear. Or the work did not really have much to say to people about the real world that they lived in. That was certainly true in the games environment, which is almost by its nature not interested in social analysis or a critical point of view. But to some degree, you can also see this technical perspective coming from people who claim to be making work that was artistically based, or based in some sort of critical context about the world. Sometimes even the artists were still much more enamored in showing what the tools could do. So we were very interested in a training approach that took the opposite standpoint, which was simply that, "Yes, these are very interesting and sophisticated tools, but in what ways do they make things that we were doing before easier?"

We teach something analogous to the writing of print. The production, if you like, as opposed to consumption. Part of literacy is the use of the tools—for us, the many software tools. It's starting from the standpoint of, "How do you produce your own material?" And then, "What are the tools that will allow you to do it?" The idea is as the tools get easier, then people can tell their stories—and they all have stories. If you were walking them into a creative writing class, you'd say, "Here's your tool, the pen and a piece of paper," or "Here's the word processor. Do you know how to use it? Ok. you do." We're taking the same approach with what are very sophisticated machines in terms of digital video and photographic manipulation. We say, "You have a story inside you. Here are the tools. Let's put those aside and focus on your story." Hopefully we've simplified these production issues to the extent that they don't feel burdened. On the one hand, burdened by using them, and on the other hand, intimidated by all the things they can do. (J. Lambert, personal communication, January 18, 1997)

The San Francisco Digital Media Center hosted a youth program called D*LAB, as in Digital Laboratory. D*LAB was based in the Center's ideas about storytelling as the training metaphor for learning new media skills and was specifically targeted to youth. It conducted a summer program for 50 students called the "The Tapestry Project," which involved making digital movies. The Tapestry Project evolved into a project called "The Story Place" on the World Wide Web for middle and high school students. Again, the use of tools was turned to purposes of diverse representation in a variety of forms.

In 1996, the Center partnered with a corporate consortium called The Bay Area Multimedia and Technology Alliance (BAMTA). BAMTA created an access center called the Digital Clubhouse in Santa Clara, California to develop a program based on digital storytelling in an environment that would encourage multigenerational collaborations. The Clubhouse conducts large community workshops for 30–50 people of all ages to facilitate digital storytelling. In addition, the Digital Clubhouse partners with local public schools—approximately six K–6, three middle schools, and one high school to pilot a program to create community digital media centers in the context of existing K–12 "tutoring" labs in public schools.

> We've done large workshops with 30 to 50 and we've seen the effectiveness in really generating some interesting and wonderful stories, but this has also proven to be a great strategy for disseminating digital literacy. The young people have skills to help their parents, their teachers, and their grandparents to learn to use these tools and to get over computer-phobia issues that, frankly, the more middle generation and the older generation suffer from much more than the young people. Now, the idea is to take that model of making a clubhouse, which is a community-based social environment, into places where computer labs already exist. The obvious place is in public schools where labs are used roughly from eight in the morning to four in the afternoon Monday through Friday, but not much outside of that. The idea is to help schools who want to create a kind of multiconstituency, multigenerational training center based on this storytelling metaphor that we have worked with through the Digital Media Center work. We assist them do that. (J. Lambert, personal communication, January 18, 1997)

CRITICAL DEMOCRATIC APPROACHES TO MEDIA EDUCATION

Another approach to media education that shows promise in moving the field toward an acquisition model is one that marries media analysis and practice with critical pedagogy for the sake of strengthening democratic institutions. The argument goes: If an informed electorate is the cornerstone of a democratic society, and, if the polls that report that most North Americans get their news and information from electronic media are correct, then it is imperative that students must learn to read and write electronic media, as well as print, in order to fully participate in a democratic society.

The problem with teaching democratic principles in U.S. classrooms is that most schools do not operate as democratic institutions, bearing a closer resemblance to minimum security prisons. Parents trust schools to provide some structure and routine for their children, and safety is of the highest priority. Because efficiency and cost are also important, school "plants," built after World War II grew larger and larger. Many older buildings are "maxed out" on the necessary wiring to accommodate technology and must be extensively remodeled to accommodate connectivity. This will likely lead to a Renaissance in school architecture, but for what purposes?

For example, the move to reduce class size is only beginning to address the need to rethink large schools and the nature of educational spaces. This provides many opportunities to redesign the physical nature of school environments to accommodate the needs of individual students. It also adds to the growing number of virtual school environments that students—of all ages—can access over geographic space and time. Smaller schools are one step in the direction of democratic pedagogy because they can provide more individual student attention. However, it is too soon to say that smaller classrooms translate into new ways of learning. Furthermore, as the trend to smaller classrooms accelerates, states are beginning to feel the strain on financial and human resources. Whether small schools can address the competing demands of efficiency, cost, safety, and student performance remains to be seen. Pedagogy is only one more competing demand to reconcile. In the meantime, new schools and new tools do not mean that democratic teaching strategies will suddenly be employed.

Teacher-centered instruction is the rule, and in many communities, the expectation. Critical media education teaches students to question ideas, but it remains to be seen if communities would be comfortable with students who appear to "talk back" and challenge authority figures, or even to challenge the authority of a school-sanctioned text. In spite of years of school reform, the ideal in the public mind is still students in rows, sitting quietly, either reading or listening to teachers talk.

Those who practice media education from a critical perspective have an affinity with the literacy and education theory bases. Just as policy specialists in Washington are called "wonks," because of their endless fascination with the minutiae of their field, these media educators are "pedagogy wonks." Critical pedagogists are wonks who delve into the arcane complexities of teaching and learning for the purposes of strengthening students' critical thinking and questioning abilities. Within this paradigm, critical pedagogists would presumably take a broader view of literacy as discourse. They would be more likely to co-investigate media with students and to encourage them to individually explore the meaning of texts.

Ira Shor, deeply influenced by the critical literacy theories of Paulo Freire, proposed a movement toward critical literacy in education. He defined his ideal concept of literacy as:

> *Critical literacy:* Habits of thought, reading, writing, and speaking which go beneath surface meaning, first impressions, dominant myths, official pronouncements, traditional cliches, received wisdom, and mere opinions, to understand the deep meaning, root causes, social context, ideology, and personal consequences of any action, event, object, process, organization, experience, texts, subject matter, policy, mass media, or discourse; thinking-in-

depth about books, statements, print and broadcast media, traditional sayings, official policies, public speeches, commercial messages, political propaganda, familiar ideas, required syllabi; questioning official knowledge, existing authority, traditional relationships, and ways of speaking; exercising a curiosity to understand the root causes of events; using language so that words reveal the deep meaning of anything under discussion; applying that meaning to your own context and imagining how to act on that meaning to change the conditions it reflects. (Shor, 1982, p. 129; cited in Graff, 1995, p. 335)

Teachers are working across the United States, classroom by classroom, to guide their students to think critically about the information presented to them from those far away from their communities. Many teachers would not call themselves "media educators," but critical media education is, in fact, one thing that they do. In some cases, this work is provoked by the perception that the dominant mass medium in the classroom—the textbook—either does not reflect the cultural diversity of U.S. society, or represents an ideological distortion of historical events (Tyner, 1992). Dissatisfaction with the textbook has moved many teachers from a technicist "teaching through" approach to one that investigates the nature of media, its purposes, and its uses by specific audiences.

For those teachers who are comfortable with a student-centered, open-ended classroom, a constructivist approach opens the opportunity to teach students critical thinking skills through dialectic, dialogic, discursive techniques. They hope that these techniques will provide students with the intellectual sinew and strength of character to effect social and political change. They would argue that because media education can lead to critical, independent thinking, it could not be taught any other way. For educators who believe that the teacher, as an adult with more life experience, is the expert and that values are fixed, the constructivist approach to media education looks far too vague, negative, and relative. Such a teacher would be more comfortable working from an approach that teaches students to discern and evaluate media against an established standard of taste. That teacher might also argue that because the research contains plenty of citations about the harm caused by media, it is the duty of teachers to inform students about the perils they face and to arm them against media's influence.

How far are educators willing to go with critical literacy? When taken to its most logical conclusions, critical literacy puts us right back on the horns of Plato's Dilemma, that is, who is qualified to interpret texts? Obviously critical literacy cannot be instilled or sustained without major changes in schooling and some working consensus about what a broad public wants education to accomplish. Furthermore, even critical literacy is a concept in transition—exploding into a multitude of literacy purposes, competencies, and practices.

Although there are entrenched constituencies for each media literacy approach, most practitioners do not lean heavily on any one approach, yet pick and choose from among the strategies, depending on their own assumptions about the purposes for media education. Nonetheless, in order to achieve the status in U.S. schooling that is seen in other countries, media education advocates must find ways to bridge their differences. The resolution between protectionist and critical pedagogical approaches is problematic, because fundamental beliefs about *who* should use *what* information for *what* purposes are at odds. Certainly, if educators cannot work together to reconcile the surmountable challenges of media education in the United States, they cannot hope to be successful in their struggle to achieve anything as daunting as democratic schooling. As in all discussions of literacy, the devil is in the details.

Representing Diversity— Media Analysis in Practice

When aligned with critical literacy principles, media education presents unique opportunities for teachers to meet the challenges of cultural and linguistic diversity in U.S. classrooms. In particular, texts that originate in popular culture and mass media can provide points of commonality for cross-cultural readings by students who engage with classroom information resources from a diverse range of cultural perspectives. By contributing multiple perspectives based on diverse cultural readings of popular culture texts, students who are inundated with mass media forms also bring a great deal of common prior knowledge of mass media narratives. These codes and conventions themselves constitute distinctive discourses. Thus, sophisticated readings of familiar texts, coupled with experiences in media-making, are powerful tools for teachers of diverse classrooms. Once students have more range of expression available to them, image-making tools of expression enable students to refine their own voices, and to tell their stories with mastery, from an informed, focused and student-centered perspective. Such uses of media in the classroom can contribute to cross-cultural understanding through deeper understanding of the difference in readings, as well as their shared meanings among wide, diverse audiences.

> Once teachers confront the popular culture of young people, they find media-generated issues are one of the best bridges to the world of their students. Since access to media [content] is egalitarian, and young people are its biggest consumers, teachers and students are on an equal footing. Particularly with general and basic level students, mutual media experiences may be their only common ground. (Duncan, 1988, p. 8)

Arguments for the uses of media in culturally responsive pedagogy have been well documented (Cortés, 1995; Estrada & McLaren, 1993; Giroux & Simon, 1989; King, 1990; McLaren & Hammer, 1992). In order to exploit the potential of media education in the culturally and linguistically diverse classroom, educators must be willing to experiment constantly with an array of media and question and revise their assumptions about the uses of information resources for teaching and learning. Furthermore, students and teachers must continually explore both their individual as well as their collective relationships to media. This begins with a conscious effort to understand and to reflect upon individual modes of discourse and to extend that understanding to the analysis and cross-cultural reading of a wide range of discursive styles.

DIVERSITY AND THE MYTH OF EDUCATIONAL FAILURE

In the not-so-distant past, the public school system in the United States did not even attempt to educate all children, let alone to encourage high standards of excellence for students who were not identified as insiders to majority, mainstream culture. Prior to World War II, about 50% of all students dropped out of high school before graduation and only 20% actually entered higher education. In those years, students were "tracked" into programs in which a quarter of their students were selected for college preparation and another quarter for vocational education. The rest were tracked into general education and it was widely assumed that most of them would drop out (Berliner & Biddle, 1995, pp. 130–131). Also at this time, norm-referenced, standardized tests began to take hold of education so that this "sorting" of educational winners and losers could be done more efficiently (Lehman, 1995). Enrollment began to change after World War II. A booming economy brought on a 50% increase in American high school and college enrollment. Education for the "masses" was becoming a reality.

> The popularization of American schools and colleges since the end of World War II has been nothing short of phenomenal, involving an unprecedented broadening of access, an unprecedented diversification of curricula, and an unprecedented extension of public control. In 1950, 34 percent of the American population twenty-five years of age or older had completed at least four years of high school, while 6 percent of that population had completed at least four years of college. By 1985, 74 percent of the American population twenty-five years of age or older had completed at least four years of high school, while 19 percent had completed at least four years of college. . . . It was in many ways a remarkable achievement, of which Americans could be justifiably proud. Yet it seemed to bring with it a pervasive sense of failure. (Cremin, 1990, pp. 1–2)

Curricular adjustments were made to accommodate the burgeoning and diverse school populations. Entrance requirements were relaxed, a broader range of courses was offered, and legal mandates addressed historical inequality in education for minority students. By 1995, the national dropout rate for public school students was at a low of 4.5% (Hatfield, 1996). As Berliner and Biddle detail in their book, *The Manufactured Crisis* (1995), the dominant social groups who had been best served by public education in the past saw these changes as a direct affront that had the potential to demote their position in society. Although educational opportunity was made available to more students, a backlash of school critics orchestrated criticism of schools that would result in a "back to the basics" approach that sought to restore pre-World War II educational opportunity for selected groups in society through mandates of sanctioned curricular activities (Berliner & Biddle, 1995, pp. 131–132).

Criticism of American education has been a national pastime for over 100 years. But according to Berliner and Biddle, in recent years, it has been orchestrated through blatant political propaganda, the false or misleading use of evidence about educational achievement, the collaboration of the media in manufacturing the idea of an educational crisis, and the blaming of education for a host of social ills that have very little to do with education (p. 172). While schools are reeling from criticism that makes so little sense they scarcely know how to address it, politicians periodically make a grab for school funding, in a political shell game that attempts to shift it to other purposes on the specious grounds that public schools are wasteful and incompetent. These "other purposes" often represent a host of social programs, themselves underfunded, such as homelessness, welfare, community health, and so forth. They also include private sector reallocation schemes such as charter schools and corporate schools. Taxpayers have been willing to shoulder the burden for public education—indeed public education is consistently one of the highest government expenditure categories—but cost-benefit in education, as in health care and welfare, is a slippery concept. Free market schemes for school funding have not yet proven to be any more beneficial to teaching and learning than public funding has been in the past. And no one has factored in the social value and resulting price tag for a quality education for all children, as compared to education of a select few. The problem is that schools are organized efficiently and work very well—for society in the 19th century.

If there is a crisis in American schooling, it is not the crisis of putative mediocrity and decline charged by the recent reports but rather a crisis inherent in balancing [the] tremendous variety of demands Americans have made on their schools and colleges—of crafting curricula that take account of the needs of a modern society at the same time that they make provision for the extraordinary diversity of America's young people, of designing institutions where well-prepared teachers can teach under supportive conditions, and where *all* students can be motivated and assisted to develop their talents to the fullest; and of providing the necessary resources for creating and sustaining such institutions. (Cremin, 1990, p. 43)

TEACHING IN THE DIVERSE CLASSROOM

The legacy of the American Civil Rights Movement of the 1960s contributed to the ideal of equal opportunity in a way that encouraged fairness and pride in diversity and that undermined the assumption that there is one American "melting pot" of common cultural understanding based on European culture and a canon of texts from classical Western culture. Instead, a post-1960s vision of the American Identity, if there is such a thing, consists of a patchwork of discrete cultures that have the potential to come together into a harmonious whole. There is much dissent about this vision of American culture from both the political left and the political right. American social commentator Todd Gitlin (1995) shocked the political left with his criticism of the politics of identity, that is, strong cultural identity with a specific cultural community and the making of political decisions on the basis of one's identification with an ethnic, linguistic, or cultural group. In *The Twilight of Common Dreams: Why America Is Wracked by Culture Wars*, he questioned the continued usefulness of the politics of identity, as it was originally conceived in the 1960s, as a means to promote the general social good. He explores the possibility that the politics of identity is increasingly anachronistic and clouded with the nostalgia of another era.

Although Gitlin has certainly not called for a return to the past dominance of one mainstream American identity, strongly associated with the language and culture of a few, he cites the impracticality of asking individuals to profess loyalty to specific communities when in fact, people self-identify with many overlapping and even sometimes conflicting, cultural perspectives. Gitlin stresses that diversity *is* the defining commonality of the American experience and calls for a balanced focus on some of the commonalities between Americans and less emphasis on the politics of difference (Gitlin, 1996, p. B-1).

For the teacher who is committed to student-centered classroom instruction, in the belief that students learn best when their prior knowledge is honored within the appropriate cultural context, the relationship between diverse student interest and some common curricular content becomes a logistical nightmare. Public school teachers, especially in urban areas, already face classrooms bulging with an average of 28 newcomers whose first language is not English. An urban U.S. classroom might consist of students who identify with Southeast Asian, Indian, Arabic, African American, Chinese,

Guatemalan, Mexican American, Cuban, Puerto Rican, Native American, and European-American communities, to name only a few examples. Then there are issues of gender, race, class, and even sexual orientation that further particularize the needs and orientation of each student. To add to the task, as Gitlin noted, students increasingly transcend the boundaries of their first cultures to identify with more than one of these "communities."

On top of all of the complexity of language and culture, teachers hope to identify each student's preferred learning style or styles. The teacher is caught between the desire to use a student-centered approach and the realistic constraints of time and resources that would result from the fractious multiplicity of such an approach in a diverse and crowded classroom.

There is also the issue of "content delivery" vs. a more interactive relationship with classroom information. The more complex the information sources and the more complex students' responses to them, the more difficult and mind-boggling the teacher's role becomes. Diversity of this magnitude raises significant questions about the nature of school activities, the texts, the approaches, the cultural contexts, and the assessments that are appropriate for a multicultural classroom. The goal of the teacher is to turn the "problem" of classroom diversity into an opportunity for growth that authentically honors students' individual cultures and prepares them for a society that will demand that they can navigate both the diversity and the commonalities of American society with a high degree of sophistication. Media and technology can help.

DIVERSITY AND THE POP CULTURE CANON

The concept of student-centered learning (or learner-centered teaching) is founded on the belief that students benefit from activities rooted in their home cultures and preexisting knowledge. It isn't that students do not want to learn about the cultures around them, or about the culture of schooling— there is early awareness that mastering the language of schooling represents a key to opportunity. It is just that they are still struggling to become conscious of their own intellectual processes, a task made harder because that kind of metacognition is often not an explicit goal of schooling. When new ideas are tied to known ideas, contexts and foundations are laid that can foster discovery outside the student's immediate experience.

Without the bridge to student knowledge, the traditional canon of information, sanctioned by most schools, has not shown much promise in reaching students whose first language is not English and who may not identify with the dominant, mainstream culture honored by the traditional literary canon. In addition to its initial irrelevance to students, the canon of traditional curricula may even prove problematic for English-speaking children whose home values may come in conflict with the values preferred in the culture of schooling. The textbook model of learning, whereby classrooms employ one text for all students in the classroom, makes it exceedingly difficult for teachers to find texts, that is, actual classroom resources, that appeal to the multitude of perspectives in their classrooms.

The solution to providing multiple information sources can be found in both the form and content of new media. Networked computers enable students to access a much richer database of information than ever before. But the teacher who sticks with *educational* media at the expense of *mass* media passes up the opportunity to use engaging and culturally appropriate information resources that can contribute to learning. The addition of popular, "nonsanctioned" texts to the classroom information pool has the potential to bridge classroom diversity.

The codes, languages, and conventions of popular culture texts such as movies, comic books, videos, and music are well known to students from a wide array of world cultures. Unlike many texts from the sanctioned canon, the codes, conventions and narrative structures of mass media and popular culture texts are widely understood across cultures and can be used to ground discourse around a central text that offers a high potential for broad understanding. By working in groups to "tease out" the meaning in texts that already retain some familiarity, students can move on to more sophisticated readings of increasingly complex texts in a variety of classical and popular forms.

Resistance to the inclusion of such texts in school contexts comes from both conservative and liberal perspectives, from those who want to conserve the traditional canon, but also from those who resist the commercialism of contemporary culture and who resent its intrusion into school culture. Those who believe that schools should be cloistered from the intrusion of popular culture come from essentially a protectionist perspective, that is, one that believes that such texts do more harm than good. The appeal of media to students from diverse cultures and the pleasure they derive from it is explained by protectionist critics as the negative result of blatant Western commercialism—a sort of populist version of "false consciousness," the belief that young minds are being hypnotized and manipulated by mass media.

The argument that commercial or mass media fare have little or no place in schools also limits the availability of classroom information resources. Given the prolific availability of popular culture texts, if mass media products are *verboten*, the teacher is forced into a gatekeeping role with media. Further, the implied need to gatekeep media implies that teachers do not question information and that students are passive recipients of it. In fact, the goal of teachers of media and their students is to explicitly question and challenge the intended meaning of texts as they enter the classroom environment.

The exclusion of popular culture from schools also represents a naïve understanding of the symbiotic relationship between modern readers and mass media texts. Teachers and media producers see ample evidence that student use of texts goes far beyond the commercial intentions of the media industries. With or without mass media, each generation carves out private modes of expression appropriate to prevailing social conditions and purposely keeps the expression coded and veiled to obscure the meaning for adults. This is common across cultures and across languages. Because it mimics natural speech, mass media texts do exploit this generational tendency for commercial purposes, but students use these texts in an array of ways both intended and unintended by the media's producers.

Just as media industries attempt to exploit students' engagement with popular messages for commercial purposes, the teacher of media can also exploit the texts for learning purposes. Popular texts serve as a strong and engaging point of departure for the purpose of provoking critical inquiry and even for leading the students back to the texts sanctioned by the dominant culture. The critical teacher can encourage sophisticated, "against the grain" reading of all texts, including those that students know and like well, in order to prod students toward a constant evaluation of their own personal relationship to media and information.

The key to the use of popular texts to enhance teaching and learning in diverse classrooms is to stick with the student-centered focus. It is important to note here that "student relevancy" is not only about teaching subject matter that is central to the lives of students and therefore engaging. More importantly, it is a strategy to use students' prior knowledge to lead them far beyond their limited perspective and to broaden their horizons beyond home, school, and community. Learner-centered education is not about "turning the asylum over to the inmates." It is about exploiting learning opportunities in a formal, structured, and rigorous way.

Nor is it enough to begin media teaching by simply exploring the "message" of a media text. A good place to begin the process of critical inquiry that can enhance learning outcomes is to engage students in the analysis of their own modes of discourse, both oral and written, so that they begin to understand that there are many discursive styles to choose from for presenting information—even the discursive modes that are rewarded in school. After students have some experience in recognizing discourses, they then have some foundation to discuss the discourses of various media, including those sanctioned by traditional canons such as textbooks and classic literature. As students begin to analyze their own discursive styles and to play with new and different discursive modes, they enter into a realm of metacognition that can help them to create a context that enhances the understanding of the discourse of others who may speak from a different cultural perspective.

This approach to metacognitive analysis is most useful when students begin to mine their own cultures for the roots of expression. The teacher can provide mentored opportunities for such an investigation through the use of traditional inquiry-based approaches such as problem-solving, dialectic strategies, and apprenticeships that are both experiential and cognitive. These teaching methodologies are especially appropriate to media teaching activities.

THE CASE FOR COGNITIVE APPRENTICESHIPS IN LANGUAGE AND LITERACY LEARNING

In the search for teaching approaches that would prove effective for contemporary schooling, researchers have noted the "spectacular" learning of young children at apprenticeships in developing countries (Bransford, Stein, Arbitman-Smith, & Vye, 1985; Pea, 1989). Through the study of traditional apprenticeships, researchers found that students were learning in culturally meaningful contexts with ongoing activities and immediate feedback on the success of their actions (Berryman, 1992, p. 30). Children's learning in the traditional apprenticeship mode is marked by some specific characteristics: Learning takes place in context; learning is guided; learning is useful; and learning is not only shown, but is explicitly stated in terms that spell out the needs and purposes of the learning (Bransford et al., 1995; Pea, 1989).

Other characteristics of apprenticeships include: (a) Activities happen in the course of daily life and may not even be recognized as a teaching activity; (b) "work" is the driving force; (c) there is a temporal ordering of skill acquisition, in "bundles" of tasks. For example, a tailor's apprentice would not necessarily work on a garment from start to finish, but would instead master simple sleeve construction on a garment cut out by someone else before going on to the next task, such as collar construction; (d) tasks are skill-based and focus on bodily performance; (e) standards of performance and evaluation of competence are implicit and based on the work accomplished rather than a marked event, such as a test; and (f) teaching and learning are largely invisible (Berryman, 1992, p. 31; Jordan, 1987).

Traditional apprenticeships offer a vision of effective, contextualized learning and teaching, but the concept of apprenticeships is not entirely transferable to the needs of modern education. For one thing, many of the domains that contemporary students must learn are processed internally, unlike the explicit modes of traditional apprenticeships. This is especially true of knowledge and information-based economies. The construction of meaning, analysis and synthesis of information, and systems design are examples of the kind of tasks that are creative, intellectual, and nonexplicit. As information becomes more of a commodity in the marketplace, displacing skill-based manufacturing jobs, the need to perform cognitive tasks for purposes of job readiness puts even greater pressure on schools. The task is to make internalized knowledge external in a way that some researchers have called "cognitive" apprenticeships (Collins, Brown, & Newman, 1989).

Traditional apprenticeships revolve around concrete tangible artifacts and visually observable practices that can be modeled and mentored for students, whereas cognitive apprenticeships work with largely symbolic materials. The task of the teacher is to set up ideal learning environments along the lines of those used in traditional apprenticeships and then to exploit them for the explicit purposes of strengthening cognitive activities.

Although cognitive apprenticeship strategies have important implications for the service and information economies of modern work, they are not to be confused with the applied curriculum of vocational education. Even though vocational curricula use real-world problems, the kind of teaching seen in apprenticeships, that is, "teaching in context," differs from vocational teaching, where the context of learning tends to be highly specific and applied (Berryman, 1992, p. 30). Instead, teaching in context means that the teacher arranges opportunities for learning experiences through a combination of observation, coaching, and practice (Lave, Smith, & Butler, 1988) so that students interpret their own experience and make sense of their own learning in a way that is far more flexible and less prescriptive than the kind of learning that applied vocational curricula traditionally fosters.

Cognitive apprenticeships play an important role in language and literacy learning, because discourses are not mastered through overt instruction, but through a kind of apprenticeship (Newman, Griffin, & Cole, 1989; Tharp & Gallimore, 1988). Literacy scholar James Gee (1996) noted that discourses are mastered through:

> enculturation (apprenticeship) into social practices through scaffolded and supported interaction with people who have already mastered the Discourse. . . . This is how we all acquire our native-language and our primary Discourses. . . . If you have no access to the social practice, you don't get in the Discourse. (p. 139)

Building on research about teaching and learning by Pinker (1989, 1994), Gee made the distinction between acquisition and learning as poles on a continuum:

> *Acquisition* is a process of acquiring something (usually, subconsciously) by exposure to models, a process of trial and error, and practice within social groups, without formal teaching. It happens in natural settings which are meaningful and functional in the sense that acquirers know that they need to acquire the thing they are exposed to in order to function and they in fact want to so function. This is how people come to control their first language.

> *Learning* is a process that involves conscious knowledge gained through teaching (though not necessarily from someone officially designated a teacher) or through certain life-experiences that trigger conscious reflection. This

teaching or reflection involves explanation and analysis, that is, breaking down the thing to be learned into its analytic parts. It inherently involves attaining, along with the matter being taught, some degree of meta-knowledge about the matter. (Gee, 1996, p. 138)

Acquisition can go on in the classroom, but Gee claims it does this only through apprenticeship and social practice, not through overt teaching. Acquisition, then, must precede learning and apprenticeship must precede teaching. Children who have not begun the acquisition process before they come to school are at a significant disadvantage. Gee (1996) noted:

Classrooms that do not properly balance acquisition and learning, and realize which is which, simply privilege those students who have already begun the acquisition process outside the school. Too little acquisition leads to too little mastery-in-practice; too little learning leads to too little analytic and reflective awareness and limits the capacity for certain sorts of critical reading and reflection. (p. 139)

A person's primary, or home discourse is the foundation for the acquisition and learning of other discourses later in life. Discourses obtained later in life also have an effect on the primary discourse:

good classroom instruction (in composition, study skills, writing, critical thinking, content-based literacy, or whatever) can and should lead to meta-knowledge, to seeing how the Discourses you have already got (not just the languages) relate to those you are attempting to acquire, and how the ones you are trying to acquire relate to self and society . . . the classroom must juxtapose different discourses for comparison and contrast. (p. 141)

Acquisition that leads to learning is the goal. Where acquisition is weak, teachers can apprentice students in a master–apprentice relationship and then provide the scaffolding—the underlying knowledge and skill foundations for incremental success, that will build a student's growing awareness of a discourse. After acquisition is sufficiently mastered, teachers can then break a wider range of material into its smaller bits and juxtapose various discourses, investigating with students how discursive styles are alike and different. By building on apprenticeships that lead to learning, students can begin to develop metacognitive awareness of a wider range of discourses from which they can master, pick, and choose.

COGNITIVE APPRENTICESHIPS
IN THE DIVERSE CLASSROOM

Cognitive apprenticeship approaches have particular relevance for the culturally and linguistically diverse classroom. Carol Lee, a researcher at Northwestern University, has conducted empirical studies with students to analyze ethnically diverse literature in an approach that she calls "culturally-based cognitive apprenticeships." She works from the research foundation that demonstrates that reading comprehension strategies can be explicitly taught (Fitzgerald & Speigel, 1983; Palinscar & Brown, 1984; Pearson & Dole, 1987) and then ratchets up the classroom activities toward a goal of making her students "expert readers" who dig below the surface of a text to discover its deeper meanings. She does this by working with "schemas for literary communication" suggested by de Beaugrande (1987) that "include a wide array of prior knowledge of genre, rhetorical and literary techniques, and knowledge of the author and of the social world of text" in ways that are culturally responsive (Lee, 1995, p. 611).

The idea is to engage students in useful cognitive work that can then lead them to explore the primary discourse(s) of their own cultures, as a form of metaknowledge, and then to provide the scaffolding for students to branch out into the analysis and production of a variety of texts. After conducting a number of classroom research studies, both quantitative and qualitative, Lee (1995) remarked, "Their prior knowledge of signifying had been a bridge over which the students had traversed to aesthetic territory of great promise" (p. 625).

> Culture provides a matrix through which meaning is created and negotiated. Natural language is among the most powerful mediators of knowledge, values, and thinking processes. Thus attention to characteristics of language capabilities of ethnically and linguistically diverse students may yield significant information on which to base instruction. (Lee, 1995, pp. 617–618)

Teachers in her studies used modeling and coaching strategies as they monitored small group activities with classroom texts. Students were required to base their conclusions on evidence from the texts or from their real-life experiences. The teacher's role was to challenge students, even playing the devil's advocate by offering contradictory information and making students defend their interpretation of texts. Lee (1995) proposed an instructional framework for the reading of texts that:

1. structures a learning environment for students in which through active investigations they can unearth and articulate otherwise tacit strategies that they use to construct inferred meanings in oral speech events;

2. apply those strategies to literary texts in which the patterns of discourse studied in the oral context are appropriated for literary effect; and

3. sequence future series of texts within units of instruction so that the first texts are ones for which students initially have greater social and linguistic prior knowledge while they learn to master task-specific reading strategies and the second texts are ones for which students

now have greater mastery of task-specific reading strategies and less social and linguistic prior knowledge. (p. 627)

COGNITIVE APPRENTICESHIPS FOR MEDIA EDUCATION

The work has important implications for teaching about media texts. Lee likes to begin this process of metacognition with oral modes of communication, a strategy in harmony with the oral aspects of electronic media, not only the audio components of broadcast radio and television, but also printed computer screens that mimic "authentic" speech: "Within a highly literate society such as the U.S., the uses of cognitive strategies to understand communication in oral contexts are likely to be more embedded, more automaticized, and ultimately more sophisticated for more people than their use of cognitive strategies to understand communication in print, especially highly specialized genres such as those within the domain of complex literature ... attention to reasoning in oral contexts, with special sensitivity to the significance of language variations within a nation state, may offer meaningful sources for conceptual modeling of reading strategies" (p. 627).

Her work with cognitive apprenticeships and culturally specific texts has been so far confined to literary works where students are the recipients of printed texts created by others. For Lee, the central problems are still "how to make public and visible to novice learners those powerful problem-solving strategies and heuristics that more expert readers practice flexibly and use strategically" (p. 627). Nonetheless, she recognizes some implications for culturally based cognitive apprenticeships for nonprint media, although she placed an emphasis on the visual nature of media:

> For the first time in history, teachers are charged to apprentice the vast majority of U.S. citizenry into very high levels of print literacy ... while the most pervasive medium of communication is visual. (p. 628)

Teachers do not always know how to incorporate the visual and moving image media into the traditional discourse of schooling. Although the use of computers is becoming increasingly familiar, computer texts are still dominated by alphabetic/text literacy modes, and their use is generally for purposes of content delivery. This is changing as audio modes, in particular, become more common in electronic and online media. Broadcast media, in particular, models a limited range of discourse for students—a style that has traditionally found little transference in classroom work. It is not only that the discourse of schooling is overwhelmingly print-based. More problematic is that the range of discourse considered appropriate for schooling—in any medium—is so narrow.

The following excerpt from a videotape of student work is an example of the difficulty of breaching traditional school discourse with the new discursive modes demanded for nonprint media:

> Kid Witness News Team (Fall 1990) presents *Making Choices: Kids of the 1990s.*

> Kids of the 90s. Choices. We have plenty of choices. Drugs, gangs, suicide, pregnancy, homelessness and drop-outs are all issues facing us daily. Are they barriers to our future? Are they obstacles to our success?

> Kids of the 90s, it's your choice. My generation must overcome the potential issues of today and move forward. They don't have to be negative hopeless or helpless. It's your choice. . . .

The video goes on in this vein for several minutes. In the late 1980s, Panasonic Corporation, through its philanthropic foundation, provided schools across the United States with high-quality cameras and equipment. *Making Choices* was made by junior high school students and their teachers through this program. Panasonic also offered a showcase for student work and prizes for the best work. But in spite of their well-intended and generous contribution to schools, the Panasonic video program did not emphasize the need for the teacher training and time necessary to explore the classroom potential of video and its unique discursive style. The designers of the Panasonic program did not fathom the formidable barriers to integrating nonprint media and hands-on production in public schooling.

The oversight is evident in *Making Choices.* Although no one would disagree that the litany of social ills mentioned in the video are dangers to children, the discourse of this video is obviously not a student-generated one. The children in the videotape are seated in rows on bleachers in the auditorium as if for a class picture. The camera is locked down on the kids and there are few edited segments, that is, in-camera cuts, or other transitions. There are a few slow zooms, apparently for no purpose. The video is produced as if a still camera were pointed at the students. This is to be expected, since a snapshot camera is probably the medium that students and teachers have the most prior experience in using.

As schools and teachers are barraged with criticism from all sides, it is no wonder that they must be very cautious when recording, and thus documenting for replay, a school-produced message for the public. There is a strong sense that the audience for the *Making Choices* video consists of those beyond the classroom. Extreme care is taken not to produce a message with controversy or ambiguity. In fact, the script is hyper-vigilant, even sanitized, for a critical public. There is no question that the videotape is rendered "appropriate" for viewing by parents, principals, and the general public. But the authenticity of the students' discourse on the social ills enumerated in the tape is questionable. The Panasonic example says less about the moral teachings of schools and more about the inauthentic and cautious discourse of adults in school settings. It raises serious questions about the educational value, purposes, and possibilities for student production of their own messages.

COGNITIVE APPRENTICESHIPS
WITH STUDENT-PRODUCED WORK

The students in the *Making Choices* video might have benefited from work that broadened their range of potential discursive modes and later, from more exercises to explore the way that specific media, such as text, video, and multimedia, might be used to complement their message. The first place to engage the notion that there are myriad ways of telling a story is to begin by encouraging students to be aware of discursive and narrative styles in their home cultures. Educational activities that heighten awareness of speech patterns and other oral modes can be attempted in any number of ways. Students can be asked to tell stories they know and to analyze how they are best told and why. Literature rooted in the students' familiar culture can be introduced and investigated for dialogue. Students can collaborate to script and record audio segments and tell the same story in different ways.

In addition to improving students' abilities to make sense of information created by others, culturally based cognitive apprenticeships have implications for student media production of stories that they generate on their own. Through scaffolding that provides incremental interventions and feedback, students can bring metacognitive awareness to bear as they explore rhetorical devices, discursive styles, and figurative language. In particular, students can use the concept of *voice* to "try on" their evolving public and private personas. The skill of representing themselves, instead of being represented by others, is particularly crucial for students whose cultures may be underrepresented, or misrepresented in mainstream, commercial mass media.

For example, in her work with African American adolescents, Lee (1995) found success by beginning with a form of discourse familiar to African Americans known as *signifying*, also sometimes known as "the Dozens," a tradition that is "full of irony, *double entendre*, satire, and metaphorical language" and ritual insults that go "across geographical and even class boundaries." Many African American adolescents routinely participate in signifying speech events in which they must immediately interpret accurately the *double entendre* and ironies of each turn of phrase. Lee argued that "the strategies these adolescents employ to process turns of talk within signifying dialogues are similar to those used by expert readers to identify and process passages in literary texts that are ironic and that are intended by the author to be interpreted figuratively rather than literally" (p. 612).

The following video transcript represents a nonliterary use of the culturally based, discursive convention of signifying. Branda Miller, a video artist and teacher at Hunter College in New York, works with children in a variety of alternative school settings. During her work with teenage mothers in a teen pregnancy prevention and parenting program at the Henry Street Settlement in New York City, Ms. Miller provided mentored opportunities for hands-on video production so that her students could explore a number of themes of concern to their particular community of learners, in this case, students who are also teenage mothers. Because media production involves two levels—the actual media product itself and the content conveyed by the medium—it lends itself to the skills (mastery of the medium) seen in traditional apprenticeships, but also to the kinds of implicit knowledge (narration, aesthetics, discourse style) seen in cognitive apprenticeships.

Branda Miller provided a great deal of scaffolding to her students along the lines of both traditional and cognitive apprenticeship approaches. She structured a video production exercise for her students that is much like a traditional apprenticeship activity. The production values are simple, and inexpensive, yet they get at important video production concepts: framing, in-camera editing, narrative structure, and focused concept. Her approach to content, on the other hand, uses a student-centered strategy that asks students to master production based on their own knowledge of how to tell a story. The girls worked from their personal contexts as teenage mothers and employed a familiar, informal discursive style that they might use with friends. Their production uses the names of popular candy bars to tell the facts of life. Their highly risqué video is an example of adolescent sexual humor that the teens called *Birth of a Candy Bar* (Miller, 1989):

Boys! Ready? Ok!
On PAY DAY
MR. GOODBAR wanted a BIT O'HONEY
So he took Ms. HERSHEY behind the MARS on the corner of
CLARK and FIFTH AVENUE
He began to feel her MOUNDS. That was pure ALMOND JOY.
It made her TOOTSIE ROLL.
He let out a SNICKER and his BUTTERFINGER went up her KIT
KAT and caused a MILKY WAY
She screamed O HENRY! as he squeezed his TWIX and it made a
NESTLE'S CRUNCH.
Ms. Henry said, "You are even better than the THREE
MUSKETEERS!"
So she was a big CHUNKY and nine months later she had a
BABY RUTH!

This video raises questions about student awareness of the appropriate contexts for public and private discourse. It is significant here that this video was produced in an alternative school program. It remains to be seen if the girls would think that this discursive style was appropriate for a formal classroom setting or for viewing by an audience of parents and community members in a public setting. Obviously, the sexual content of *Birth of a Candy Bar* would not "fly" in every community setting, but outside of school, the candy bar story is a popular chant that preteens use when jumping rope in the playground. In the context of this activity the *double entendre* represented by the candy bars is a clever, bawdy exploration of the facts of life. Teenagers all over the world engage in this indecorate, goofy, not-so-subtle behavior and the teen producers of *Birth of a Candy Bar* recognize the *double entendre* as a way to play with language and to talk about taboo subjects with their peers. This video served as a beginning exercise to apprentice students in the skills of video production techniques such as in-camera editing and framing, but also in the cognitive power of narrative storytelling. In the process, the video exercise makes explicit the otherwise subtle discursive style from the students' own local culture. From this video, students can go on to study proverbs, poems, and stories that celebrate this discursive tradition. They can also be encouraged to point out other modes of discourse that they recognize in daily life, in literature, and in media. Once students understand that there are a range of ways to use their modes of expression, and to appropriate other styles, they are on their way to investigation of different styles that may be more academic, literary, or problem solving in purpose.

As their production skills become more sophisticated, students can begin to broaden their communication to a wider and wider audience for the purpose of social action. The following video was produced by Sara Safford for the Brooklyn Perinatal Network in New York. *Self Protection: Teen Moms Expand Their Options* (Safford, 1990) is a rap music video in which Public Enemy's 1989 hit recording *Self Destruction* is appropriated (with the rap group's permission) by a group of teen moms in the GED/Job training program at Brooklyn College. They perform their own rap commentary on their experiences with social service institutions, birth control, and pregnancy. Performances are intercut with discussion and advice about their experiences as young mothers confronting public institutions. Following is an excerpt of the 12-minute video. It opens with the girls "rapping" about their plight:

Just sit there for years and years
Holding back the pain and tears
The pain gets worse, times runnin' out
Nothing left to do but scream and shout

They ask you "How you gonna pay your bills?"
You pull out your Medicaid and feel the chills
They mistreat you! They don't treat you right!
The next thing you know you'll be there all night.

There's no explanation for the delays
The less money you have, the longer you stay
It's at their convenience, never at yours
Who cares how many times you go through that door?

But times are changin' we're getting smarter
When things get rough, we just try harder!

Refrain:

Stress reduction, We need some stress reduction.
Stress reduction, We need some stress reduction.

[The video cuts to an earlier shot of the teens negotiating the words that will go into their script for the final video]:

Teen 1: "The less money you get the more you stay." What's that mean?
Teen 2: It means that if you ain't go no money you stay in the clinic and if you got money they'll see you and get you the hell out of there! That's what that means!

[The video cuts back to the girls acting out their experiences taking their sick children to a welfare clinic for treatment]:

Everywhere you go in life, you have to wait . . .

Receptionist: Ms. Sharilyn Briggs? Do you have your Medicaid (welfare medical insurance)? Your social security number?

Teen Mom: My Social Security card isn't here yet. I don't have my Medicaid. That's what I'm here to get.

Receptionist: I see. Well have a seat. I'll call you in minute . . .

[Much Later]

Receptionist: Ms. Sharilyn Briggs? [As the fictional Ms. Briggs approaches with her baby] Make sure you bring your social security card and your Medicaid and this W26 Form and come back on March 26.

[Cut to - Teen mom talks on camera about the message they are trying to convey to the audience in the clinic scene]:

A lot of the people who go in there are young and a lot of the people serving you are older and automatically they're trying to tell you that "you shouldn't be here" and "You're too young for this" and "You're too young for that." And they are trying to give you the whole rundown on the situation you're in when *YOU* are in the situation and you realize all this. But as a result of that, they tend to treat you with less courtesy or kindness than an adult would receive. They talk down to you or in a degrading fashion. (Reprinted permission Brooklyn Perinatal Network, Inc., 30 Third Avenue, Brooklyn, NY 11217. (718) 643-8258)

From here, the girls learn important information about health care, family planning, relationships, support organizations, and even celibacy. More importantly, they learn to speak up for themselves and their babies.

THE CASE FOR VIDEO PRODUCTION
IN THE DIVERSE CLASSROOM

Just as popular media texts engage students by working with the discourse of media, that is, familiar narratives, aesthetics, and conventions, the use of media production offers an opportunity for experiential, collaborative problem solving that enhances media analysis skills. Media-making also takes a refreshing approach to media representation as an entry point for the discussion of a range of aspects inherent to the construction of media. Although critical analysis exercises that model the construction of media and a range of styles are important to the production of student media, production is not necessarily intended as the "carrot" to hoodwink resistant students into reading the classics in print formats. Instead, it offers a space for students to define and redefine their own "problems" with media and to explore their own relationship with media. It may very well be that classical literature is a part of the equation for some, as students begin to broaden their range of discourse.

VIDEO AS A SCAFFOLDING MEDIUM

Although all media have great potential for production, video is particularly useful as a starting point, that is, as a scaffolding device that builds production sensibilities and skills in small and incremental ways that can later be transferred in increasingly sophisticated applications. Video production allows students to learn immediately how to work with the frame, image, and sound in ways that can later be employed to construct on the computer or on paper. The equipment is simple to use and activities can be designed as short, "media-readiness" tasks that guide students in the step-by-step practice of media construction. Video uses reading, writing, calculation, and encourages research, collaboration, and problem solving. Feedback is immediate and evaluation can be done easily, either individually, or as a whole-class activity.

In contrast, beginning student production on the computer is tricky. Although it is easier to support traditional skills such as reading, writing, and calculation on the computer, at this point, software that allows students to use the computer for graphics, video, audio, and multimedia production requires sophisticated and intricate skill-building—especially for small children. Furthermore, the best way to apprentice children in the aesthetic use of the "frame," that is, the video or computer screen, is to structure classroom tasks for skill-building in the placement of graphics, color, shapes, and text toward various choices in shot composition, transitions, and uses of audio. Novice media producers build expertise through trial and error and modeling. On the computer, a high level of skill is necessary even to begin production of multimedia products and the labor-intensive nature of the machine makes students reluctant to experiment, throw work away, and try again. Students must render projects for hours before they are ready for feedback from their peers.

For that reason, video is the perfect tool for scaffolding the composition, transitions, narrative, and aesthetics of the moving image. The tools are sturdy, simple to use, and feedback is immediate. Students can explore narrative structure without a great deal of prior skills in videomaking. Compared to film and digital reproduction, low-end consumer video provides relatively low cost and ease of use for students, factors that explain video's popularity as the medium of choice for hands-on student production in the K–12 classroom.

Because the focus is on strengthening cognitive skills, the quality of student video productions is a secondary issue. Many projects can be easily edited in the camera without sophisticated video editing equipment and accomplished in a standard 50-minute class period. When editing equipment is available, students have an even greater opportunity to learn about the constructed nature of media. Hands-on opportunities come full circle as students enhance their understanding of the way media are constructed, through the construction of their own products.

After students learn to handle the frame in the relatively easier medium of video, they are ready to sit down at the computer and apply their knowledge of design, sound, movement, and narrative to digital production. In this way, video is the perfect "scaffolding tool" for students as they become proficient in the use of more sophisticated technology tools.

When students move from video to the computer, they know much more about how to handle text, image, and sound. On the computer, a greater universe of creative possibilities becomes open to them. Students can compose media from a rich database of online resources. They can link resources in order to create new narrative possibilities. They have access to ever-wider audiences of peers and experts for critical feedback, information, and debate. With their skill in manipulating the moving image, students can now move beyond print and take advantage of the full potential of digital technology.

The important "glue" that holds analysis and practice together is pedagogy. By way of example, Table 2 illustrates the use of the video medium to foster both traditional and constructivist approaches to education (Tyner, 1994, p. 18). The table has implications for student use of a range of multimedia tools, including both analog and digital student publications.

REPRESENTATION AND REPRODUCTION

In addition to the aesthetic study of form, video is a useful place to address content issues such as the social and political implications of media representation. Those who practice hands-on video production with children argue that encouraging students to represent their own experiences through media making broadens the discourse about representation in media to accommodate new aesthetic codes, conventions and discourses. They argue not only for more and different representations in media, but for more kinds of media discourse that go far beyond commercial broadcast, or even beyond conventional notions about independent media production.

The central objective for the study of media representation as a cognitive approach to media production is that of *voice*. Voice is a concept that transcends the vagaries of the image or even the politics of identity. Specifically, media production gives voice to students who are otherwise silenced in their schools and communities. It allows students to represent their experiences and their communities as cultural insiders, instead of the incessant representation and misrepresentation of them by media producers outside their communities. It allows them to see the ethical dilemmas presented by representation and media from a much broader perspective than simple watching, criticism, and evaluation can provide. And by emphasizing the power of their own voices to redress social inequality, it encourages students to participate actively in problem solving as vital members of their communities.

In their budding awareness of the range of discourses available to them, teenagers and young children must go through the process of "trying on" identities so that the full mosaic of their personalities can emerge and a wide range of the many identities that contemporary children negotiate are encouraged to emerge through expression and experimentation. As "Birth of a Candy Bar" demonstrates, the experimentation often results in narratives that are outside the conventionally accepted discourse of schooling. Video encourages students to choose carefully the discourse that is most appropriate to their intended audience.

Students' first productions are often highly personal. Note the use of video production with a teen whose first language is not English, in this short video done by a Maria Herrera, a young mother in Branda Miller's program

TABLE 2
The Way Video Is Used in the Classroom

Function	Traditional Approach	Constructivist Approach
Access and analysis of information	Prepackaged programming delivers information to students.	Students and teachers produce their own instructional content.
	Video is an expert, a "substitute teacher" that presents one-way knowledge to students.	Students learn codes and conventions of video to express themselves. Their knowledge is valued and they have outlets to express it.
	Video is considered a "window on the world."	Video is a manufactured construct with inherent values and biases.
Hands-on production	Video is used to document other real-time classroom or extracurricular projects.	Video productions that derive from original concepts are encouraged.
	Video replicates broadcast formats.	Students see a range of independent and experimental pieces from which to model and practice a variety of formats.
	Teachers choose the themes and concepts for student productions	Students work with teachers to choose themes, content, and concepts for classroom information and hands-on production.
	Teachers are experts, students learn.	Students are sometimes experts. Teachers are sometimes learners.
	Emphasis is on job readiness, that is, production skill-building.	Emphasis is on critical thinking skill building.
	Video themes are based on rigid disciplines.	Students and teachers work in interdisciplinary teams. Students are encouraged to make connections between disciplines.
	Teachers talk, students listen.	Students talk, move about in an orderly way and challenge one another, based on agreed upon rules of discourse.
Assessment	Teachers establish assessment criteria.	Students and teachers establish assessment criteria together.
	Assessment is based on teacher judgment.	Assessments are based on explicit standards and authentic classroom activities.
	Students compete as individuals.	Students are assessed both as individuals and as collaborative team members.

(Continued)

186

TABLE 2
(Continued)

Restructuring		
	Teachers assess student work.	A variety of assessment strategies include self-assessment, peer assessment, and opportunities for community feedback.
	Emphasis on "right" answers and "correct" ways of working.	Emphasis on pertinent questions and responses based on viable evidence.
	High-stakes assessments that rank students based on arbitrary tasks.	Low-stakes assessments based on actual classroom tasks.
Restructuring	The school day is divided into rigid time periods.	The school day has flexibility for block time, team teaching and collaborative planning.
	Classroom products are intended only by teachers and student(s).	Classroom products are produced for a wider audience.
	Media studies is a separate class or unit.	Students are encouraged to question media every time it is in the classroom environment as an approach, not a discipline.
	Media analysis and production are separate courses of study.	Media analysis and video production are cross-curricular and interdisciplinary and integrated.

Note. From *Arts Education Policy Review*, 96:1, September/October 1994, pp. 18-26. Reprinted with permission of The Helen Dwight Reid Educational Foundation, Published by Heldref Publications, 1319 18th St. NW, Washington DC, 20036-1802. © 1994.

at the Henry Street Settlement. It is significant that second-generation kids in the United States live in at least two cultures and may identify with many subgroups of their peers. They fluently navigate back and forth between their various languages and cultures in a way that linguists call "code switching." In the following video segment, the demarcation between the world of Maria and that of her mother is marked by language. Maria's mother, who is an immigrant to the United States from Mexico but who can speak in English when necessary, prefers to speak in Spanish. Maria, whose preferred language is Spanish, but who fluently switches back and forth between English and Spanish, depending on the circumstances, speaks in English for the video. As the video unfolds, it is evident that the use of English affords Maria a small space for privacy while she lives under her mother's more powerful authority.

Excerpt from *Maria Herrera* (Herrera & Miller, 1989)

Baby Cries . . .
Go! Go! Hurry Up!
Bathe! Run! Wake Up!

Cut to:

Mother (in Spanish):

I married at 14. I had my first child at 15. In Mexico, in those days, contraception was never used. In 5 years I had three children. 11 years later after I had my 3rd child, I had Janet [Maria's Anglo name]. Then, I had no more. I've always lived here alone and worked here alone in this country. I thank God it's gone well.

Cut to:

Go get the milk! Hurry!

Maria (in English):

When I found out I was pregnant I was 13 years old. My mother was the one who took me to the hospital and they gave me a urine test to find out if I was pregnant or not or if I had an infection. And they told me that it was positive that I was pregnant. . . . And I felt bad.

Go get the little girl's clothes! Hurry Up!

[My mother] started to cry, telling me how could I have done that to her . . . that she always gave me everything that I want . . . and how could I bring this to her now?

Mother (in Spanish):

I felt much resentment and pain and my thoughts. . . . I don't like discussing it because it makes me feel bad. I wanted her to study. For one, to come out of poverty. I wanted her to be somebody before she had a baby. In any event, she says now she will study. Nothing will change. [She sighs]. But I know the problem.

Maria (in English):

I got pregnant. I finished the whole year of the seventh grade and then my belly started getting bigger and I didn't go for a whole year. . . . I wasn't in love. It was like curiosity. I don't know. I wasn't in love with the guy. . . . I followed the first guy I went to bed with and I regret it. . . . I told him I wanted to see him, but he only came by a couple of times. I don't really have any high love for him, but . . . I hate him.

Maria's Mother (in Spanish):

One should allow the young girl to have the child so that she can feel and experience the reality. That she suffers this reality of motherhood.

Right now, she is suffering. She can't go out. She can't dress the way she used to. She has to change Pampers (diapers), clean bottles and heat milk. So she sees what it is to have a baby.

Maria (in English):

I don't have the same freedom. I used to not think about the future. I didn't like school that much. I was absent a lot. I used to cut [class]. But now I want to have a career. I want to be a computer programmer. . . . I want my daughter to have the best. (Herrera & Miller, 1989)

The video allows Maria an important place to reflect on her situation through personal self-expression. Even so, self-expression alone cannot improve her life chances. The role of the teacher is to provide the skills and knowledge, in incremental steps, for students to move from personal reflection to plausible action steps that can improve the conditions of their lives. Furthermore, students who have been historically underserved by education and who may not have access to the life chances enjoyed by their peers who feel at home in the dominant culture, are in most need of such academic opportunity.

It is important to stress again that student expression, although charming and productive, does not absolve the teacher of the responsibility to provide academic rigor and challenging educational opportunity for all students. Media production must be justifiable to the core curriculum, linked to some standards that are explicitly understood by both teachers and students, and authentically assessed in order for it to be valuable to students' educations. Media education that includes both analysis and practical work provides the opportunity to link cognitive work with skill-based work in a way that supports strong academic standards for all students. It has the potential to lead students back to a range of print and electronic texts that can be better understood because of the heightened cognitive awareness provided by the media work.

Even though engaging, the examples of student videos excerpted here arose from learning objectives that sought to strengthen narrative, problem solving, and research skills in addition to skill-based learning with media equipment. The videos provided structured apprenticeships for students to present a project to a wider audience. Finally, the students' use of static graphic elements based on personal themes can be employed for video book reports and research projects based on more traditional academic themes. The following video produced by a middle school student in Houston is an example of the kind of research work that can be initiated with video. The student used graphic elements and animation, built a diorama, and used in-camera editing and audio-dubbing techniques to report about the Caddo Indians. He keeps his narration short and appropriate to the video format.

The Caddo Village
by Alex Hanschen (Dallas, 1994)

The Southeastern tribes in Texas lived in the eastern part of the state. The Caddos lived in scattered villages that stretched along the creeks and rivers of East Texas and western Louisiana. Historians considered the Caddos to be the richest and most advanced of all the Texas Indians. The forests and streams of East Texas provided the Caddos with many kinds of food, both plant and animal.

Caddos lived in a house shaped like domes made from tree limbs, grass and reeds. They wove colorful rugs, baskets, hangings and bedding materials from reeds and tree limbs. The Caddos were known for their useful as well as beautiful pottery.

The main food source of the Caddos was corn. In addition to corn, the Caddos grew beans, squash, sunflower seeds and tobacco. The Caddos used a number of modern farming methods. Among these was crop rotation.

The Caddos were great fire worshipers. They believed that fire had a strong power. They always kept a fire going.

The Caddos fished in streams and rivers. They were one of the first Texas Indians to use a trout line. They placed bait on a series of hooks and then strung the line across a creek or river.

The Caddos were friendly people. Their methods of farming allowed them to raise enough crops to support a large population. They were able to trade their forest products with the Spanish and other Indians for flint and turquoise which they used to make tools and weapons.

They built sturdy homes and produced a beautiful pottery.

The information in *The Caddo Village* is simplistic and shows a naïve cultural bias, common to students who may not have had immersion in cultures different from their own. The phrase "Texas Indians" is just one example. Because food, crafts, and dance are politically safe topics for the discussion of culture, teachers often limit their multicultural education strategies to these elements. Critics have derisively called the use of these non-controversial cultural topics "chomp and stomp" and challenge teachers instead to use them to help students take a hard look at the brutal history of cultural assimilation and inequality in U.S. history. Teachers are forced to find a space for classroom work that enables students to learn about other cultures in an authentic and unflinching way, but that does not dissolve into blatant ideological didacticism, a virtual soapbox for adult ideologies. In short, just because media production is a useful tool for expression, incremental discovery and complexity cannot automatically be expected from a student's first productions. In fact, a teacher who expects hands-on video to provide some respite from reading torturous student essays will be sorely disappointed by their first viewing of beginning student videos.

In spite of its ease of use and its potential to experiment, discard and re-do, hands-on use of electronic media is such a rare and powerful event in educational settings that the productions can take on an unnecessary sense of urgency. If students have the feeling that this is the only chance they will ever get to display their knowledge and tell their stories in electronic media, their productions run the risk of becoming unnecessarily precious. More storytelling, more reflection, and more opportunities for mentorship, that is, both cognitive and traditional apprenticeships, will yield more sophisticated and less parochial results.

For example, the sensitive teacher can use the Caddo video to lead students beyond a parochial context of the Caddo story to one that challenges students to explore their own assumptions about the place of the Caddos in history. Through peer discussion and structured research projects, the teacher can ask the students to answer the questions, "Why do you call the Caddos 'Texas' Indians?" and "What happened to the Caddos in the mid-1800s?" Additional hands-on projects might include exercises in tool-making, gardening, fishing, and crafts-making, or having students plot on a map the demise of the Caddo villages over time as encroachments on their land, subjugation, and disease overtook their culture. Subsequent videos about the Caddos could include more sophisticated uses of historical photographs, diaries, and anecdotal interviews with historians and descendants of the Caddos. A look at documentary forms that use a variety of techniques, such as voice-over, still photographs, or the use of stock footage, would open a wider range of possibilities. Such use of documentary formats would also provide important scaffolding for analysis of the documentaries produced by others.

By using video to investigate and address issues in a broader social context, students can become active in their communities as a media advocacy strategy. This is a method that has true potential to correct inaccurate media stereotypes and to call attention to the need for solutions for explicit social problems. In the following video, a gay teen reaches out to other gay teenagers. The video is an excerpt from a reel produced by gay and lesbian teens in workshops at Eagles Center in Los Angeles and the Hetrick–Martin Institute in New York City. The teens call their reel *Divas in Training* and it consists of a number of clips that showcase gay and lesbian discourse and perspective. In this video, the teen producer is just beginning to look beyond the boundaries of personal self-expression to explore the potentials of media discourse to promote wider social understanding across cultures:

Always There (1995, VHS, 6 minutes)

[Boy walks on a city street]

I'm 16 years old. I'm a junior in high school My parents are separated this year. I was kind of upset about that at first, but now I'm used to it.

I live with my mom in an apartment. My sister stops by a lot. Basically I have a big family, but they're all scattered all over and I have one really best friend and it's my sister, Devanna. And she's like the only person who has really been there for me besides my few slut friends.

Me and my mom left our little suburban perfect picket fence sort of life and moved into a less posh neighborhood and I had to learn how to budget. And I wasn't a spoiled brat anymore. And I had to really come down to earth, because it was a totally different way of living and totally different kinds of people.

I told my family [that I was gay] at the beginning of the summer. And it really had a hard effect on my dad. We weren't really close to begin with and my parents are separated and I live with my mom. We were just starting to get close again, me and my dad, and I came out to him. I guess I was really disappointed in his reaction, because he was really hard on me and he basically disowned me and I don't really have a father anymore because of it.

But at least I have my mom and my sister. They're really great and they're there when I need them. Whenever I want to talk to them about it or about anything else in my life, they're always there for me.

When my parents separated, I can remember one time I was just like having a terrible day and this was soon after people found out about me and I was just walking down the hallway and a big group of jocks, I mean, you know, assholes, screamed, "Fag!" at me down the hallway and screamed some disgusting things. And just threatened to kill me. And I just wonder what goes on in people's heads when they have to act like that. I mean when they have to prove themselves, like their manhood or something, by screaming obscenities at me or threatening my life. Because it seems like those people are the most insecure about themselves.

Gay people aren't out to convert the world or to make everyone gay or try to turn their straight friends gay. They just want to be accepted. We all want to be accepted. If you can't accept it, then at least give us respect—enough respect not to scream something at us on the street, or to discriminate against us in the job field. We just need equal opportunity and for all those teenagers out there who are gay and they're scared to tell anybody and they're just living a lie. . . . You really should [tell someone], because the sooner you do, the sooner you can really come to terms with yourself and the kind of person you want to be. (Williams, 1995)

The use of popular culture texts in the diverse classroom offers a promising intervention strategy that explores the nature of discourse, bridges cultural understanding, and enables students to realize the full range of expression available to them. Student knowledge of discursive modes and their relationship to media through a combined production and analysis approach is intended to lead to a deeper understanding of the more traditional, sanctioned texts that are valued in the cultural canon of the dominant culture. Student readings of such texts may be "against the grain," but will at least result from a reasoned approach to appreciation. Media education also makes students aware of the prevalent modes of expression, that is, mediated discourses, peculiar to each medium. It allows students to rethink the uses of a wider variety of artistic expression.

In his study of the uses of textbooks for international, cross-cultural education, Gopinanthan (1987) remarked on the need to rethink the use of print as the dominant, all-purpose classroom learning tool. Although of particular relevance to international education, his study resonates in the contemporary, arts-starved U.S. classroom:

> It needs to be noted that in many cultural contexts the textbook is an alien tool. When one looks at the African context one notes that song, dance, drama, and poetry associated with traditional African rituals and festivals were the primary media of communication. With these media went valuable content-myths, legends, proverbs, and a store of data on the environment, social relations, and a moral code. This national educational resource was kept down during the early years of missionary-sponsored education, but even today there is by no means unanimous support that they should be reintroduced into the school curriculum. (pp. 193–194; Eisemon, Hallett, & Maunda, 1986, pp. 232–246)

As previously noted, digital media provide tools for the educational use of audio, text, and image. But digital media are by no means superior to more familiar tools of expression such as paint, performance, oral storytelling, and so on. When skill is coupled with cognitive work, that is, when literacy is seen as explicit through an understanding of discourses, the ability for students to use a wide range of media, including computers, to their fullest potential can be realized. In addition to the construction of online personas and the strengthening of alphabetic literacy communication, an expanded view of literacy can open up the use of computers to a much wider student population—an issue that goes far beyond access to the "engines." Bernard Hibbits, a professor of law at the University of Pittsburgh, sees the use of new literacy tools for multiple modes of expression as a positive one. In his study of the relationship between law, media and the senses, Hibbits (1996) found that:

> Computer technology is not inherently biased against women, African-Americans, or native Americans. What really disfavors them is text, the traditional code for communicating with that technology. Text has appealed to white American males who've historically had ready access to books and literate learning. It's been less attractive to members of other gender and racial groups which, in the face of prejudice and delimited educational opportunities, supplemented their literacy with strong oral traditions. Today, however, sophisticated forms of human-computer interaction are replacing text with speech. The World Wide Web is offering a multimedia experience that's both seen and heard. In these circumstances, people can use computer technology to

reclaim, extend, and emancipate their voices. This suggests that the interface—not the medium—is the message. (Hibbits, p. 130)

The incorporation of student-centered teaching methodologies into media
teaching also offers fertile ground for successful learning interventions for
diverse classrooms. Cognitive apprenticeships, student-centered learning, inquiry-based and project-based instruction and the re-introduction of arts
education are compatible with media analysis and practice. All of these help
teachers to meet the challenges of divergent student knowledge, interest,
and orientation and to extract the best opportunities from diversity, the
classroom's richest asset.

Toward an Interactive Education

If access to information is the first plateau of the Information Age, application of information looms over the horizon as the next challenge. Application, that is, how education integrates the use of electronic communication tools into school culture, calls into question the usefulness of the one-way commercial model of content delivery, as it seeks out the most compelling and life-enhancing uses of literacy in a digital world.

Several scholars have noted that educational technology has been used in the past to replace and de-skill teachers; to inculcate and reinforce the values and interests of dominant forces in society; and to promote education as a commodity instead of as a process for lifelong learning (Apple, 1982, 1987; Cuban, 1986; Ellsworth, 1987). At the same time, new literacy tools also have demonstrated the ability to overcome time, space, and distance in order to ensure access to education to students who may be isolated by geography, poverty, or disability. Technology has been seen to enable a more diverse range of student expression and to open the door to a wider array of diverse viewpoints—far beyond teacher and textbook. In short, digital communication enables students to go beyond the four walls of the classroom in order to have access to mentors, resources, opportunities, and alternate perspectives (Woronov, 1994). Given its ability to serve enlightened—or darker—purposes, it is clear that the role of technology in schooling is a surrogate for the role of literacy in schooling. Both have little to do with specific technologies and everything to do with the way they are used.

> The point then is not to incorporate media and new technology into traditional modes of schooling, but rather to use media to transform the schooling in which it is incorporated. (Goodman, 1996)

Teaching and learning in an age of information can be at its most liberating when literacy, technology, and pedagogy are aligned toward a common purpose: a democratic education that improves the life chances of all children. These include: (a) critical literacy that teaches *about* information, as well as *with* information; (b) experiential education that employs communication tools for student use in experimental and investigatory ways; and (c) critical pedagogy that supports constructivist, inquiry-based, and democratic practices.

The terms used to describe such a vision of education are highly inadequate. Perhaps *design curriculum* or *project-based learning* will embody and unite the principles of those who want to teach *about* as well as *with* information resources. Perhaps one of the multiliteracy terms will prevail to unite literacy, technology, and education. In this book, the term *media education* has been privileged, but with the implicit understanding that it is a transitional concept. Media education expands literacy to include reading and writing through the use of new and emerging communication tools. It is learning that demands the critical, independent, and creative use of information. It is learning that speaks to the social contexts of literacy and encourages a range of discourse. It holds the promise of an expansive, diverse, and efficient education. Media education is intended as a strategy to accommodate a world marked by both the challenges and the promise of technology:

> What we teach is determined by a vision of the future. We want students to be competent and critical users of media—not competent and critical for one school year and long enough to pass the examination, but people who will continue to be competent and critical users of the media long after they have left our care. Therefore the texts we give students to analyze at school are simply vehicles—a means to an end—and that end is the development of critical skills which can be applied to any aspect of the media in the future. (Quin & McMahon, 1993, p. 22)

Media education offers the potential to respond to social, economic, historical and cultural realities of the times. In contrast, schools that use literacy to reflect a narrow discourse of schooling are increasingly out of step with a diverse, technological society. Mass technologies that continue to promote the type of literacy that hearkens back to the Industrial Age are destined to promote the same social inequities that were seen in schooling of the past. Access to more and better communication tools, within limiting and anachronistic conditions of communication systems, is pointless. In contrast, the use of technologies to promote the goals of a diverse and meaningful kind of literacy, that is, critical literacy, hold the promise of transforming schools in a way that have potential for improving the life chances of all students.

When the purposes for literacy are clear, the choice of tools that promote critical literacy can follow.

COMING TO CONSENSUS

Schools are buffeted by a number of competing demands on their resources: shorter school years or longer school years; smaller class sizes or consolidated school plants; lengthening the school year or dropping the senior year of schooling; the list is endless. Technology has often been touted as a solution to these conflicting visions of school reform. As the equipment depreciates, without resulting gains in student achievement, educators who have turned to technology under these conditions are right to wonder if technology is a zero sum game. Initial reactions to the failure of technology to make a difference in public schools is that "there was not enough equipment," or that the school "purchased the wrong equipment," or that "there was not enough money to support the use of technology."

If schools stick with technology long enough, they find out very quickly that the problem is not with the equipment, or lack thereof. Meeting contemporary challenges to teaching and learning involves much more than tinkering with technology. A retooling of the whole system is in order. At the heart of the failure to integrate technology in the classroom is a stunted vision of both literacy and education:

> Although the state of the *art* in instructional technology has gone far beyond the provisions of on-screen workbooks, the state of *practice* in many places has not kept pace. Many uses of technology either support the classroom status quo or occur at the margins of education, rather than the mainstream academic program. (Means, 1994, p. 3)

American education is essentially pragmatic, perceived as a means to train a productive workforce that will serve the needs of each community. As such, it emphasizes skill-based, rote learning that is teacher-centered, a method so hierarchical that it is sometimes referred to as the "factory model" of education. This model is even reflected in the architecture of school buildings, monolithic concrete structures designed for economy, safety, and the specializations of tasks.

In 1997, the U.S. Department of Education released *Building Knowledge for a Nation of Learners*, a report that outlined priorities for educational research into the 21st century. The report acknowledged that public schools teach with increasing amounts of information, but provide few skills to effectively use it:

> The vast majority of high school seniors cannot synthesize and learn from specialized reading materials, nor can they solve multi-step problems . . . in

short, they lack precisely the skills that will be more highly valued and more highly rewarded in coming decades. (p. 2)

In order to meet new challenges in the workplace and in civic life, America's learners will need a firm grasp of basic competencies, a broad general knowledge of the their world, and the skills to respond to the rapid generation of new knowledge. (U.S. Department of Education, 1997, p. 1)

Since the 1960s, the trend toward consolidation of small, community-based schools into larger, more cost-efficient facilities has exacerbated the adherence to the factory model of education in the United States. The top-down, authoritarian pedagogy associated with the factory model is in direct conflict with the democratic, student-centered pedagogy of critical literacy and, as such, still presents a formidable barrier to the optimum integration of new technology tools across the curriculum in the United States. The recent trend toward smaller schools and smaller class sizes is a reversal, but smaller learning environments do not necessarily ensure that the factory model will change.

It is fashionable to rebuke this model of education, but its roots in education are deep. Many parents expect it and many teachers are still rewarded by a system that is rigidly hierarchical and isolated from authentic social structures in the community. Although they might acknowledge that the system is "broken," educators must be convinced of the concrete benefit of yet another round of change. Those who still operate within a factory model of education are right to question school reformers with "What's in it for me and my children?" In order to justify the introduction of media education in schooling, it will be necessary to reframe the debate on a number of fronts in order even to begin to answer that question.

THE MARRIAGE OF ANALYSIS AND PRODUCTION

Pedagogy—how teachers teach and how students learn—is at the heart of school change and serves as the linchpin for incorporating new literacy practices into the classroom. Pedagogies that show promise in new uses of information technologies have been called constructivist, inquiry-based, student-centered, project-based learning, and experiential. There are doubtless many others. Pedagogy is the "glue" that unites media analysis and practice.

Constructivist education recognizes that meaning is not fixed, but that people produce their own meaning from a wide range of contexts, a form of knowledge construction. Teachers build on this tendency to construct meaning by exploiting a variety of methods, including hands-on, learner-centered, interdisciplinary, collaborative, and inquiry-based processes to create learning opportunities that encourage students to think for themselves.

Inquiry is vital to the constructivist use of new technologies. Inquiry may come under the guise of problem-solving, or project-based work, or Socratic dialogic investigations. As students produce information resources in an inquiry-based environment, they can practice questioning information produced by others under the guidance of their teacher. Classroom analysis of information is investigatory; the important thing is not to have one "right" answer, but to come up with a range of plausible and reasoned solutions to problems. Yet inquiry-based education does not deny that occasionally there is only one right answer. Nor does it deny the usefulness of memorization. Inquiry-based education is much more useful than rote memorization for problem solving that is situational and complex. When teachers question with students, they encourage the ability to know how to ask questions and to have the research skills necessary to find information that is useful to address problems as they occur.

Although factual knowledge is still important, the goal is to stimulate the questioning process. Thus, speculation about possible answers to questions is the first step. Posing questions in response to questions is the goal. This is especially important to media teaching. Because the answers to questions about authorship, production processes, costs, and origins are not always readily available, students can still draw from their knowledge of media codes and conventions to predict answers to questions. They can then broaden their understanding of media form and content by posing new questions. Possible questions are suggested in standards rubrics that British teachers use to teach about media in elementary education. The use of questions as the basis for standards is also a clever way to reinforce the importance of inquiry-based modes to the teaching of media:

Who is communicating and why?
What type of text is it?
How is it produced?
How do we know what it means?
Who receives it and what sense do they make of it?
How does it PRESENT its subject? (Bazalgette, 1989)

As students practice questioning media and other information with their teachers and each other, they begin to internally question information *every time it appears in the environment,* without prompting from the teacher or parent. It is the hope of critical pedagogists that this habit of questioning information, developed through classroom practice, will create critically autonomous citizens, who question information and authority as a matter of course.

Analytical skills are important keys to independent thinking, but British media educator, Len Masterman (1985) stresses that analysis alone, uncoupled from experiential student use of tools, is half a program at best. At its worst, strict media analysis has the potential of creating cynical student attitudes about commercial media, without the outlet for change, expression, and citizen feedback that hands-on production provides. He says, "Media education consists of both practical criticism and critical practice. It affirms the primacy of cultural criticism over cultural reproduction" (Masterman, 1990, p. 8).

Students have already informally learned to "read" electronic media forms, although they may not yet have the vocabulary to articulate their specific codes and conventions. Hands-on student production demonstrates levels of understanding about the way print and electronic media construct popular culture, as well as a deep understanding of various genres and they way they overlap.

The challenge of the critical media teacher is to bring the highly symbolic sounds and images of electronic texts into the realm of rational discourse, so that students have the skill and vocabulary to analyze and evaluate the meanings and the usefulness of all information resources. The most effective way to accomplish sophisticated analysis, critical literacy, and metacognition of various discourses is to encourage students to produce their own media, in a reprisal of the symbiotic relationship between alphabetic reading and writing.

The goal of student production is not creative self-expression, nor vocational "job readiness" for future jobs in media industries, although these may be important by-products of production in the classroom. Media educators recognize that although some of their students will go on to become artists, producers, and media workers, most will not. Even so, all students are ardent consumers of media. Therefore, the primary emphasis of hands-on production is to inform analysis of the information produced by others—especially commercial or governmental information products. In turn, students analyze their own products and other media products in order to create more satisfying productions, thus strengthening their knowledge of media codes and conventions. The analysis–production formula creates a spiral of success: analysis informs production, which in turn informs analysis.

IN SEARCH OF MEDIA EDUCATION STANDARDS

The challenge for media teachers who work from a critical literacy perspective is to guide students through practical, authentic, "real-world" tasks and to look closely at the way students accomplish these tasks in order to assess the amount of learning that takes place. If the student performance on the task indicates that he or she needs more challenge, then the teacher can provide it. If a student's work looks as if the task was too hard to master, then the teacher can go back and provide more scaffolding and remedial help. In other words, authentic education implies that tasks are meaningful and that the assessment of students is based on the things that they have actually had the opportunity to learn. Although students have had ample opportunity to learn about media informally, the goal of the media teacher is to make such learning formal and structured enough to recognize it when it takes place.

Standards that are explicit and agreed upon by learners, teachers, and schools are meant to ensure that opportunities for a comparable, quality education are available to all students. In spite of the fact that students have various teachers with diverse expertise and interests, standards help to ensure that everyone in the school system is working toward similar goals. When teacher teams within schools develop tasks based on standards, every child can have access to "the basics," without redundancy or gaps in their relative educational experiences. Standards are especially important for media education, because of its *ad hoc* and fragile status in the curriculum.

When standards, classroom tasks, and student assessment are aligned, teachers can better recognize when learning takes place. If students are not making progress in their learning, or if they are falling behind, a standards-driven curriculum provides teachers with a kind of "map" that helps them to identify the appropriate remedial or customized intervention that enables the student to succeed and go on to the next learning challenge.

At least in theory. Arguably every teacher has personal standards for what his or her own students should know and be able to do. But standards are meant to equalize educational opportunity for all students. Therefore, in order for standards-driven education to address the wide range of quality that each student is likely to encounter behind the closed door of the classroom, standards must be instituted systemically. Historically, teachers have a great deal of autonomy to decide how they teach and what they teach. Working under trying conditions, with mounting public criticism, the classroom is sometimes the only professional domain where the average teacher is still in control. In order to revitalize classroom practices, standards require teachers to give up some degree of autonomy for the greater good and to reach consensus with their colleagues and communities about what to teach. It requires the whole school to prioritize the vast universe of potentially valuable, interesting and enriching subject matter and to answer the question: What do we want our children to know and be able to do?

Teachers have seen so many fads come and go that they are nearly "reform-proof." In order for teachers to buy in to the concept of standards, they must see how new reform-minded rhetoric immediately benefits their students and their own working conditions in the classroom. Otherwise, it is safer—for both themselves and their students—to stick with their existing expertise around topics of personal interest and expertise, that is, the devil they know versus the devil they don't know.

One thing that teachers *do* know is that norm-referenced standardized testing is what drives elementary and secondary education. Norm-referenced tests as a measure of student progress often have little to do with the actual teaching and learning that takes place in individual classrooms. Minority students traditionally have dismal group scores on such tests and to frustrated educators, it sometimes seems that standardized tests were devised to separate children into educational winners and losers. Standardized scores are used to publicly humiliate schools, to transfer teachers, and to generally reconstitute schools. Because standardized tests are used in a punitive way by school administrators, politicians, the media, and the public, teachers feel a responsibility to teach to standardized tests. Such high-stakes consequences as funding, local real estate values, negative media attention, community pressure, and student advancement hang in the balance.

At the same time, classroom teachers are canny about what can be called "low-stakes" assessments. This kind of classroom assessment is between teacher and learner and has little in common with high-stakes, norm-referenced tests. For one thing, assessment of this kind is nonpunitive. It doesn't rank one student against another. It is simply a way for teachers to recognize when individual learning is taking place and then to provide the necessary scaffolding to ensure that it does. It is here—in low stakes, classroom situations—that standards hold the most promise to improve student learning.

It is common in education for reformers to decry the fact that schools "re-invent the wheel" every decade. But with standards-driven education, re-inventing the wheel is a fruitful way to proceed. Because of the long history of strong local control over education in the United States, reform efforts are introduced idiosyncratically. Standards that are responsive to low-stakes assessments of teaching and learning can only be created within the specific contexts of each community. When teachers and communities create and "own" standards, standards-driven education can begin to fulfill the promise of educational improvement. Attempts to introduce totalizing versions of academic standards, created by those far away, are of little use to classroom teachers. Although they may serve as models for locally customized standards efforts, national standards created by professional committees on a national level, are still only the latest in a long line of high-stakes impositions from outside. Accordingly, national standards in the United States are voluntary. They do, however, offer schools and districts a place to begin creating their own standards.

EXEMPLARY MEDIA EDUCATION STANDARDS IN THE UNITED STATES

The U.S. Speech Communication Association created national standards for speaking, listening, and media literacy in K–12 education in 1996. The goal of the standards are to ensure that the "effective media participant can demonstrate":

1. the effects of the various types of electronic audio and visual media, including television, radio, the telephone, the Internet, computers, electronic conferencing, and film, on media consumers; and

2. the ability to identify and use skills necessary for competent participation in communication across various types of electronic audio and visual media. (Speech Communication Assocation, 1996, p. 6)

Defining media education's place in education is a problem that many educators have already solved by including it in their daily classroom practices. Although these educators may not have begun by teaching from standards, the standards are useful as a way to justify media education in the curriculum. Standards are increasingly required for all coursework, but even when implemented in an ad hoc manner, they prove useful as low-stakes classroom assessment tools. To maintain its credibility as a rigorous subject for study, media education must organize standards committees and hammer out standards documents that can inform the tasks and assessments for media education.

It depends whether media studies are implemented as a course, or across the curriculum, in which case, standards would be incorporated as part of a larger subject. This is the case for media education standards in Ontario, Canada, where media literacy is represented by a "viewing and representing" strand within the province's Language Arts curriculum for Grades 1–9 (Ontario Ministry of Education, 1995). The document is then used to customize tasks and create assessments at the local level.

The language arts discipline is a logical place to embed media education within a discipline. One example can be seen in the use of the Media Education Institutes, an in-depth professional development opportunity for educators designed by arts educator Deborah Leveranz and media educator Kathleen Tyner. During formative evaluation of the Institutes in Texas, Deborah Leveranz gathered feedback from teachers to develop a "viewing and representing" strand that could be aligned with state standards for the Language Arts. The viewing and representing standards provide "scope and sequence," that is, content and performance standards, for the incorporation of media education across all grade levels. The rubrics that Leveranz created for the Language Arts are compatible with the state's frameworks, *The Texas Essential Knowledge and Skills (TEKS)* for the English Language Arts and Reading and are familiar to language arts teachers in Texas. Media education is represented as a viewing/representing strand as essential elements of the English Language Arts and Reading standards and embedded in every grade level (Texas Education Agency, 1997).

In addition, the Texas Standards contain technology application standards with four strands that are fruitful for critical literacy teaching: foundations, information, acquisition, work in solving problems, and communication. The strands incorporate definitions from information literacy, media literacy, computer literacy, and visual literacy. They also balance information analysis with hands-on practice:

> Through the study of technology applications foundations, including technology-related terms, concepts, and data input strategies, students learn to make informed decisions about technologies and their applications. The efficient acquisition of information includes the identification of task requirements; the plan for using search strategies; and the use of technology to access, analyze, and evaluate the acquired information. By using technology as a tool that supports the work of individuals and groups in solving problems, students will select the technology appropriate for the task, synthesize knowledge, create a solution, and evaluate the results. Students communicate information in different formats and to diverse audiences. A variety of technologies will be used. Students will analyze and evaluate the results. (Texas Education Agency, 1997)

The demarcation of "viewing" and "representing" incorporate the concepts of both "reading/analysis" and "writing/practice." The scope and sequence of the viewing and representing structure are compatible with international media education standards. In addition, the rubric builds on the definition of media education familiar to media educators, that is, "media literacy is the ability to access, analyze, evaluate and produce communication in a variety of forms" (Tyner & Leveranz, 1996, p. 1).

Tables 3, 4, and 5 provide details of the standards developed by the Texas teachers in the Media Education Institutes. An overview of the viewing and representing strand is represented in Table 3, which summarizes the viewing and representing strand in the English Language Arts and organizes it by the media education definition of "access, analyze, evaluate and produce." Table 4 presents a useful overview of the strands. Table 5 is a content and performance rubric that teachers can use to assess learning. It details progress checkpoints each K–12 grade level. Tables 3 through 5 demonstrate how teachers at the local level can use state standards to inform the curriculum.

Incorporating media education within the standards of existing disciplines, such as language arts or technology application is one strategy to further its legitimacy and formal recognition in the curriculum. The TEKS English Language Arts and Reading standards also include a stand-alone elective for Media Literacy in a Speech/Communication strand.

Because they help teachers to recognize learning and to provide the help and challenge that students need, standards are powerful tools for classroom teachers to assess the learning of an individual student. At their most positive, national and state standards can be used as models to inform the development of local standards. However, there is a concern state and national standards have the potential to fuel high-stakes assessment that may be

TABLE 3
The English Language Arts Essential Knowledge and Skills:
Viewing and Representing Strands At a Glance

K-3	4-8	9-12
The student accesses print, visual and electronic media for varying purposes	The student accesses print, visual and electronic media for varying purposes	The student accesses print, visual and electronic media for varying purposes
The student accesses terms related to techniques, technologies and institutions involved in media production	The student accesses terms related to techniques, technologies and institutions involved in media production	The student accesses terms related to techniques, technologies and institutions involved in media production
The student recognizes that all forms of media contain messages.	The student recognizes that all forms of media contain messages.	The student recognizes that all forms of media contain messages.
The student acquires skills to decode and analyze media messages.	The student acquires skills to decode and analyze media messages.	The student acquires skills to decode and analyze media messages.
The student gains an informed understanding of media through critical analysis.	The student gains an informed understanding of media through critical analysis.	The student gains an informed understanding of media through critical analysis.
The student critically examines and interprets media messages in an historical, social and cultural context (understands the relationship among audiences, media messages and the world).	The student critically examines and interprets media messages in an historical, social and cultural context (understands the relationship among audiences, media messages and the world).	The student critically examines and interprets media messages in an historical, social and cultural context (understands the relationship among audiences, media messages and the world).
The student is able to assess and articulate personal media use and speculate on the media use of others.	The student is able to assess and articulate personal media use and speculate on the media use of others.	The student is able to assess and articulate personal media use and speculate on the media use of others.
The student uses knowledge of various media to solve problems, communicate and produce self-selected and assigned projects.	The student uses knowledge of various media to solve problems, communicate and produce self-selected and assigned projects.	The student uses knowledge of various media to solve problems, communicate and produce self-selected and assigned projects.

Note. Reprinted by Permission, Deborah Leveranz, Media, Analysis and Practice, 1996.

TABLE 4

English Language Arts Viewing and Representing Strands: Access, Analyze, Evaluate, and Produce

Access	K-3	4-8	9-12
The student accesses print, visual, and electronic media for varying purposes	• uses media for information and entertainment • uses media to investigate an issue • uses viewing as a tool for learning and research • views for enjoyment and appreciation of language • identifies media forms, e.g., news, drama, cartoon, advertising, entertainment	• uses a wide range of media for information, entertainment, and communication • Accesses media resources to define, investigate, and represent questions, issues, and problems • accesses library databases to discover primary and secondary sources and select those appropriate to research projects • views for enjoyment and appreciation of language • identifies some major genres and categories, e.g., soap opera, sitcom, action, adventure, tabloid	• selects viewing materials from a wide range of forms and reflects critically on choices • accesses media resources to define, investigate, and represent questions, issues, and problems • accesses library databases to discover primary and secondary sources and select those appropriate to research projects • views for enjoyment and appreciation of language • identifies a wide range of media forms and categories
The student accesses terms related to techniques, technologies, and institutions involved in media production	• names the important parts of basic equipment, e.g., still camera, video camera, laser disk, computer, photocopier, slide projector, etc. and be able to perform basic operations • distinguishes one shot from the next in the sequence • identifies shot types, e.g., close-up, pan	• observes, identifies, and discusses features of audio/visual text, such as: — different camera angles & distances — arrangement of people and object within the frame — color, black & white, variations — different sounds and levels of amplification — different transitions from shot to shot, e.g., fade, dissolve, cut, wipe — camera movements, e.g., pan, tilt, dolly, zoom — variation in writing, print size, and typeface — variation in size and quality of paper	• identifies and discusses postproduction and distribution terms and processes, e.g., editing, printing, email • defines occupations involved in making a media product, e.g., preparing a newspaper, a political campaign, or a marketing campaign for a product

K-3	4-8	9-12
• describes basic production roles, e.g., writer, director, camera operator, floor manager, graphic artist	• describes basic production roles and work performed by specific people in the media industry, e.g., agents, actors, producers, public relations	• describes specialist roles involved in the preproduction, production, postproduction, distribution, and marketing of media products.

Analyze

K-3	4-8	9-12
The student recognizes that all forms of media contain messages		
• researches how stories occur in the media (narrative) and compare these stories to the types of stories they already know	• recognizes devises for controlling narrative, e.g., voice over	• identifies narratives as a series of constructed conventions such as character motivation, sequence, hierarchy of events and characters rather than being a "natural part of a story"
• draws on prior experience and knowledge	• follows multiple/parallel plots within a narrative	
	• asks questions about he intended message of a media text and state opinions about the content (accuracy, relevance, bias) and form	• identifies implicit as well as explicit messages and biases in media texts
• examines the choices made in the production of media products	• describes how different elements in media texts help to create atmosphere and shape meaning	• identifies that meaning is conveyed in media texts through a combination of elements (e.g., sound, sequence, and perspective together can convey a specific mood)
• identifies and describes different stereotypes in the media, e.g., hero, heroine, villain	• compares their own experiences with those attributed to their age group in the media	• analyzes the stereotypes used to portray certain groups

(Continued)

TABLE 4
(Continued)

Analyze	K-3	4-8	9-12
The student acquires skills to decode and analyze media messages	• differentiates between media, e.g., print and electronic	• identifies some stereotypes in media text depictions of various children in their age group and explains how they imply judgments of various social, racial, and cultural groups	• compares gender, social and occupational stereotypes from across cultures
	• identifies some ways of organizing material in media texts	• differentiates between specific genre, e.g., entertainment, news and information, advertising	• understands how genre shapes an audiences' expectation of media content
	• examines how visual and verbal symbols communicate meaning (traffic signs, advertising signs)	• identifies a range of ways of organizing and presenting material in media texts	• identifies a range of ways of organizing and presenting material in media texts and critically examining the reactions of others
	• looks at the types of advertising in different media forms	• identifies symbolic codes used in the media, e.g., different shots in a film, framing devices in photography	• examines how different symbolic codes can operate together to create meaning
		• explains what information is being communicated by media codes and conventions, e.g., fade to black close-up	• examines the effects of advertising
The student gains an informed understanding of media through critical analysis	• researches how stories occur in the media by considering advertising, news and documentaries, as well as fictional forms	• examines how media forms are affected by the presence or absence of advertising	• considers the importance of advertising to commercial media
		• considers how the same story can be adapted to different audiences	• compares the way in which different media present the same topic or story

K-3	4-8	9-12
• identifies and explains beginning, middle, and end of a story	• identifies narrative patterns and how they are used in the presentation of fictional and nonfictional material in the media	• compare and contrast media products either or the same or different types, e.g., news reports in different newspapers, on television, and over the internet

Evaluate

K-3	4-8	9-12
The student critically examines and interprets media messages in an historical, social, and cultural context (understands the relationship among audiences, media messages, and the world)		
• identifies the difference between an event and the representation of that event in media form	• identifies and discusses differences between an event and the representation of that event in media form	• identifies and discusses differences between an event and the representation of that event in media form
• asks questions about the content of the media text and connects to own knowledge and experience	• asks questions about issues raised in a media text, e.g., characterization, validity of factual material, and listens to others' opinions and states own ideas	• provides examples of the social outcomes of particular media representation
• recalls some details of a media text and describes how they make the text more interesting or enjoyable	• identifies and analyzes the interpretations made of a media text by viewers who are of varied cultures, ages, or backgrounds	• responds to concrete and abstract meaning in a media text, recognizing that people interpret texts differently depending on many factors, e.g., age, gender, race, experience

(Continued)

TABLE 4
(Continued)

Evaluate	K-3	4-8	9-12
The student is able to assess and articulate personal media use and speculate on the media use of others	• examines the ways in which media can affect the individual • expresses preferences when discussing media productions • views media deliberately and critically • views different media texts for pleasure, recognizes the main idea of what has been viewed, and responds to presentation and content • examines the effects of the media in their environment (family, home, school) • identifies audiences for media products	• uses media tests to explore human relationships, new ideas, own and other cultures • evaluates the effectiveness of different elements used in media texts • expresses preferences when discussing media productions and justifies choices • views media deliberately and critically • makes conscious viewing choices and describes how the content is presented to provide entertainment or information • examines the influence of the media in the workplace and in leisure activities (how people spend their leisure time) • examines how media messages are designed for different audience groups	• uses media texts to explore human relationships, new ideas, own and other cultures, analyzes presentations critically and explains how text influences and controls the viewer • judges the effectiveness of different elements used in media texts and gives reasons • expresses preferences when discussing media productions and justifies choices • views media deliberately and critically • views a variety of entertainment and instructional media texts, describing the elements of the text as well as the issues raised by it • examines the impact and effect of the media on people's beliefs and values, and the power of the media to both reinforce and change attitudes and behavior • considers the amount of influence and control audiences have over the media products which they receive

Produce	K-3	4-8	9-12
The student uses knowledge of various media to solve problems, communicate, and produce self-selected and assigned projects	• selects a medium and form (e.g., photographs, drawings, magazine pictures) and develops a simple theme for a story	• creates a variety of different narratives from the same images controlling the message by changing the form or elements	• experiments with a variety of forms and technologies to explore how they can be used to communicate specific messages
	• identifies and creates story line or message in visual texts (e.g., photograph, video, drawing, computer graphics	• makes decisions about the use of available media (e.g., photograph, video, drawing, print, computer graphics) and discusses and justifies choices	• uses a range of techniques in planning and creating a media text, reflecting thoughtfully and critically on the work produced
			• creates a media product to engage specific audiences, and predicts how audience will respond to the product
	• arranges a presentation of the project	• arranges a presentation of the project; or, tests the project	• arranges a presentation of the project; or, tests the project

Note. Reprinted by permission, Deborah Leveranz, Media, Analysis and Practice, 1996.

TABLE 5
English Language Arts: Viewing and Representing Strands

Basic Understanding(s)

The ability to access, analyze, evaluate, and produce communication in a variety of forms, including visual and electronic media, is an important part of language development. Viewing is not just the act of looking at a media product, but also the entire range of critical and analytic activities in which a class or an individual engages. Media texts are a major source of information about the world, and they have the power to influence thinking and behavior. Students need to be critical viewers, consumers, and producers of media texts.

Progress Checkpoints: Kindergarten Through Grade Three

Essential Knowledge and Skills		Performance Descriptions
1. The student accesses print, visual, and electronic media for varying purposes.	1a.	The student uses media for information and entertainment.
	1b.	The student uses media to investigate an issue.
	1c.	The student uses viewing as a tool for learning and research
	1d.	The student views for enjoyment and appreciation of language.
2. The student accesses terms related to techniques, technologies, and institutions involved in media production.	2a.	The student identifies media forms, e.g., news, drama, cartoon, advertising, entertainment.
	2b.	The student names the important parts of basic equipment, e.g., still camera, video camera, laser disk, computer, photocopier, slide projector, etc. and performs basic operations.
	2c.	The student distinguishes one shot from the next in the sequence.
	2d.	The student identifies shot types, e.g., closeup, pan.
	2e.	The student describes basic production roles, e.g., writer, director, camera operator, floor manager, graphic artist.
3. The student recognizes that all forms of media contain messages.	3a.	The student researches how stories occur in the media (narrative) and compares these stories to the types of stories they already know.
	3b.	The student draws on prior experience and knowledge.
	3c.	The student examines the choices made in the production of media products.
	3d.	The student identifies and describes different stereotypes in the media, e.g., hero, heroine, villain.

4. The student acquires skills to decode and analyze media messages.

4a. The student differentiates between media, e.g., print, and electronics.
4b. The student identifies some ways of organizing material in media texts.
4c. The student examines how visual and verbal symbols communicate meaning (traffic signs, advertising signs).
4d. The student looks at the types of advertising in different media forms.

5. The student gains an informed understanding of media through critical analysis.

5a. The student researches how stories occur in the media by considering advertising, news, and documentaries, as well as fictional forms.
5b. The student identifies and explains beginning, middle, and end of a story.

6. The student critically examines and interprets media messages in an historical, social, and cultural context (understands the relationship among audiences, media messages, and the world).

6a. The student identifies the difference between an event and the representation of that event in media form.
6b. The student asks questions about the context of the media text and connects to own knowledge and experience.
6c. The student recalls some details of a media text and describes how they make the text more interesting or enjoyable.

7. The student is able to assess and articulate personal media use and speculate on the media use of others.

7a. The student examines the ways in which media can affect the individual.
7b. The student expresses preferences when discussing media productions.
7c. The student views media deliberately and critically.
7d. The student views different media texts for pleasure, recognizes the main idea of what has been viewed, and responds to the presentation and content.
7e. The student examines the effects of the media in their environment (family, home, school).
7f. The student identifies audiences for media products.

8. The student uses knowledge of various media to solve problems, communicate, and produce self-selected and assigned projects.

8a. The student selects a medium and form (e.g., photographs, drawings, magazine pictures) and develops a simple theme for a story.
8b. The student identifies and creates a story line or message in visual texts (e.g., photograph, video, drawing, computer graphics).
8c. The student arranges a presentation of their project.

(Continued)

TABLE 5
(Continued)

Progress Checkpoinst: Grades Four Through Eight

Essential Knowledge and Skills		*Performance Descriptions*
1. The student accesses print, visual, and electronic media for varying purposes.	1a.	The student uses a wide range of media for information, entertainment, and communication.
	1b.	The student accesses media resources to define, investigate, and represent questions, issues, and problems.
	1c.	The student accesses library databases to discover primary and secondary sources and select those appropriate to research projects.
	1d.	The student views for enjoyment and appreciation of language.
2. The student accesses terms related to techniques, technologies, and institutions involved in media production.	2a.	The student identifies some major genres and categories, e.g., soap opera, sitcom, action adventure, tabloid.
	2b.	The student observes, identifies, and discusses features of audio/visual texts, such as:
		— different camera angles and distances
		— arrangement of people and objects within the frame
		— color, black & white, variations
		— different sounds and levels of amplification
		— different transitions from shot to shot, e.g., fade, dissolve, cut, wipe
		— camera movements, e.g., plan, tilt, dolly, zoom
		— variations in writing, print size, and typeface
		— variation in size and quality of paper
	2c.	The student describes basic production roles and work performed by specific people in the media industry, e.g., agents, actors, producers, public relations.

3. The student recognizes that all forms of media contain messages

3a. The student recognizes devices for controlling narrative, e.g., voice over.

3b. The student follows multiple/parallel plots within a narrative.

3c. The student asks questions about the intended message of a media text and states opinions about the content (accuracy, relevance, bias) and form.

3d. The student describes how different elements in media texts help to create atmosphere and shape meaning.

3e. The student compares their own experiences with those attributed to their age group in the media.

3f. The student identifies some stereotypes in media text depictions of various children in their age group and explains how they imply judgments of various social, racial, and cultural groups.

4. The student acquires skills to decode and analyze media messages.

4a. The student differentiates between specific genre, e.g., entertainment, news and information, advertising.

4b. The student identifies a range of ways or organizing and presenting material in media texts.

4c. The student identifies symbolic codes used in the media, e.g., different shots in a film, framing devices in photography.

4d. The student explains what information is being communicated by media codes and conventions, e.g., fade to black close-up.

4e. The student examines how media forms are affected by the presence or absence of advertising.

5. The student gains an informed understanding of media through critical analysis.

5a. The student considers how the same story can be adapted to different audiences.

5b. The student identifies narrative patterns and how they are used in the presentation of fictional and nonfictional material in the media.

6. The student critically examines and interprets media messages in an historical, social, and cultural context (understands the relationship among audiences, media messages and the world).

6a. The student identifies and discusses differences between an event and the representation of that event in media form.

6b. The student asks questions about issues raised in a media text, e.g., characterization, validity of factual material; and listens to others' opions and states own ideas.

6c. The student identifies and analyzes the interpretations made of a media text by viewers who are of varied cultures, ages, or backgrounds.

6d. The student uses media texts to explore human relationships, new ideas, own and other cultures.

(Continued)

TABLE 5
(Continued)

Essential Knowledge and Skills		Performance Descriptions
7. The student is able to assess and articulate personal media use and speculate on the media use of others.	7a.	The student evaluates the effectiveness of different elements used in media texts.
	7b.	The student expresses preferences when discussing media productions and justifies choices.
	7c.	The student views media deliberately and critically.
	7d.	The student makes conscious viewing choices and describes how the content is presented to provide entertainment or information.
	7e.	The student examines the influence of the media in the workplace and in leisure activities (how people spend their leisure time).
	7f.	The student examines how media messages are designed for different audience groups.
8. The student uses knowledge of various media to solve problems, communicate, and produce self-selected and assigned projects.	8a.	The student creates a variety of different narratives from the same images controlling the message by changing the form or elements.
	8b.	The student makes decisions about the use of available media (e.g., photographs, video, drawing, print, computer graphics) and discusses and justifies choices.
	8c.	The student arranges a presentation of their project.

Progress Checkpoints: Grades Nine Through Twelve

1. The student accesses print, visual, and electronic media for varying purposes.	1a.	The student selects viewing materials from a wide range of forms and reflects critically on choices.
	1b.	The student accesses media resources to define, investigate, and represent questions, issues, and problems.
	1c.	The student accesses library databases to discover primary and secondary sources and select those appropriate to research projects.
	1d.	The student views for enjoyment and appreciation of language.
2. The student accesses terms related to techniques, technologies, and institutions involved in media production.	2a.	The student identifies a wide range of media forms and categories.
	2b.	The student identifies and discusses postproduction and distribution terms and processes, e.g., editing, printing, email.

	2c.	The student defines occupations involved in making a media product, e.g., preparing a newspaper, a political campaign, or a marketing campaign for a product.
	2d.	The student describes specialist roles involved in the preproduction, production, postproduction, distribution, and marketing of media products.
3. The student recognizes that all forms of media contain messages.	3a.	The student identifies narratives as a series of constructed conventions such as character motivation, sequence, hierarchy of events and characters rather than being a "natural" part of a story.
	3b.	The student identifies implicit as well as explicit messages and biases in media texts.
	3c.	The student identifies that meaning is conveyed in media texts through a combination of elements (e.g., sound, sequence, and perspective together can convey a specific mood).
	3d.	The student analyzes the stereotypes used to portray certain groups.
	3e.	The student compares gender, social, and occupational stereotypes from across cultures.
4. The student acquires skills to decode and analyze media messages.	4a.	The student understands how genre shapes and the audiences' expectation of media content.
	4b.	The student identifies a range of ways of organizing and presenting material in media texts and critically examines the reactions of others.
	4c.	The student examines how different symbolic codes can operate together to create meaning.
	4d.	The student examines the effects of advertising.
	4e.	The student considers the importance of advertising to commercial media.
5. The student gains an informed understanding of media through critical analysis.	5a.	The student compares the way in which different media present the same topic or story.
	5b.	The student compares and contrasts media products either of the same or different types, e.g., news reports in different newspapers, on television, and over the Internet.

(Continued)

TABLE 5
(Continued)

	Essential Knowledge and Skills		Performance Descriptions
6.	The student critically examines and interprets media messages in an historical, social, and cultural context (understands the relationship among audiences, media messages, and the world.	6a.	The student identifies and discusses differences between an event and the representation of that event in media form.
		6b.	The student provides examples of the social outcomes of particular media representation.
		6c.	The student responds to concrete and abstract meaning in a media text, recognizing that people interpret texts differently depending on many factors, e.g., age, gender, race, experience.
		6d.	The student uses media texts to explore human relationships, new ideas, own and other cultures, analyzes presentations critically and explains how text influences and controls the viewer.
7.	The student is able to assess and articulate personal media use and speculate on the media use of others.	7a.	The student judges the effectiveness of different elements used in media texts and gives reasons.
		7b.	The student expresses preferences when discussing media productions and justifies choices.
		7c.	The student views media deliberately and critically.
		7d.	The student views a variety of entertainment and instructional media texts, describing the elements of the text as well as the issues raised by it.
		7e.	The student examines the impact and effect of the media on people's beliefs and values, and the power of the media to both reinforce and change attitudes and behavior.
		7f.	The student considers the amount of influence and control audiences have over the media products which they receive.
8.	The student uses knowledge of various media to solve problems, communicate, and produce self-selected and assigned projects.	8a.	The student experiments with a variety of forms and technologies to explore how they can be used to communicate specific messages.
		8b.	The student uses a range of techniques in planning and creating a media text, reflecting thoughtfully and critically on the work produced.
		8c.	The student creates a media product to engage specific audiences, and predicts how audience will respond to the product.
		8d.	The student arranges a presentation of their project, or tests their project.

Note. Reprinted by permission of Deborah Leveranz, Media, Analysis and Practice, 1966.

useful to bureaucrats and politicians, but have very little usefulness for parents, teachers, and children. National and state standards can be used to assess (or punish) whole schools.

Because media education is more an approach than a discipline, there is also the possibility that high-stakes, standards-driven education could have a chilling effect on media education and its inclusion in the curriculum. University of New Mexico Professor Don Zancanella (1994) cautions that standards development could cause "a freezing of existing subject-matter arrangement" (p. 26). Thus far, national standards "freeze out subjects which aren't part of the traditional curriculum, or, on the other hand, send such [subjects] scurrying to find a home within a traditional discipline. . . . If no traditional curricular area 'adopts mass media,' it seems likely to me that any thoughtful study in school of such influences on our lives as television, advertising and popular culture will remain rare" (p. 27).

The concern for high-stakes versus low-stakes standards and assessment makes standards work at the local level all the more valuable. Because of the difficulty of integrating new areas of study across the K–12 curriculum, individual districts have the flexibility to draft standards that create unique areas of study that address the use of media and technology in schooling. One example can be found in the Minneapolis, Minnesota public school district. Based on conversations with a broad cross-section of the community, a task force of educators at Minneapolis Public Schools drafted standards that could be used to teach about information and technology. The standards, called *Information Media and Technology Content Standards*, contain five separate strands: access, processing, media and digital technologies, reporting, and media ethics. The ethics category includes guidelines for teaching about copyright, cyberspace protocol, media representation, and so on. They represent familiar concepts that are central to visual literacy, media literacy, and information literacy.

In 1996, the Standards Study Group for the Information Media and Technology Service Department, a team of elementary, middle school, and secondary media specialists in Minneapolis, created district-wide standards for each of the five strands. Table 6 is an example of one of them: the Processing strand.

The Minneapolis Public Schools Information Media and Technology strands are unique in standards development at the K–12 level because they blend media analysis and practice with information technology in a newly conceived, yet mandated, area of the curriculum that makes the need for media and technology education explicit.

The Minneapolis Information Media Technology Processing Standards are living documents, that is, they are still in development. Classroom tasks and assessment rubrics will be created, based on the standards. The Minneapolis curriculum shows great potential as a model for other states and districts who hope to incorporate media education in the curriculum in a formal and

TABLE 6
MPS Information Media and Technology–Content Standards

Information Media and Technology Processing:
Students select research topics and analyze content and design of a variety of resources which reflect/influence diverse perspectives.

	Ages 5-9	Ages 9-14	Ages 14-18
3.1	Students apply research techniques using a variety of information media.		
3.1a	Define and choose a topic that is from a single subject area.	Determine which information is relevant to single-discipline, cross-discipline, and interdisciplinary study topics.	Establish criteria to distinguish among best information to use for single-discipline, cross-discipline and interdisciplinary study topics.
3.1b	Formulate questions and seek answers from diverse perspectives.	Formulate questions and seek answers from diverse perspectives.	Formulate questions and seek answers from diverse perspectives.
3.1c	Understand main idea.	Choose key ideas (e.g., note taking)	Choose key ideas (e.g., note taking)
3.1d	Organize information for reports (e.g., graphic organizers).	Organize information for reports or presentations (e.g., topics, subtopics, graphic organizers).	Organize information for reports or presentations (e.g., outlining, graphic organizers).
3.1e	Gather, sort, manipulate, and store data in a variety of ways (e.g., use computer to create database).	Gather, sort, manipulate, and store data in a variety of ways (e.g., use computer to determine contents of a file to be sent via telecommunications).	Gather, sort, manipulate, and store data in a variety of ways (e.g., use computer to receive and send messages via telecommunications).
3.1f	Cite sources (e.g., within text).	Cite sources (e.g., footnoting).	Cite sources (e.g., create bibliographies).
3.1g	Ask questions and critique the results of other students' work.	Ask questions and critique the results of other students' work.	Ask questions and critique the results of other students' work.

TABLE 6
(Continued)

	Ages 5-9	Ages 9-14	Ages 14-18
3.2	Students identify, analyze, interpret and evaluate the content of information media, including the mass media, from diverse perspectives.		
3.2a	Analyze real, realistic, and unreal content from various viewpoints.	Compare and contrast information with real-life situations.	Recognize diverse points of view or purposes.
3.2b	Recognize works by authors, illustrator, non print media creator.	Identify and evaluate the role and perspective of author.	Identify, analyze, and interpret the purpose or cultural perspective of the author.
3.2c	Recognize main idea, details, sequencing, cause and effect, inference in content.	Recognize differences between facts and opinions in content.	Recognize propaganda and other persuasive approaches in content.
3.2d	Compare the same topic from a variety of cultural perspectives.	Analyze and evaluate the similarities and differences in news reports and reporting techniques from various perspectives.	Analyze and evaluate how the amount and type of information can distort perceptions of an event.
3.3	Students analyze unique properties of design of various information media, including the mass media.		
3.3a	Analyze and interpret the influence of audio in non print information media (e.g., sound effects).	Analyze influence of editing in print and non print information media.	Relate script, soundtrack and visuals to the purpose of non print information media (e.g., determine whether purpose is to inform, narrate, entertain, persuade, and/or stimulate emotion).
3.3b	Analyze and interpret the influence of visuals and special features in print information media (e.g., graphics).	Analyze and interpret the influence of visuals in non-print information media (e.g., camera angles, shots, special effects).	Analyze commercial influences on the creation of information media (e.g., determine what "sells," what is popular or trendy, which cultures are appealed to).

(Continued)

TABLE 6
(Continued)

	Ages 5-9	Ages 9-14	Ages 14-18
3.4	Students analyze ways in which information media, including the mass media, reflect/influence diverse cultures.		
3.4a	Identify contributions to information media and technology by many people in various cultures throughout history.	Identify contributions to information media and technology by many people in various cultures throughout history.	Identify contributions to information media and technology by many people in various cultures throughout history.
3.4b	Establish criteria to distinguish best information media to suit purposes.	Establish criteria to distinguish best information media to suit purposes.	Establish criteria to distinguish best information media to suit purposes.
3.4c	Evaluate impact of time spent daily on mass media and entertainment technologies.	Analyze advantages and limitations of the mass media.	Evaluate power of mass media to create opinion about various cultures.
3.4d	Recognize motive and appeal of persuasive mass media messages.	Interpret inferences of words, visuals and sounds in mass media and evaluate their impact on various cultures (e.g., stereotyping, propaganda, sexual innuendo).	Analyze long-range effects on diverse cultures of mass media messages on diverse cultures.

Note. Reprinted with Permission Minneapolis Public Schools, November 1995.

structured way. Some of these assessments may include the use of student portfolios, self-assessment, peer assessment, and assessment by teams of teachers and community members (Worsnop, 1994, 1996).

The standards documents for media education modeled in this chapter provide useful tools for classroom teachers and their students. They do provide some accountability for districts to prove their effectiveness and responsiveness to the public. They also provide the opportunity to ensure quality educational opportunities for all students. But most importantly, standards work for media education offers the community an opportunity to arrive at some consensus about what is important to teach and learn.

It would be far simpler to assign one bright and motivated teacher to the task of writing media education standards for his or her colleagues and then to require their implementation in every classroom. But such an approach is entirely beside the point. The process of developing standards demands a crowd, or at least a committee. And it is, by its nature, fraught with tension, because it begs the questions, "Why do we want to educate children? And how?"

Standards work stipulates the art of compromise as hard choices are made about what is included and what is left out of a child's education. It asks that teachers and parents leave their special interests at the door. Once the document is produced, the real value of the effort can easily be overlooked. The real value lies in the process of coming to consensus about the value of education.

When consensus about underlying beliefs about the benefits of education is made explicit and clear, then the purposes of literacy emerge. Appropriate classroom tasks can be brought to bear that accommodate a broader vision of literacy. These might include the use of source documents, a balance between analysis and production activities, introduction to experimental formats, the use of noncommercial and alternative points of view, an emphasis on storytelling and narrative, the building of contexts across disciplines, and so on. These classroom tasks, in turn, will suggest the pedagogy for the purposes at hand: short, scaffolded exercises, cognitive apprenticeships, inquiry-based techniques, collaborative and team approaches, and more.

Because of the diversity in U.S. culture, standards are not a panacea for promoting critical literacy. Advocates must be prepared to accept that some communities will embrace traditional educational ideals that include a goal of critical literacy as a tangential element, if at all. But even when standards are drafted that lie in opposition to the goals of critical uses of literacy, standards will provide some direction and clarity for the visionary classroom teacher in traditional settings. The process of standards development will provide a forum for educators to present and explore arguments for divergent points of view. Such a process yields results in the form of standards documents that have the ability to change with the community.

Standards documents are living proof that consensus about education can be attained and demonstrated in a practical way. Educators and community members can refer to the standards documents as an agreement and remember that they represent a covenant to put differences aside in order to provide a quality educational experience for all students. Standards development that integrates an expanded sense of literacy into the curriculum will also go a long way toward finding some common ground among and between the various approaches to literacy.

RESEARCH AND PRACTICE

Scholarship about the history of literacy has demonstrated the value of research that looks at small, local, and authentic examples of literacy in education. This has been the purview of researchers from higher education, who research, teach, and write about elementary and secondary classrooms. Although useful as a way to disseminate information about classroom practice, research by outside observers is of limited use to teachers and students. In contrast, when classroom teachers and students conduct their own research, based on primary experience, it offers an important opportunity to reflect and grow. This is especially important when teachers venture into new areas of expertise, such as media analysis and practice. Unfortunately, schools are not structured to accommodate the research necessary for elementary and secondary teachers to reflect on their own practices and share their findings with colleagues. This is where partnerships with colleagues in higher education could reap rich rewards.

The divide that Joshua Meyrowitz (1995) observed between the two functions of the university resonates up and down the formal system of schooling. Are schools cloisters for the patient, perhaps unattainable, pursuit of knowledge, or are they worldly, dynamic partners that shape the course of social events through applied research and efficient credentialing? Or both? Although Meyerowitz writes about how the split plays out in university education, his ideas about the bifurcation of the university can also be used to explain the "disconnect" between K–12 and postsecondary education.

In spite of the fact that there is a growing "teachers as researchers" movement that encourages K–12 educators to reflect on their own practice and to build a theory base from reports, or "cases" of actual classroom observation, the yawning gap between educational theory and practice persists. In general, postsecondary researchers build theory; educational bureaucrats fund its implementation; elementary and secondary educators attempt to apply it; and school administrators enforce its application.

This can be a harmonious relationship, when all parties work from a consensus of theory and approach. But such an arrangement can also be a recipe for disaster, setting up an adversarial relationship among academic researchers, classroom practitioners, and school administrators. The gap between postsecondary and K–12 educators reflects a bifurcation of theory and practice—a significant barrier that must be breached if anything useful is to come of academic forays into the nature of electronic literacy and its relationship to schooling.

It is not enough simply to observe classroom practice as a dispassionate outside observer. Because they are involved in the actual implementation of educational theory, classroom teachers are the most appropriate people to conduct and report educational research in action. Nonetheless, the teacher-as-researcher comes up against formidable obstacles, chief among them time and isolation. Seldom do K–12 teachers have the time to experiment with various methodologies, or to write up and disseminate information about their practice. Because they work in isolation from their colleagues, teachers also have to make a real effort to find time with their colleagues for planning, problem solving, and reflection. When they do, the information yields important first-hand accounts of theory in action.

Academic scholars are confronted with another obstacle: They must justify their credibility to those who labor daily in the classroom. Although scholars may be able to carve out the time to work in teams to conduct research, they encounter questions from teachers and students about their actual knowledge of classroom practice. Credibility is important to K–12 teachers, who are reluctant to engage in new practices unless they trust that university researchers and educational bureaucrats have an authentic understanding of the conditions under which they work. When scholars are teamed with classroom teachers, they provide an important overview that informs the research and tempers the all-too-common tendency in K–12 education to predict wide-scale trends from single-case examples of particular classrooms. Whole new paradigms of evaluation must be explored before teachers see an outside evaluator as a "critical friend."

In order for theory to make sense, a research base consisting of testbeds, demonstration sites, or other field-based work must provide evidence that they can improve the conditions of the classroom—not only for improved student performance, but also for improved working conditions for teachers. Collaboration must go far beyond the external evaluation of individual programs, too often tacked on as an afterthought in order to fulfill the evaluation expectations of funders. Instead, the system cries out for creative forms of collaboration to bridge the gaps between theory and practice; K–12 and university; print and electronic cultures. These might include project-based portfolios, extensive formative work that includes tracking, open-planning methods, and enlisting project participants as evaluators who can map results along the way. When academic researchers and classroom teachers team up to become one another's *critical friend*, educators can begin to answer the hard questions about literacy and schooling in digital media environments.

SCALING UP LOCAL CRITICAL LITERACY EFFORTS

Outside reformers cannot facilitate school change without the complicity of classroom teachers who see media education in small, contained venues. Neither can the reflective teacher, no matter how dedicated, fuel school change without a critical mass of colleagues who strive to see a "big picture" for media education and its kindred multiliteracies, such as information literacy and visual literacy.

Documenting evidence about promising practices in media education at the local level is of limited use if successful efforts cannot be disseminated and tried among a broader audience of practitioners. In order to go beyond a simple, parochial view of media education, it is necessary to amass some research and then to provide a meta-analysis of the data for trends and patterns that may be useful to a critical mass of teachers and learners. This kind of meta-analysis of a whole range of media education activities, operating under varying conditions, is necessary before media education can successfully argue for its place in the curriculum and overcome inevitable resistance to new and emerging information technologies in education.

Such resistance is not peculiar to education. The private sector has seen similar resistance when technology is introduced to workers in a top-down fashion. A combination of factors provides barriers to the uses of technology in schools, but teachers' resistance to altering their traditional styles of instruction serves as one of the strongest barriers to their integration of audio and video technologies into teaching. A review of the literature about the classroom teachers' role in school change efforts indicates that barriers include: teachers' inertia; satisfaction with present methods of teaching; dislike for outside interference in planning instruction; unwillingness to yield center stage to mechanical devices; a misperception of the complexity of the technology; and fear of making embarrassing errors when attempting an unfamiliar instructional technique (Thomas, 1987, p. 117).

John Pungente, of the Jesuit Communications Project in Toronto, Canada, surveyed media education worldwide and found seven elements crucial to its implementation in schools:

1. teachers must want to teach about media in the classroom;
2. school administrators must be supportive of the program;
3. teacher-training institutions must have faculties and policies capable of training teachers who practice media literacy concepts;
4. school districts must supply ongoing in-service opportunities;
5. consultants must be available for training support and to establish communications networks with teachers;
6. media education resources must be readily available to teachers and students; and

7. support groups, preferably run by teachers, must be established to arrange workshops and conferences, disseminate media education news, and to develop curricula. (Pungente, 1987, 1993)

Disseminating promising educational practices to a broader audience is known as "scaling up" in educational "bureaucrat-ese." Scaling up is preferred to the word *replication*, in recognition of the fact that programs cannot be instituted whole, but must be customized to fit local community conditions. Because of the idiosyncratic nature of U.S. education, the problem of scaling up promising practices in education can be a nightmare. Combined with the individual preferences exhibited by each classroom teacher, the introduction of new subject matter in the curriculum becomes a Hydra of complexity. Change and adoption occurs district by district, school by school, teacher by teacher. It is difficult to know which conditions, in which configurations, will foster the kind of critical mass necessary to produce wide-scale educational change efforts.

International media education programs in Canada, England, and Australia have an advantage because they work from a central education ministry that disseminates resources, training, and information on a regional or national scale. The downside of the centralized approach is that bad educational ideas can be spread as easily as good ones. Nonetheless, the mechanisms for wide-scale educational change are in place when a centralized structure serves as a clearinghouse for concepts and resources. At this time, no comparable institutional mechanism exists in formal educational structures to support U.S. media educators. This puts the onus of support on ad hoc organizations, nonprofit, community-based organizations, professional education associations, or local teacher groups.

Mapping international success in the integration of new literacies and technology would be useful as a foundation for nurturing similar programs in the United States. Many of these successful efforts have developed along the lines of the success factors identified by Pungente. Many of them have to do with supporting the classroom teacher to explore literacy practice, broadly conceived. Others have to do with the development of policies that fill the dissemination vacuum created by a lack of central bureaucracies. Some of the needs of U.S. educators who want to expand the teaching of literacy to accommodate new technologies include:

1. a clear link between technology use and critical literacy in educational technology policy documents;
2. grassroots, teacher-led organizations that serve as centers of support, collegiality, and dissemination of information;
3. local standards for media education that are crafted by a broad coalition of educators and community members;

4. programs that take a broad view of literacy and that respect the diversity of home languages in the classroom;

5. the inclusion of experiential and arts-based aspects across the curriculum;

6. fair and equitable means of school funding that ensures access to print and electronic classroom resources for all children;

7. school restructuring that accommodates project-based work, including the flexibility of time, smaller schools, thematic, interdisciplinary approaches to instruction, and high-levels of community involvement; and

8. opportunities for media education training that nurture new teachers and refresh seasoned teachers.

WHY MEDIA EDUCATION?

Information technologies have changed the face of economic and social institutions, but schools remain at a loss to deal with them, creating a disjuncture between school's relationship to home, work, and play. Part of the problem is that the focus on digital tools, instead of on liberating and democratizing processes in schools, has stunted the debate about the role of technology in education. Before anything as ambitious as media education can become a priority in U.S. schools, society must first answer the broader question: "Why education?" As literacy needs for the workplace change rapidly, it is difficult for educators to track and serve business interests alone. Perhaps the public will arrive at a greater vision of education, beyond practical job training. Media education, with its reformist pedagogies, close relationship to emerging communication forms, and goals toward strengthening democratic structures, is in a central position to support educational reform that is responsive to learners and in harmony with the world outside the classroom.

No discussion of education can take place out of context of the culture of the country, a diverse, multicultural landscape in the United States. The culture is, by its nature, contradictory, changeable, and contentious. The trick is to look for strengths and commonalities afforded by this rich cultural diversity and to use those strengths to create visionary forms of education that accommodate the needs of society and reward the kind of flexibility that can weather rapid technological changes.

Americans love technology and technology is widely recognized as an important factor in educational reform. Every state is in the process of adopting model technology plans. These model plans stress communication forms and information access, but rarely address the educational strategies that inform the analysis and evaluation of the information that flows through the media channels. In other words, educational policy seems unified in the belief that technology is good for education, but beyond a vague notion of "job readiness," it is otherwise unclear about *why* technology is necessary. Technology plans are needed that not only address access to information, but also teach media education principles and strategies that help learners decode, analyze, evaluate, and produce communication in a variety of forms. These plans can best be accommodated by integrating them into the processes for creating local standards documents that inform the uses of information.

An informed public has always been seen as the cornerstone of democratic societies. Although some schools interpret this goal as a nationalistic, patriotic duty to teach students a hollow respect for their country, many others have seen this as a need to encourage critical autonomy and social participation in government. Unfortunately, the ideal of citizen democracy is in conflict with the repressive and undemocratic education that students receive daily in the school environment. Civil liberties taken for granted by adults, such as freedom of expression and assembly, have been denied to students in U.S. courts of law. Classroom policies that respect the democratic freedom of the learner are essential if the ideal of democracy is to continue into adulthood. Media education can demonstrate and model practical strategies for the democratization of the classroom by exploring the rights and responsibilities of communication in society.

Creative self-expression, an outlet for the individualism that Americans admire, is given short shrift, if the decline of art and music programs in public schools is any indication. As communication forms merge in digitized, multimedia formats, new relationships between visuals, texts, and graphics call for creative expression, as well as logical displays of knowledge. The relationship between fine art and popular culture art forms is blurred, ushering in a rich renaissance of artistic expression and scientific achievement. Furthermore, computers and video are merging with multimedia, making digital formats an important entry point for media education in classrooms. Policies that place an emphasis on art as well as science would go a long way toward ensuring that students have opportunities to grow and explore their full creative potentials. Media education is intended to revive, and not to displace, the fine tradition of storytelling and oral history.

Americans respect equality and justice, qualities that can simply be called "fairness." They want all children to live happy, productive lives. As governments wrestle with issues of copyright protection, information access, and the availability of technology for all, policies that insure fair and equal access to the tools necessary for education must be crafted for schools, as well as businesses, so that everyone has the right to the same quality educational experience.

The 20th century ushered in cultural and technological upheavals that called into question the relationship between literacy and schooling. As much as the public might wistfully long for the little red schoolhouse of times past, there is no going back to a world defined only by the printed and spoken word.

Educational strategies that blend critical literacy, experiential education, and critical pedagogy can do much to explain the relationship of literacy, technology, and society. Such a blend, called *media education*, for want of a better phrase, has the potential to shape the course of modern education. Once contemporary education finds its footing, with clear policies and wide societal consensus about its goals and outcomes, media education is inevitable. As Hollis Frampton, an American experimental filmmaker, once remarked, "Once you can read, you cannot *not* read."

A Tale of Two Cities

In the course of writing this book, I conducted interviews with a number of teachers about their integration of new technologies into education. I talked with teachers in rural, urban, private, and public school settings. I talked with teachers who worked with adult learners and with young children. The similarities in these teachers' experiences were more striking to me than their differences. The teachers all had a sense that literacy was an important measure of a learner's integration into society, employability, and general social success. Nonetheless, access to computers and other digital technologies is still very problematic for educators who work in poor, or geographically isolated communities. For that reason, analog technologies such as video or radio are only beginning to be used in the classroom. Teachers are still struggling with the uses of electronic tools, in general, and are only beginning to envision what they will do when they have access to multimedia digital networks. In the meantime, there is optimism that many of the concepts they explore in working with a wider range of media beyond print, will serve them well as digital media becomes more ubiquitous.

A central focus that emerged from conversations with teachers of new media was the use of storytelling for literacy teaching in a variety of ways. The emphasis and importance that these teachers placed on narrative structures cut across all cultural and geographic spaces and united the oral, alphabetic, and digital uses of literacy mentioned throughout the book. Here, I present the points of view of two teachers—one from a rural perspective and one from an urban perspective—in the belief that a good way to gauge the response of schools to the literacy needs of a digital world is to let master teachers speak for themselves.

LITERACY IN A RURAL SETTING

Robert Gipe has worked throughout the southern United States in rural educational efforts. A native of Tennessee, he was an associate of the Rural School Challenge, a nonprofit organization that fosters school change efforts in rural schools. Gipe also worked for many years as Director of Education for Appalshop, a media arts organization in Whitesburg, Kentucky founded in 1969 as an experiment in community-based filmmaking. Appalshop is dedicated to supporting mountain people to tell their own stories. It hosts a world-class theater company, a record label, a radio station, arts activities, and school-based media education for children and teachers. It often partners with the Eastern Kentucky Teachers Network, a Foxfire group. Every summer, Appalshop conducts the Appalachian Media Institute (AMI), a video and radio "camp" for kids and teachers, founded by mountain educator Jeff Hawkins, Appalshop Executive Director, Dee Davis, and directed by David Sturgill.

KT: Why do you think we should bother to educate people at all?

RG: When people don't have it, education and literacy is access—in a real tangible way—to more power, over themselves and the ability to participate in the power structure. In a coal field you had a lot of people recognize just how much power was embedded in the educational process, and just how much control you could exert over people by denying them education, in a lot of subtle and not-so-subtle forms. Just growing up in that environment and working in that environment couldn't help but shape and direct me to understand education, and also the denial of education, as a tool of power.

I think the other equally important thing for me was the capacity for joy in education. It's one of the most joyous parts of life—to transfer understanding from one person to another, both the giving and receiving of it. So, education is basically an act of joy. That is something that—especially in the media education teacher workshops that we did—that we directly and indirectly try and communicate to teachers that powerful and joyful process.

KT: Tell me more about what you've observed at the Appalshop workshops.

RG: At Appalshop, we like the Eastern Kentucky Teachers Network, which is a network of Foxfire teachers. The first project that I did with them was with about 50 or 60 teachers who were all committed to the Foxfire process. Sometimes it had to do with media, but it always had to do with democratic pedagogy.

Appalshop works with a network of teachers to take the body of documentary video that we have produced over the years, which is all about Appalachia and the culture, politics, environmental issues, and social justice issues of Appalachia. We offer the workshops to teachers in eastern Kentucky to explore how they integrate our archive of documentaries into their work with kids. We ended up doing developmental workshops for teachers on video production. Our main emphasis was really on hands-on production, so in that way it was kind of an arts–space approach.

AMI began as a 6-week summer video production program in community-based documentary for high school kids. Some of the students have come back as Institute teachers. Appalshop ran the program and paid the kids. It was a summer job for them, but their responsibility was to make a 15 minute video documentary. Some of them produced video animation, too. Then they were supposed to commit to working with their school to institutionalize community-based video production at their school. We had a kind of auxiliary teacher program where we were trying to do training for them. Appalshop was real successful in having students and teachers collaborate to where students were teaching courses in video production in their schools. What came out of the Appalshop Media Institute, AMI, was a lot of really good documentary work by the students— almost 10 years' worth now.

The thing was, we always had trouble with our content concerns and our philosophical concerns making the jump back to the school building. You don't want to be too hard on people; they're trying, it's all new, and they are trying to figure it out. We were trying to figure it out, too.

KT: What did you find to bridge the summer Institutes with school?

RG: We had a common understanding about the importance of storytelling. We're very narrative-based. I think that most of the artists at Appalshop were pretty well convinced that they would never exhaust the potential from narrative in terms of video-making or in radio-making. Their commitment to the Appalachian culture, to the Appalachian story and its capacity to carry a video or a radio report, was just so unwavering and complete that you just never saw much reason to look beyond narrative. At least I didn't, because the voice of the people and the drama of the story was so compelling. In 6½ years in eastern Kentucky, I never found the limit of it. I never ceased to be excited by being engaged with the history and culture of that region.

KT: Let's break down narrative a little bit. What about narrative? It's dramatic, you said, it's compelling, but what kind of narratives? Are they more traditional, are they just traditional to Appalshop? Do teachers understand some more experimental kinds of ways to put stories together? And how do they scaffold storytelling a little bit for the reader?

RG: In eastern Kentucky, where I worked—I think a lot of it is true for southern and western Appalachia, too—is a place with a great narrative tradition, a place where folklore collectors for the whole 20th century have gone to understand traditional English folktales and stories. It is a region that was very late to get highways. Now I'm talking about the 1930s and 40s and 50s. Even 10 years before I arrived in eastern Kentucky, it was an 8 hour trip to the nearest major city in Kentucky, which was Lexington, from where we were, and now it's only 2½ hours to get there. So even into the 1950s and 60s, it was a place unto itself in ways that lots and lots of America is not. In many ways, that place was preserved. It created a shelter for old traditions.

You have a kind of folktale history. You also have an amazing— despite its physical isolation—dramatic connectedness to the whole sweep of American history in the 20th century. Appalachia was one of the strongholds of yeoman farmers into the 20th century, and people who lived off the land, hunting and fishing, and developed a very self-sufficient, or individually family-based people who were suddenly run over by the Industrial Age in the early 20th century, with the coming of the industrial-scale coal mine. That led to horrible conditions for workers.

One of the most amazing stories, and the larger back story, is of union organizing. Here you had these people who were very independent and very much interested in people being allowed to do what they thought was right as individuals coming together. To me, that is one of the most amazing stories in American history—how bad it must have been in the coalfields for people to organize these unions, against all their own natural inclinations. It's a testimony to how difficult it must have been working there.

The community contained a lot of people who believed that people should be allowed to follow their own inner light, or at least to be left alone—that everyone should have his or her own mind. It's real important and I think ended up as being a strong tradition in narrative. Because people were allowed and encouraged to have their own minds, they were very interested in the mind. I always found Appalachia to be a very sophisticated place to talk to people. Everybody you talked to was at some level a sophisticated speaker and story teller. The analysis and contexts emerge in the storytelling process that explain how things were and how they came to be the way they are now.

I was surrounded by people rich and poor, formally educated and not formally educated, who were kind of fascinated by the life of the mines, this historical sweep that had happened in front of them. All of those things combined. You had a great respect for narrative; just the construction of a story. And, you had a great attention to craft, period. Throughout the culture there was this attention to craft in all kinds of different areas. And, on top of that, you had kind of amazing content. And then finally, you also had this recognition that all this was threatened, and that one of the institutions that threatened it was the public school. So, you had this kind of cultural clash between people's interest in developing their minds and the destructiveness of public schooling, on some level, to culture.

Then, you lay on top of that, in the years that I was teaching in Kentucky, 1989–1995, they were in the middle of a comprehensive state school reform. That reform placed a big emphasis on educational technology. It was hard on the poor districts, many of them in eastern Kentucky coal counties, because of the inequities of the funding system of the state schools. The state, the legislature, required a whole new system for schooling kids that then had to be somehow implemented in these places. Sometimes it was good, sometimes ill for Appalachian kids. Sometimes it was both ill and good for the mountain culture. So it made for this very fascinating time.

KT: To jump ahead a little, how does digital media contribute to the educational goal of power and joy? How did you take advantage of the cultural knack for storytelling that was there and pull it over into a different construction with technology?

RG: I believe one of the reasons to educate people is to "learn the ropes" in a cultural context. I grew to feel really deeply that there were some larger cultural trends that schooling was promoting and that these trends were threatening what was strong about the culture. The general sense in the mountains is that people gain more than they lose by being rooted, and that generally, people in the United States have to move around too much. Also reinforced was the urge that education has to be in bigger schools. And also, that school creates its own community, rather than communities creating schools.

I had to look at digital technology, computers and video, in the context of all that. It was a delicate balance for introducing and using it, because TV and Internet and mass media are potentially as destabilizing to this culture as it is stabilizing. The main efforts that we made at media literacy were not so much trying to figure out what people were saying to you in this commercial or that commercial, what was the subtext, etc. Rather, it was how do you take hold of these things to bolster rootedness? How you take hold of them to bolster smallness: And, how do you use them to stabilize a place rather than destabilize? I think that television—not the Internet yet, but you just see it coming—television is just such an attachment of corporate power, with its powerful impulses to consolidate, to define people's culture for them. It is more than just about sex and violence on TV. It's more the sense that mass media defines what success is. That's what concerns me about what corporate culture tries to implant in us.

A lot of what we did with media was to use its potential to excite kids. You could pick it up and just go do it. As adults, we use that as a lever to get kids to understand all of what we (as adults with our hidden agendas) think is the real stuff—the pageantry and the pride. We want them to see the drama and the history of the place and the pride that these kids should take in it and the sophistication that it takes to understand it. We wanted to add to the schools' ability to communicate that degree of sophistication of understanding to the kids. We want them to define success the way they want to define it.

KT: How does media education contribute to this?

RG: It wasn't really a matter of ever telling kids to turn the TV off. It's like the other literacy efforts. We always wanted them just to be able to approach it with their own resources, with their own core of strengths, whether that be critical thinking about the media or in the case of Appalshop, through their hands-on work through the Appalachian Media Institute.

Appalshop worked with high school kids. We worked with an alarmingly high percentage of kids that thought they were second class citizens, culturally speaking. I did not work with the Institute directly that much, but I observed the two ways that teachers worked to counter that. One way was to inspire the students to discredit the witness, that is to discredit the mainstream culture. They would say, "Look, when they came here and did a *48 Hours* piece about eastern Kentucky, what did they get wrong? And "How wrong were they?"

What I always enjoyed more was the more proactive response: "Say listen, let's just start from scratch with video. Let's create our own way of using it, and let's use our own local resources to make statements about it, and as much as possible focus on what's in front of you, not the other kind of media." To focus on what this person that you're interviewing or this social condition that you're witnessing needs in terms of media, rather than what the media needs from that phenomenon that you're observing.

KT: How do you make sure that your basic concerns are being met: that kids engage Appalachia as a subject for their school work.

RG: The summer workshops were conducted to kind of steer the focus back to content. What does this subject matter demand? What was harder was, kids want to play around with the forms that they've inherited, and I think to some extent that's good.

KT: You mean from broadcast, commercial media?

RG: Yes. They want to do a game show, or network news. It's a great teaching opportunity, because when kids get back in school and they're asked to do the school news instead of a 15 minute documentary on something. The teaching opportunity was always there to say, "Ok, how does this change the way you have to deal with your material now that you're on a deadline and you're in a structure that's more like a broadcast structure."

KT: Which is getting less like a broadcast structure in real life, anyway. Do you find that the more they see alternative kind of work, the more open they are to form, the more experimental they are with form? Or do they just think independent media is schlocky?

RG: What we were always able to do at AMI was always to get kids interested in the subject matter. What they were being taught and what they were being reinforced to do in the Institute was documentary style production. The kids are always motivated. They were on their own for subject matter and scheduling interviews. There were a lot of givens that had to do with documentary. The kind of genre that we were working in was not up for debate. [Laughs]. Well, I mean, that wasn't where a lot of their creative input was requested.

KT: Can you explain a little bit about the Appalshop process of documentary making?

RG: Appalshop documentaries are famous for not having a narrator, or being constructed strictly on the words of the people who are the story. It's a fairly conscious reaction to the fact that when people in the coal fields were in documentaries or in the news, in the kind of feature documentary or the kind of lone format documentary that the news networks used to do more of, that invariably you'd have Walter Cronkite or Charles Kuralt in the voice-over explaining what you were supposed to think of these people. So for the young filmmakers at Appalshop in the early 1970s, it was the reason that it was necessary to leave out that voice-over narration, to let the rest of the country come to an understanding of Appalachian people on their own. So in the Appalshop videos, you'll see people talking to the camera, but you won't have voice-over. Usually you won't see anybody asking them questions as an interviewer, either.

In working with teachers I always thought this was kind of funny—that it's always been a bit of a problem with the videos. They never just came out and summarized what they were trying to say in a straightforward kind of way. But to me, this style was a built-in media literacy component of Appalachia film and video. Its construction forces you to reconstruct it yourself. You had to figure out what it was talking about. It required more kind of cognitive activity than a lot of other stuff. There was an ornery resistance to spoon-feeding in almost every video we have in the Appalshop archive.

KT: So the media teacher sets up the environment—the parameters.

RG: Yes. The given was that this was a documentary workshop. We also did some video animation. Some kids produced an animation short and most of them did folktales. There was heavy reinforcement for the selection of that kind of form and content.

It's a negotiation. I think that's probably better than giving kids free reign. It's like, "Ok, here's where you get to make decisions, and here are the givens." That's part of Foxfire philosophy too, and Jeff Hawkins, the founder of AMI, is trained in Foxfire. A lot of Appalachian Media Institute method is Foxfire inspired and derived. What's good about the process is it's all explained and all on the table, and the kids understand and get it, and they understand they're being negotiated with by the teacher.

Most of the way we communicated content was through expression; that kids were in the process of making a statement of their own. Our job was to direct them back towards content—that they were making a statement about something substantial, and that they were making a substantial statement about it. We really tried to push them to make a more considered statement.

One of the inherent limits of video is that it's so production driven. We need 30 seconds of voice here, and we need pictures here, and it's almost like the voice and the pictures get a little abstracted. The push for understanding the issue can get lost. We have to slow the kids down and say, "Are you sure you're ready to make a statement about snake handling? Don't we need to talk about this some more?" It's not about the perfect response, it's about understanding what you're talking about. I think that's something that it's easy to let kids get away from with media. So we stay focused on the content.

KT: It's sort of like the cognitive craft of it. The production skill part is a lot easier to teach.

RG: That's right. It's easy to teach them how long a paragraph should be; it's not that easy to teach them how to say something that people will remember. That's hard with any media. But the oral culture all around them functions in that way. That stuff is memorable. People were saying things that made a difference, that people could remember, so that you could remember it to tell it the next time.

KT: In this shift from the oral culture, do you bypass print? In terms of story telling, do you use electronic tools to bypass print? In some cultures it goes from an oral culture to an alphabetic print culture to an electronic culture, not in a linear fashion, but all three are there.

RG: One way that print and video are the same is that once you get it down, you don't have to remember it. You can always reference it after that. No, we have plenty of print in Appalachia. Eastern Kentucky people are very proud of their literary tradition and there are lots of writers and poets, but the way they do it here is a little different.

It's funny, but there are lots of readings. People like to get together and read their scribblings and there are lots of writers' groups. People love language here and I think it translates pretty well to print. But again, one of the places people are very communal is around their language and around their stories. So no, I wouldn't say that the way we work with media bypasses print, at all. But I will say that I see kids from all over Appalachia take to video. That's kind of interesting to me and this is something that needs to be researched. When asked to choose between lots of art media, there's something about video that they respond to. So now I'm wondering what is it about the Appalachian kids that makes the respond to video.

KT: One idea that comes to me is Walter Ong's theory of secondary speech. He thinks that the speech we hear in media mimics authentic speech and therefore it's really not so much about pictures as it's about authentic vs. inauthentic orality The narrative of alphabetic print is a little more conventional in its own defined sort of way. So there's something about people who value oral traditions and the way that radio and video pick up authentic speech in a way that reading print silently to yourself just can't do.

RG: I think that makes sense. Another part of my theory about it is that I met a lot of kids and adults who really like to edit, and they like the repetitiveness of editing—what some people would think of as dwelling in the prison house of language. But I've seen a lot of people in the mountains that really got into that process of really breaking down the language and rearranging it, and working to construct narrative that way. They have the patience to think about. They have that kind of interest, the interest in the language gives them the patience to deal with that process. There's that savor for the language that allows you to spend those endless hours fooling with it in a way that someone who is not as attached to the ins and outs of language would not bother to do.

KT: You've worked in informal arts-based and community-centered spaces. How do you think that education differs in formal vs. informal spaces?

RG: I think the best schools don't really quibble over formal vs. informal. They don't worry that kids are out of their seat. What's becoming the best of formal practice involves a lot of what you think of as informal, getting kids out of the building, having kids work with nontraditional teachers, having kids doing hands-on or group work. A lot of that was considered informal education, now that's become more a part of formal education. At the teacher workshops, we make a big effort at Appalshop to make everything that we do educationally rigorous but casual. We tried to recreate what really is the best about informal educational setting and that is, you're able to access it.

We're doing it because there's nothing we'd rather be doing. Everything that *fun* is, *this* is: Out running around, out being with your friends, out doing stuff that challenges *the status quo*. All of that is education. When you get into that in a formal setting, you're challenging the very basis of what's wrong with school—that it's a system for communicating to kids who's going to win and who's going to lose, and it's a system for communicating to kids the risks involved in speaking your mind in this culture. So there's always that tension if you're going to work in public schools that you always want to butt up against it to the point that you're pushing the envelope and not to the point that you're jeopardizing your capacity to work.

I think that school is such a powerful teacher of how content and process are linked that if you're challenging the status quo in one way that you're going to challenge it in even more fundamental ways at some point—if you follow your challenge to the logical conclusion. So how are formal educational spaces still viable and how does technology contribute to that? For me and for most people who are on the outs in this society, public education is generically considered as the last best hope for people. The fact is public schools are structured so that, if you're for power sharing, if you're for re-distributing power within a society, that you are naturally going to get in trouble with your public school. Unless, of course, you are in a really lucky spot. People who are enemies of power sharing are showing up now—correlate them with the same crowd who's the enemies of public education right now. I think that there's a pretty good correlation.

Tied into this more for me is that the presence of technology correlates real strong with the presence of money. Poor schools have to approach technology in a different way.

KT: How does that relate to the technologies that schools use? For example, computers. Kentucky has a lot of computers, right?

RG: Right. In Kentucky, of course, you have a gigantic state school reform and a gigantic allocation of technology money and an infusion of computer technology. What's going to happen when they start tearing them up and wearing them out and the political will isn't there to replace them? I think that's a big question for rural school technology integration. It became a big question when the quality of the work you could do is limited directly by the amount of money you could spend, and on a scale that is quite different than, say, a literature program. Or in a media program, or the arts in general—even a painting program. But all arts programs are expensive to do right. You can't deal with technology without dealing with that issue of class and money in it.

KT: Why do you suppose that school bureaucracies spend so much on computers and neglect the video production?

RG: That's a good question. My guess is that on some kind of inchoate level and on some level that they could speak is that the instinct is that computers are going to teach you something and video's going to give you the power to express yourself. That video's going to give you the power to record what's happening, whereas heretofore computers haven't been seen as that kind of tool of expression, they were kind of . . .

KT: Information delivery systems?

RG: Right. They were just an advance on notebooks and chalk and blackboards.

KT: You've already talked about how Foxfire and a lot of the Institute's ideas are derived from Foxfire. Is there anything else you want to say about that? What about traditional lecture—teacher telling? We talked about student-centered education, but teacher-centered discourse has been pretty much sidelined or even denigrated nowadays. Do you think it's appropriate to straight teacher talk?

RG: I admire Foxfire. I think teacher talk is appropriate when the teachers are smart and when they're good communicators and when they care about what they're talking about. I think you have to go back to that basic point: Is the teacher communicating the joy of education? Most kids would rather figure it out themselves than listen to the ham hock who's standing in front of the classroom. When the teacher is interesting and worth listening to, that's just storytelling. Teachers have to decide whether they should be talking to kids or not. I'm very improvisational, in everything. I think that teachers should plan on never doing teacher talk, and do it when the kids ask for it.

That's the other kind of great pedagogical thing that I learned from Foxfire, that kids are capable of reflecting on educational process, that the kids are capable of talking about pedagogy, and you can ask them. You've got to build a relationship with whoever you're teaching. What I like about the good Foxfire teachers is that the class is just a constant series of choices. We could do this or that. We could do this or the other. The kids, once they get into it, you don't even have to ask them after a while. Lecturing or modeling, it's more like you've got to do a Foxfire approach the whole time, with everything you're doing, so that you build up that relationship, where it's an open democratic place, where you can say, "Well do you just want me to tell you this?" And the kids can tell you, "Yeah" or "Let's get down to work on something else." I've heard that happen in class and it's kind of cool when the troops ask for a lecture.

KT: What do you think the kids expect from hands-on media work?

RG: The more I was at it, the more I realized that all you can really do is stand as an example of how to live your life. This is kind of big picture stuff, but those kids are going to take what skills out of it that *they* want or need. The best thing you can do as a teacher is give a child a capacity for their own mind. The more I was at it, the more I became conscious that what was important was that I be an adult who cares about certain things. That those kids understand what's important to me, because they have the roles from corporate culture that are oftentimes so bad.

Just so that they know there are adults who care about something—beyond money. That there are adults who understand their work as having meaning and leading to something that might be better; that you can be cynical and disgusted and still get and be proactive in work and be happy and enjoy people. Even though you might think a lot of folks behave like asses a lot of the time. Kids need to see this. You don't want to give them anything, you just want to be, and let them take what they need. I think it's very important to treat them as people too, trying to figure out the same things we're still trying to figure out.

KT: You're a reflective teacher, then.

RG: Hopefully, yeah. Truly believing in your heart that you don't know what you're doing and that at the same time, you know a lot of stuff. It's kind of funny. You want to project control and lack of control at the same time, You want to project ignorance and wisdom at the same time. I want to stand up there and be complicated in a way. I remember that was what I always liked. If someone came in and they were kind of complicated, I'd pay attention. To me, that meant they were real people.

LITERACY IN AN URBAN LANDSCAPE

Steve Goodman is Founding Director of the Educational Video Center in Manhattan. EVC is worlds apart from Appalshop, but the two programs have much in common. Media teachers in the United States consider the two as flagships for successful media teaching. From 1984 to 1995, EVC was a thriving nonprofit organization that worked with children in an after school program to produce documentaries about their lives in New York City. In 1995, EVC became a formal part of a secondary alternative school called the School for the Physical City on 25th Street in Manhattan. The School for the Physical City is part of the New Visions Initiative, which was a spin-off of the larger Annenberg Network for School Renewal. The School for the Physical City belongs to a new small schools' network and is a public school, supported by the New York City Board of Education. Students at EVC are beginning to work with digital cameras and editing systems and to participate in online networks.

KT: Let's start with a big picture issue. Why should we educate people at all? Why should people be literate at all?

SG: For one thing, literacy enables all children to participate fully in society—to be able to be critical of the world around them as well as to be able to express themselves and to articulate their ideas and thoughts. So, if we believe that we want 100% of our children to be educated regardless of class or race, and that this is really a participatory democracy, then that means that all kids have to be able to have access to information and to be able to make sense of it, and to be able to contribute to the national conversation. Education enables everyone to be able to realize the potential they have within themselves—their imagination and creative capacities. And that, I think, is not very often a goal of education as much as the economic or vocational goals that I think are too often put as the reason we want to educate kids: "To compete in the global marketplace."

KT: To follow that, how does new media, or electronic media, contribute to your vision for education?

SG: It contributes in the sense that so much of the information in our society now originates outside of the classroom, through mass media. That includes TV, films, billboards, magazines, as well as the more interactive variety—the Internet and Websites and computer games. I think that kids have to learn to critically read those media that are visual, aural, as well as print. I'd like to see them able to be fluent in writing and creating and authoring those media and to be full participants in the culture. It shouldn't be just those who have the means—who own the best means of production—who can make the Disney movies and influence the way the stories are told. That is such a one-way kind of conversation. I think it should be that all kids have those capacities and skills for a two-way conversation.

KT: At Educational Video Center, you work with both kids and adults. How does your training differ for these two audiences?

SG: Let me start with some of the similarities, and then I can go to the differences. In terms of similarities, we have both kids and teachers who learn to use media for exploration and research into communities—their own communities. We learn to tell stories of those communities, or to explore institutional issues, or personal issues, and to do it through first person, face-to-face interaction, through interviews, as well as to do research in more traditional ways. With teachers we have the added responsibility of talking about how a teacher would incorporate or teach media exploration in the classroom. In other words, it's not just bringing in technology to do the same things you've always been doing, but it's changing the classroom, and changing the way they teach. It changes things so that the teacher is not necessarily the repository of all the information, nor is the textbook the main source. We encourage our students and teachers to have confidence that they can locate people out there in the neighborhood for information. And we help them learn how to use these community experts to their best advantage. We show teachers how to handle multiple perspectives on a question and to be comfortable as a learner, right along with the kids. This flips the teacher–learner equation. For example, information might be in different languages, and so the student is the expert when they're doing an interview in Spanish, if that's their native language, and if that's their own neighborhood. This is only one example of how a teacher could learn from a student. It's a change in the way that teachers think about their craft and about schooling. And so, that's the important added dimension that we think about when we work with teachers. The skill-based technology work is a lot the same with kids and teachers, but the pedagogy is an added piece.

Another piece of our teacher work is assessment. Everyone tells teachers about how technology offers important tools for learning. But we ask them, "How do you know?" Teachers have to know when learning takes place and so they need to think about assessing learning from multiple forms of communication that might be visual, video, or aural means, as well as textual. Our program also demands that teachers know how to assess individual kids in a group project, so that they can be sure that learning is taking place in a collaborative situation, too. Assessment is a very important part of our work with teachers.

KT: Let's talk a little bit about the pedagogy. Do you have names for the style, or approach, that you favor when you teach teachers?

SG: We didn't at the beginning! We thought we were just showing them the "natural" way that you would do any kind of journalistic or documentary approach to media-making. But now we've come to use some terms from the educational arena, mostly from what might be called "constructivism." A lot of it comes from Dewey's work, so it's concepts like "experiential" approaches to learning, or "inquiry-based" ways to make media.

KT: Are there networks of teachers whose educational philosophies you admire?

SG: I think of the Foxfire network approach as something that is very close to what we do, and we've learned a lot from. I think of the Coalition of Essential Schools as being a network that has principles for how school can be different, and centered on the student. There are lots of other networks that—the National Writing Project I think is a useful network that takes a look at print literacy in a way similar to the way we work with electronic media. Breadloaf has a network of teachers that do excellent work. Actually, Breadnet is their community of teachers network that communicates through the Internet. There are common themes that are shared by all these networks which look at putting the student at the center of the work, and respecting the culture and the experience that the student brings to the work, to the classroom. These networks also support collaborative work. They encourage the students to monitor their own work and to be successful through portfolios and other kinds of alternative assessment.

KT: These approaches are satisfying to teachers and students, but why technology? The question of efficacy keeps coming up and the research-based for the efficacy of technology such as computer networking or multimedia, or even video, is just not all that convincing yet. There are a lot of single-case descriptive kind of qualitative stories. But in terms of a little harder evidence, or a little longitudinal evidence of those qualitative stories, there isn't much there. So it begs a question: Given that constructivist, experiential, inquiry-based pedagogy has an ability to change schools and teaching and learning, what does technology have to do with this. I mean, you could build a birdhouse with a caring adult, or you could do writing, or public speaking. Why digital technology? What's all this hype around this new technology? What does it contribute that is so special?

SG: First of all, I think you're right that there is a lot of hype—which is a word that comes from hyperbole. It's not the technology itself, but how it's used, and how teachers construct their classroom and school. Educational scholar Larry Cuban talks about how technology has been thrust upon teachers over the last century in various ways and they then try and fit it into ways that make their life easier, meeting the demands that are already placed on them in a more efficient way. For example, a school administrator might use computers to help with attendance, or to place computerized phone calls to the home when the kids are absent, or other ways that routine tasks might be automated.

KT: Business applications, in a way.

SG: Exactly—for control and efficiency, but not necessarily to enhance real understanding or learning. I'm afraid that has happened in the past. Distance learning is another example. In many cases, education via satellite or phone lines replicates the one-way talking head lecture of a teacher, but does it in a way that is even less satisfactory—the teacher is not even there in person to take in the student response firsthand. Another example is when the computer is used as an electronic workbook, fill-in-the-blank, kind of thing.

KT: You might as well have a textbook, then.

SG: Right. It's new technology doing the old approach. So for these reasons, researchers aren't necessarily finding a lot of innovative uses or changes in kids learning. But I think if you can have designs of the use of new technologies with an underpinning of the practices and principles of a more progressive education, then you'll see a difference. The technology can be used to foster deeper inquiry that could not have happened without technology. Collaborative work, or really getting kids to be independent learners, can also be made possible with technology. But it is clear that technology has to be married to some of the same principles and approaches you might find in a Foxfire project of building a birdhouse.

KT: Is there something different—in terms of the learning that takes place—about image technologies, and/or the confluence of image, text, and moving images, etc.?

SG: I think it's different in that it's the kind of the sea in which kids swim—we all swim—now, in terms of the dominance of the image. And also the fluidity of image and text now, through mass media. So I think it's really important that those media forms are used in the classroom for kids to be able to use what they already know so well, to further academic progress. And they don't have to learn the alphabet to understand it, or to be part of it. I know that Amelia, my 1-year-old, is looking at TV and her older brother Theo began watching it at about that age, too. They are very knowledgeable about the way that media works, in some ways, but it's partly a false sense of knowledge. They really do need to go deeper, beneath the surface. They're very interested by the image technologies. After all, media relates to their personal experience outside of school. But there's a great need to expand their knowledge and understanding of it by teaching them to be critical viewers and producers of it.

KT: I'm also thinking about something that media teacher Deborah Leveranz says about kids she works with in the juvenile justice system in Texas. She says that some of these kids have never before even seen a snapshot of themselves. They've never had someone say to them, "You look good in blue." It's poignant, really. She talks about how it's somewhat startling, but also reflective for them to see their own image and the image of those things around them, in a distanced kind of way.

SG: I don't know if it's startling, but I find that some kids certainly enjoy it and feel pride in seeing themselves. You know, they sometimes ham it up in front of the camera. But there's also a real sense of wanting to shy away from the self-image—of it never being good enough.

KT: So it's got a dark side to it.

SG: Well, teenagers are so down on each other. If they have a pimple, or if they're overweight or whatever, it's a big, big deal and they can be cruel to each other. So I work with both kinds of kids—there are kids who just can't get them away from being in front of the camera, and then there are kids you have to shove in that direction. But yes, there is a real capacity to be reflective and that it is a kind of reflectiveness that is subtly different from any other kind of, teaching, in any other kind of media. The kids can record something and then watch it back multiple times, and see different things each time. It has a built-in critical distance. You walk down the street in your neighborhood every day and you're not as aware of what's going on around you, but if you videotaped it as you walked, and watched it, you might be able to see things as if you're kind of a stranger to that place—seeing it for the first time. I think that's really a great use of video. But that can only happen if the teacher allows that kind of reflection, or promotes that, or allows space or time for that kind of reflection. So there is that great potential for video in learning, but again, the context of its use is key.

KT: What are some step-by-step methods that you think are essential to getting the student to competency, or to mastery?

SG: First, I would ask. "What competency and in what area?" You're talking multiple intelligences and learning strategies, à la Howard Gardner, and with technology, there are so many things going on, in terms of learning and skill-building. If I were to focus on being able to critically analyze an image, for example, we would want students to ask the deeper questions. We'd talk a little bit about how to begin the process of producing a documentary piece and then we'd go from there.

They begin production by looking. They look at a whole range of media, including independent documentaries. They look at photographs. We pick apart a photograph. They like to look, but the hardest thing for them is to just describe what they see. So we have to break down a lot of tasks to get them to the place where they have the vocabulary and the discourse to describe what they see on a deeper level. Those are some of the early activities: to develop their capacity for observation, and to name what they see. That's only one step along the way. Just because they're watching TV, or playing video games, or they're watching things through the eye piece of a camera, doesn't mean they're really seeing things carefully, closely.

Another step is to learn to look at the different interpretations of documentaries: What is the audience? Who is the audience? What is the filmmaker trying to say here? How do they use the medium to say that? They get a little bit of introduction to analysis of documentaries, as well as still images. Then they begin to make connections to their own lives, and their own communities and begin to generate questions based on their own concerns. They have a brainstorming activity and they spend a couple of days as a group writing about, talking about the issues that they think they would want to explore in a documentary. They end up debating and voting and coming down to one issue and they then have to say, "Well, what about that issue? What are we going to say that's different or new? Why is it of importance to us? What's been said before on it?" This leads us to a whole research strand.

First they look at tapes that other kids that have produced at the Educational Video Center that have approached the same issue. Then they begin to formulate their hypotheses, generate and sharpen their questions, and gather evidence. They start deciding, "Where do you have to go to answer this question?" And this is a very important part of the process: to be able to ask their own questions, and find answers to their own questions. They decide that they might want to go to a newspaper, or book, or to interview a person. They start developing a list of places to go for research. They break into teams to begin to do that.

Simultaneously, they have to learn more about the equipment. We have an informal principle about equipment skill teaching that I'll just call "information on a need-to-know basis." We don't start out and lecture "this is a camera and a microphone," or "this is a library," or any of that until there's a reason to use it as a tool. Once they need to, they go out and do practice interviews on their theme. And they learn how to use an audio recorder, or a camera. They'll rotate roles so that the person who used the camera the day before might be the interviewer today, or might monitor sound, or might help with getting people in the crowd to come in and be the next person to be interviewed. Rotations ensure that different jobs are assigned and that everyone gets to try different roles.

Of course, the beauty of video is the ability to instantly rewind, or reset, and immediately see what you did—whether it's a mistake, or a really great shot, it's visible for everyone to critique. That presents another opportunity for learning both how to shoot and how to critique. And also how to offer criticism and still be kind to one's colleague! And conversely, how to develop a thick skin for criticism and to see it as a positive thing.

And there are smaller, incremental steps in between, of course, that are too numerous to mention. After some skill and cognitive building foundations are established, they do a practice project. They learn to work in groups to edit. Each group then edits different versions from the same raw footage that was shot. They make copies of the tapes. They see how you can edit, take the same material and make different decisions, and make it come out with different points of view, or even completely different meaning. They begin to learn the media literacy principle, "all media are constructed." They learn it by doing it and by having it pointed out to them. What they're actually doing now, when they're at this phase in the project, is to work in groups.

When they get involved in their major project, they repeat that process, but in a more extensive, sustained way for the rest of the semester. The process of asking questions and going out and conducting interviews, and watching the materials and forming an edit plan, and how you're going to put it together, and what's missing, all have many classroom tasks attached to them. They learn to generate questions that can be applied to media throughout their lives. They make a rough cut and screen it to an audience for feedback. Then they edit a final version based on that kind of feedback.

KT: Does the drive to complete an end product interfere with the learning process? How do you balance that?

SG: Throughout the whole process, they keep a portfolio which would include things like the articles they read, or the questions they asked, or the photographs that they analyzed, or about why certain selections are included in their video. They keep journals. The journal is divided into sections and is intended to help them become aware of their own learning in a variety of different ways. This kind of authentic assessment approach is a hard thing to do: The students have to do the project and keep aware of the skills and habits they're developing. It's easy for the product–process dynamic to get in the way. That tension crops up throughout the semester. But the assessment is critical. It is so valuable to watch back what they're doing and then refer to what they talked about 3 months earlier, in terms of being critical of an image, or how you look at an image. It really depends on the teacher to make that connection if the students are not making the connection. Each piece builds on what they did before.

KT: Let's talk some more about the way you know that learning takes place.

SG: At the end of the documentary workshop each student goes through a roundtable—a portfolio roundtable. This is a time when the student looks back on all material in their portfolio, and all the tapes and kind of evidence they've collected to reflect on what they've learned. They are asked to demonstrate what they've learned and to explain it to a panel made up of parents, media-makers, teachers, and other students. We foster the idea that our work must be accountable to the broader community. And that the standards are not just set by an individual teacher or media-maker or a principal, but that it really is something that's collectively agreed upon by a broad range of people in the community. So the kids pick two areas that they have in their portfolio. It could be technical arts, or writing, or research—critical viewing, communication, interviewing—any of those areas. Then they might show, perhaps, the first time they went out and used a camera, and compare it to the most recent time, in order to show their growth. Then they have to talk about what it is that they learned: "Why is this a better example of their skills. What is this evidence—what counts as evidence, and what is does this evidence of success look like?" They might show their research notes, or their interview questions, and how they revised them over time. And then they could show a tape of themselves conducting an interview. Or they might put together editing decks and demonstrate their ability to do an edit. It's some kind of in-depth demonstration of their skills. Then, there's time for questions from the panel. The panel gives what we call "warm" and "cool" feedback. It's a very structured protocol.

KT: Warm and cool? It sounds like McLuhan. Did you mean it to do that?

SG: No. It's actually something that Joe McDonald from the Coalition of Essential Schools developed. It's a structured protocol for this process, but it's structured in a way where they can respond. People go around and say what they thought was really strong about what they showed, what they liked. They also comment on what things are missing and could be developed more. It's about helping the student—drawing the students out and helping them think about these skills and how they might develop them later in other course work, or maybe after they graduate. That's the portfolio roundtable.

KT: When you started out, you were a nonprofit organization outside the formal school structure. How is it different working in a more formal, educational space, such as a school and more of an informal space, like an after-school program?

SG: When EVC started, we were in an old firehouse that was part of a media center called Downtown Community TV. And now we are in an alternative public school called the School for the Physical City on 25th Street in Manhattan. A big part of why we moved here was because we share a common philosophy about education with this school. One of our partners is Outward Bound. It's an expeditionary learning center and they believe in learning through going out on expeditions and experience and trips and that kind of thing. And we were saying, "Well, we think kids learn by going out into the world with cameras."

We converted two classrooms into offices. The library that was going to have books, the media library, is now where we have our workshops. One of the really nice things about this is that we're surrounded by kids and teachers. Yesterday, I was asked to sit in on a presentation by some of the seniors in this school, to be what's called a "critical friend," as I've asked some of the teachers in this school to do for our program's portfolio roundtables. So there's an exchange and I was there to comment and ask questions of the kids in their classes, and they do the same for our kids.

One of the problems is that we always felt it was a great thing for kids to be able to leave their school and come to a space that was clearly identified as not being a school, so we could have a sense of a different kind of culture where kids could feel like they're treated as professionals and media makers and surrounded by adults who were doing the same kind of thing. For some of our students, *school* had such a negative connotation. So we felt we wanted to create a space within a school that didn't feel like a regular classroom. And that's been our challenge. The kids can't hang out in front of the school, or break school rules, like smoking in front of the school, because we are part of a larger institution here. We can't come and go as we please and have the kids edit until midnight like we did in the other space. Although we have very flexible and generous use of the space, it is different.

But overall, this is a positive move. For one thing, the school has a rather well-established electronic network and we can tap into that. We can use the server, or contact all of our teachers via email.

KT: You can leverage their infrastructure, in other words.

SG: Yeah. And they can leverage our resources. Together, we can talk about building a media center with both of our resources. We bring in all of our video and we have nonlinear editing, but they also have a lot of computers that we're talking about doing all our kinds of nonlinear editing with digital software and hardware. That is a really nice thing about this. The other thing is just to be in a place where you can test out theories and approaches and strategies. It's an educational laboratory—right in the school. And I'm consulting with some of the teachers here who incorporate media in what they do.

KT: Educational Video Center has always been associated with analog video. What are you doing to combine video with other media such as video-conferencing, or Photoshop, or e-mail, etc. Have you experimented with those?

SG: What we want to do is to incorporate digital video technology and computer technology, with the same principles of students creating their own work, doing research, and using digital media as a delivery system to get their information out there, through the Internet.

They have digital cameras and they can do documentaries in the way they have gathered information in the past, but then they can layer in other kinds of visual texts, such as photographs. They can create graphics with the computer, they can bring in audio or other kinds of music or interviews, or sound bites from other sources. So they'll have a richer range of material to draw from once they're fully connecting with the Internet and the Web to their work. They can get their work to a wider audience in new ways over the Internet. This is becoming a reality real soon. The challenge will be to make sense of that information and still tell a story that is interesting and engaging. We haven't really explored digital media enough yet to know what this might do to narrative structures. I know that the possibilities for revision are really great, and we have done that with our digital editing system.

KT: What about collaboration with others outside the four walls of the school? I notice the similarities between you and the Appalshop program in Kentucky.

SG: This is one thing we want to explore. Kids in rural Kentucky could work with EVC students on a project together. They can have a common theme, for example—kids and music, or something else about youth culture and how it plays out in a rural area and in an urban area. They can communicate with e-mail about the issues. Then they could do storyboards with commentary. The possibilities of doing something long-distance that way is something we want to explore—but always trying to be mindful of the connections between the virtual community and their own social community. And not forgetting that both are possible and important.

KT: If someone were to give you $50 million and tell you to build your dream school, what do you think that would look like?

SG: It would be small. I'd probably build a couple of schools with that much money, but they would be small. They would have technology that kids would have access to across their day, and across subject areas. I think that kids would be doing projects that, they'd be learning by doing projects, and they would be having the opportunity to travel, not just in their own neighborhood but elsewhere to meet with kids or adults who are involved in. There would be budgets for kids to travel as well as using technology for that. I think whenever possible we would broaden their horizons beyond their local view. I think it would be a school that—I'm trying to think of how we would be spending the money! We would bring in people who are working in the field that kids aspire to or are learning about so that there isn't that great chasm between school and actual work. I want kids to have a sense of the reason—you know, talk to a real historian and see how they do their research. Or to an engineer to find out why in hell they are studying this math! That kind of school would really contribute to a clear reason and a path to what they're learning and a sense of high standards. Maybe there'd be an honorarium for people to come in and participate, from the professional world, from the arts world, so that the school is really drawing on those resources and the community is really feeling committed to contributing to the school. I would make connections, too, so that anyone who doesn't have a computer would get one and have it connected to the school so that the move toward digital portfolios online would progress? If they were hooked up, the parents could be up to date on the conversations that are happening in the school, and could participate in it, contribute to it. If they don't have the time to come and visit during the working day they can log on and communicate, anytime, and participate that way as well as through a digital portfolio. They could find out—in depth—the kind of work their kids are doing in classes. Instead of coming home and saying, "What did you do today?" and the kid says, "Oh, nothing," there should be some tangible way, on an ongoing basis, for the parent to participate with the school and with each other so that even in the poorest community that question of access wouldn't be an issue. That's my dream school.

Appendix:
Global Multiliteracy Networks

Fortunately there are some attempts to network, in a collegial and professional sense, between various literacy constituents who look for opportunities to broaden and rethink literacy in an array of contexts. These include international efforts such as collaborative literacy research from The New London Group; The Bertelsmann Foundation's media education efforts in Germany and the United States; the International Visual Literacy Association; and the World Council on Media Education, a Spanish-English research and publishing effort. In Europe, the British Film Institute collaborates with other European agencies such as CLEMI in France to host joint publishing and conferencing ventures. In addition, national organizations that work together to promote cross-disciplinary study of multiliteracy issues in North America include: The National Association of Media Educators (NAME) and the National Forum on Information Literacy in the United States; and the Canadian Association for Media Education Organizations (CAMEO) in Canada. In Australia, the Australian Teachers of Media (ATOM) has emerged as a seminal organization for research and publishing about media education and the development of media education standards and assessments.

In Spain, international media educators met for three years for *Pé de Imaxe*, a media education conference in Galicia that resulted in joint English and Spanish publishing efforts exploring the theory and practice of media literacy education (Quin & Aparici, 1996). The executive committee of this effort is the World Council on Media Education. The Council meets yearly at media education conferences around the world to plan English–Spanish publishing, teaching, and conferencing opportunities.

The International Visual Literacy Association (IVLA) hosts international conferences and has published journal articles about visual literacy in a number of languages since the 1960s. Located in Blacksburg, Virginia, the group holds an annual international conference (Braden, Beauchamp, & Baca, 1990; Silverblatt & Eliceiri, 1997, p. 102). IVLA represents a cohesive, if eclectic, international group of educators and artists who are open to international, collaborative studies about the relationship between images and literacy. The group embodies broad expertise about the uses of images and their nature that can expand the discourse about literacy beyond text.

In addition, the British Film Institute (BFI) publishes for an international audience of media educators (British Film Institute, 1995). In 1991, the BFI, UNESCO, and the CLEMI organized a number of international conferences, including "New Directions in Media Education" in Toulouse, France (Bazalgette, 1993). The BFI has also collaborated with other film institutes and media education organizations in Europe, Africa, and Russia.

The Bertelsmann Foundation, the philanthropic arm of the Bertelsmann media corporation, has also sponsored German–American retreats for the purpose of discussing communication technologies' role in schooling (Bertelsmann Foundation, 1995). Since 1990, the Bertelsmann Foundation has sponsored a partnership between the Athens Academy in Athens, Georgia and a high school in Gütersloh, Germany in order to work toward an understanding of how new technologies can be integrated into the secondary curriculum (Bertelsmann Foundation, 1994). Bertelsmann Foundation was also the founding contributor to the Media Workshop in New York City, a nonprofit organization that conducts research, development, and training about the integrated use of media and new technologies across the curriculum. In addition, the Australian Teachers of Media (ATOM) serves as an international point of contact for conferencing, publishing, and resources for media educators in Australia, New Zealand, and other countries in southeast Asia. The quarterly magazine of ATOM, *Metro*, welcomes international contributors and is peer-reviewed by media educators (Australian Teachers of Media).

In North America, the National Alliance for Media Educators (NAME) is a cross-disciplinary coalition of media artists and educators who have created a national directory of those who research and practice media education across academic disciplines in the United States and Canada (Sherarts, 1996; Silverblatt & Eliceiri, 1997, p. 138). In Ottawa and Montreal, Canada, the Media Awareness Network (1996) offers a range of off- and on-line services in English and French for media educators, producers, and distributors in North America. It is a member of the Canadian Association for Media Education Organizations (http://www.screen.com/mnet/eng/med/class/support/cameo.htm).

In the United States, a similar coalition of organizations is the National Forum for Information Literacy initiated in 1989 with seed money provided by the American Library Association. Dozens of library and literacy organizations came together to focus national attention within the United States on the importance of information literacy to individuals, to the economy and to citizenship (http://www.nald.ca/fulltext/report1/rep01.htm). In addition, The Center for Media Literacy in Los Angeles and the National Telemedia Council in Madison, Wisconsin have hosted a number of national media literacy conferences in partnership with a variety of organizations consisting of health professionals, media artists, media professionals, governmental agencies, and educators. These gatherings are important forums for finding common ground and sharing ideas. Similarly, the National Council of Teachers of English and the National Speech Association have well-developed media education committees.

Some promising U.S.-based programs that partner media arts with critical literacy approaches include: Albuquerque Academy in New Mexico; Appalshop and public school teachers in Eastern Kentucky; Berkeley High School (CA) Communication Arts and Sciences program; Community TV Network in Chicago; Dearborn High School in Dearborn, Michigan; Educational Video Center, located at the School for the Physical City in New York (Educational Video Center, 1995); the Herald Project, a collaborative effort of San Francisco Unified School District and Southern Exposure Gallery in San Francisco; the L.A. Mobilization Project and Los Angeles public schools (Lamb, 1994); the Media Workshop in New York City; Southwest Alternate Media Project in Houston, Texas. Some of these programs are more fragile than others, but all have contributed to a vision of media education in action. In higher education, important media education efforts have been started by Appalachian State University in Boone, North Carolina; Clark University in Massachusetts; Webster University in St. Louis, Missouri; and New York University, Department of Media Ecology. The Georgetown University Communication, Culture and Technology program is another promising graduate program established at the CCT Media Center in Washington, DC. The Georgetown University program attempts to breach the gap between the sciences and humanities (http://www.georgetown.edu/grad/CCT). These programs represent only a few of the growing number of successful educator–artist literacy partnerships across the United States. They provide the nexus for a new generation of formal and informal teacher training and can provide important foundations for integrating an expanded sense of literacy in the classroom.

References

Adams, G. D. (1996). Space at S.F.'s new library is scarce, its chief admits. *San Francisco Examiner* (4 September), A-1.

Allen, R. L. (1993). Conceptual models of an African-American belief system: A program of research. In G. L. Berry & J. K. Asamen (Eds.), *Children & television: Images in a changing sociocultural world* (pp. 155–176). Newbury Park, CA: Sage.

Altheide, D. L. (1974). *Creating reality: How TV news distorts reality.* Beverly Hills, CA: Sage.

Althusser, L. (1971). *Ideology and ideological state apparatuses, Lenin and philosophy and other essays.* London: New Left Books.

American Library Association (1991). *American library association handbook of organization and membership directory.* Chicago: American Library Association.

American Library Association (1994). *Fact sheet* (January). Arlington, VA: American Library Association.

American Library Association Presidential Committee on Information Literacy (1990). *Final reports.* Chicago: American Library Association.

American Psychological Association (1993). *Violence & youth: Psychology's response. Vol. 1.* Summary report of the American Psychological Association Commission on Violence and Youth. Washington DC: American Psychological Association.

Amey, L. J. (1976). *Visual literacy: Implications for the production of children's television programs.* Halifax, Nova Scotia: Dalhousie University School of Library Services.

Anderson, D. R., & Collins, P. A. (1988). *The impact on children's education: Television's influence on cognitive development.* Washington, DC: U.S. Department of Education.

Anderson, J. A. (1980). The theoretical lineage of critical viewing curricula. *Journal of Communication, 30*(3), 64–70.

Anderson, J. A. (1992). The role of theory and research in the design of media literacy programs. In J.-P. Golay (Ed.), *Proceedings of the symposium on media education: June 27th to 30th, 1988* (pp. 11–21). Centre d'initiation aux communications de masse: Lausanne, Switzerland.

Anderson, J. A., & Ploghoft, M. E. (Eds.). (1981). *Education in a television age: The proceedings of a national conference on the subject of children and television.* Athens, OH: The Co-operative Center for Social Science Education.

Aparici, R. (Ed.). (1996). *La Revolución de los medios audiovisuales: Educacion y nuevas technologias* (2nd ed.). Madrid, Spain: Ediciones de la Torre.

Aparici, R., & García-Matilla, A. (1989). *Lectura de Imágenes*. Madrid, Spain: Ediciones de la Torre.

Apple, M. (1982). *Education and power*. London: Routledge & Kegan Paul.

Apple, M. (1987). *Teachers and texts: A political economy of class and gender relations in education*. London: Routledge & Kegan Paul.

Arizona State University West (1994). *Information competencies for students*. Phoenix, AZ: ASU West Library.

Armstrong, T. (1994). *Multiple intelligences in the classroom*. Alexandria, VA: Association for Supervision and Curriculum Development.

Arnheim, R. (1967). *Toward a psychology of art*. Berkeley, CA: University of California Press.

Arnheim, R. (1969). *Visual thinking*. Berkeley, CA: University of California Press.

Aufderheide, P., & Firestone, C. (1993). *Media literacy: A report of the national leadership conference on media literacy*. Queenstown, MD: The Aspen Institute.

Australian Teachers of Media. (1988). *Metro*. Metro Editorial Office, PO Box 204, Albert Park, Victoria 3206, Australia.

Baker, K. (1992). Against 'cultural relativism'. *San Francisco Examiner* (5 April), p. 9.

Baker, N. (1996). The author vs. the library. *The New Yorker* (14 October), pp. 50–62.

Bandura, A., & Walters, R. H. (1963). *Social learning theory and personality development*. New York: Holt, Rinehart & Winston.

Barr, T. (1988). *Reflections on media education: The myths and realities*. Keynote address delivered at the Ox Media 88 Conference. Brisbane, Australia.

Barthes, R. (1973). *Mythologies*. London: Paladin Press.

Baruch, R., Stutman, S., Benjamin, M. L., Rayder, T. Z., Grotberg, E., Livingstone, J. B., & White, C. B. (1996). *TV violence: Parents under the gun*. Washington, DC: Institute for Mental Health Initiatives and Turner Broadcasting.

Bazalgette, C. (Ed.). (1989). *Primary media education: A curriculum statement*. London: British Film Institute and the DES National Working Party for Primary Media Education.

Bazalgette, C. (1992). The politics of media education. In M. Alvarado & O. Boyd-Barrette. *Media education: An introduction* (pp. 140–149). London: British Film Institute.

Bazalgette, C. (Ed.). (1993). *Proceedings of the 1992 UNESCO conference on media education*. London & Paris: British Film Institute, CLEMI and UNESCO.

Bazalgette, C., & Buckingham, D. (Eds.). (1995). *In front of the children: Screen education and young audiences*. London: British Film Institute.

Beentjes, J. W., & Van Der Voort, T. H. (1988). Children's written accounts of televised and written stories. *Educational Research and Development, 39*(3), 15–26.

Behrens, S. J. (1994). A conceptual analysis and historical overview of information literacy. *College & Research Libraries* (July), 309–322.

Benton Foundation. (1996). *Buildings, books, and bytes: Libraries and communities in the digital age* (November). Washington, DC: Benton Foundation.

Berenfield, B. (1996). Linking students to the infosphere. *T.H.E. Journal*, 76–83.

Berg, I. (1971). *Education and jobs*. Boston: Beacon Press.

Berliner, D., & Biddle, B. (1995). *The manufactured crisis: Myths, fraud, and the attack on America's public schools*. Reading, MA: Addison-Wesley.

Berryman, S. E. (1992). Apprenticeship as a paradigm for learning, *Youth apprenticeships in America: Guidelines for building an effective system* (pp. 25–39). Washington, DC: American Youth Policy Forum.

Bertelsmann Foundation (Ed.). (1994). *Media as a challenge: Education as a task*. Gütersloh, Germany: Bertelsmann Foundation Publishers.

Bertelsmann Foundation (Ed.). (1995). *School improvement through media in education*. Gütersloh, Germany: Bertelsmann Foundation Publishers.

Boal, I. (1995). A flow of monsters: Luddism and virtual technologies. In J. Brook & I. Boal (Eds.), *Resisting the virtual life: The culture and politics of information* (pp. 3–15). San Francisco: City Lights Books.

Bolter, J. D. (1991). *Writing space: The computer, hypertext and the history of writing.* Hillsdale, NJ: Lawrence Erlbaum Associates.

Bonham, G. W. (1980). What next? *The communications revolution and the education of Americans.* New Rochelle, NY: Change Magazine Press/The Council of Learning/The Aspen Institute, 33–38.

Brabent, S., & Mooney, L. (1986). Sex role stereotyping in the Sunday comics: Ten years later. *Sex Roles, 14*(3/4), 141–148.

Braden, R. A., Beauchamp, D. G., & Baca, J. C. (1990). *Perceptions of visual literacy.* Conway, AK: The International Visual Literacy Association.

Bransford, J. D., Stein, B. S., Arbitman-Smith, R., & Vye, N. J. (1985). Three approaches to improving thinking and learning skills. In J. W. Segal, S. F. Chipman, & R. Glaser (Eds.), *Thinking and learning skills: Relating instruction to basic research* (Vol. 1). Hillsdale, NJ: Lawrence Erlbaum Associates.

Breivik, P. S. (1985). Putting libraries back in the information society. *American Libraries,* November (15), 723.

Breivik, P. S., & Gee, E. G. (1989). *Information literacy: Revolution in the library.* New York: Macmillan.

Breivik, P. S., & Jones, D. L. (1993). Information literacy: Liberal education for the information age. *Liberal Education, 74*(1), 24–29.

British Film Institute (1995). *BFI education 1995: The catalog of the British film institute.* London: BFI Publishing.

Brown, J. A. (1991). *Television "critical viewing skills" education: Major media literacy projects in the United States and selected countries.* Hillsdale, NJ: Lawrence Erlbaum Associates.

Buckingham, D. (Ed.). (1990/1992). *Watching media learning: Making sense of media education.* New York: The Falmer Press. (Republished 1992 by Falmer)

Buckingham, D. (1991). Teaching about the media. In D. Lusted (Ed.), *The media studies book* (pp. 12–36). London & New York: Routledge.

Buckingham, D. (1994). *Children talking television: The making of television literacy.* Basingstoke, Hampshire: Falmer Press.

Buckingham, D., & Sefton-Green, J. (1996). *Cultural studies goes to school: Reading and teaching popular media.* Basingstoke, Hampshire: Taylor & Francis.

Burke, P. (1972/1978). *Popular culture in early modern Europe.* New York: Harper and Row. (Reprinted 1978 by Harper and Row)

California Department of Education (1995). *Connect, compute and compete. The report of the California Education Technology Task Force.* Sacramento, CA: California Department of Education.

California State University Commission on Learning Resources and Instructional Technology. (1995). *Information competence in the California state university: A draft report.* Long Beach, CA: CSU Office of the Chancellor.

Campbell, J. R., Voelkl, K. E., & Donahue, P. L. (1996). *Report in Brief, NAEP 1994 Trends in Academic Progress* (November). Princeton, NJ: Educational Testing Service and the National Center for Education Statistics.

Campeau, P. L. (1974). Selective review of the results of research on the use of audio-visual media to teach adults. *AV Communication Review, 22*(1), 5–40.

Carpenter, E. (1972). *Oh, what a blow that phantom gave me!* New York, Toronto, London: Holt, Rinehart & Winston.

Carveth, R. (1996). Communication via interactive media: Communication in a new key? *The New Jersey Journal of Communication, 4*(1), 71–81.

Cassidy, M. F., & Knowlton, J. Q. (1983). Visual literacy: A failed metaphor? *Educational Communication and Technology Journal, 31,* 67–90.

Chomsky, N. (1957). *Syntactic structures.* The Hague, Netherlands: Mouton.

Chomsky, N. (1964). *Current issues in linguistic theory.* The Hague, Netherlands: Mouton.

Chomsky, N. (1968). *Language and mind.* New York: Harcourt, Brace, Jovanovich.

Chomsky, N. (1975). *The logical structure of linguistic theory.* New York: Plenum.

Cipolla, C. (1969). *Literacy and development in the west.* Harmondsworth: Penguin.

Clanchy, M. T. (1993). *From memory to written record: England 1066–1307* (2nd ed.). Oxford, U.K. and Cambridge, MA: Blackwell.

Cleveland State University (1990). *Passages to information literacy: Your key to success. A report on the goals and objectives for information literacy.* (21 September). Cleveland, OH: CSU Library.

Coley, R. J., Cradler, J., & Engel, P. K. (1997, May). *Computers and classrooms: The status of technology in U.S. Schools.* Princeton, NJ: Educational Testing Service, Policy Information Center.

Collins, A., Brown, J. S., & Newman, S. (1989). Cognitive apprenticeship: Teaching the craft of reading, writing, and mathematics. In L. B. Resnick (Ed.), *Knowing, learning and instruction: Essays in honor of Robert Glaser* (pp. 453–493). Hillsdale, NJ: Lawrence Erlbaum Associates.

Collis, B., & Levin, J. (1993, November). *Research on telecommunications and learning: An international perspective.* Paper presented at the International Society for Technology in Education's Tel*Ed '93 Conference. Dallas, TX.

Comstock, G., & Paik, H. (1991). *Television and the American child.* San Diego: Academic Press.

Considine, D. M. (1986). Visual literacy and children's books: An integrated approach. *School Library Journal* (September), 38–42.

Considine, D. M. (1990). Media literacy: Can we get there from here? *Educational Technology* (December), 27–32.

Considine, D. M. (1995a). Are we there yet: An update on the media literacy movement. *Educational Technology Journal* (July/August). Englewood Cliffs, NJ: Educational Technology Publications, pp. 32–43.

Considine, D. M. (1995b). An introduction to media literacy: The what, why and how to's. *Telemedium: The Journal of Media Literacy (Special supplement), 41*(2), 1–8.

Considine, D., & Haley, G. (1993). *Visual messages: Integrating imagery into instruction.* Englewood, CO: Libraries Unlimited.

Continental Cablevision (1994). *TV tool kit.* VHS. Boston, MA: Continental Cablevision, The Learning Channel & Pacific Mountain Network.

Cooke, P. (1992). TV or not TV? *In Health* (December/January), 33–43.

Cortés, C. E. (1995). Knowledge construction and popular culture: The media as multicultural educator. In J. A. Banks & C. A. M. Banks (Eds.), *Handbook of research on multicultural education* (pp. 169–199). New York: Macmillan.

Cradler, J. (1995). *Summary of current research and evaluation findings on technology in education.* San Francisco, CA: WestEd.

Crary, D. (1995). Canadian network to dump U.S. shows from prime time tv. *San Francisco Chronicle* (24 November), B-1.

Cremin, L. (1990). *Popular education and its discontents.* New York: HarperCollins.

Cressy, D. (1980). *Literacy and the social order.* Cambridge, England: Cambridge University Press.

Cuban, L. (1986). *Teachers and machines: The classroom use of technology since 1920.* New York and London: Teachers College Press.

Dale, E. (1946). *Audiovisual methods in teaching.* New York: Holt, Rinehart, and Winston.

Davies, J. (1996). *Educating students in a media-saturated culture.* Lancaster, PA: Technomic Publishing Company.

Davis, J. (1992). *Media literacy: From activism to exploration.* Background paper for the national leadership conference on media education. Queenstown, MD: The Aspen Institute.

de Beaugrande, R. (1987). Schemas for literary communication. In L. Halasz (Ed.), *Literary discourse: Aspects of cognitive and social psychological approaches* (pp. 49–99). New York: Walter de Gruyter.

Debes, J. L. (1968). Some foundations for visual literacy. *Audiovisual Instruction, 13,* 961–964.

Delgado, R. (1996). Card catalog spared for the present: City residents persuade library commission to extend the life of predigital records. *San Francisco Examiner* (4 September), A-12.

Delpit, L. (1995). *Other people's children: Cultural conflict in the classroom.* New York: The New Press.

DelVecchio, R. (1996). NAACP leader announces forum on ebonics. *San Francisco Chronicle* (28 December), A-17.

Dery, M. (1993). The empire of signs. *Adbusters Quarterly, 11*(2), 54–61.

de Saussure, F. (1974). *Course in general linguistics.* London: Fontana Press.

Desmond, R. (1997). Media literacy in the home: Acquisition vs. deficit models. In R. Kubey (Ed.), *Media literacy in the information age* (pp. 323–343). New Brunswick, NJ: Transaction Books.

Dewey, J. (1938). *Experience & education.* Kappa Delta Pi. Reprinted (1963) by Macmillan.

Dick, E. (1987). *Signs of success: Report of the media education development program.* Glasgow: Scottish Film Council.

Donald, J. (1997). Media studies possibilities and limitations. In M. Alvarado (Ed.), *Media education: An introduction.* London: BFI/Open University.

Dougherty, T. (1996). The information blitz vs. truth. *San Francisco Chronicle* (2 December), A-21.

Drennan, M. (1996). *Technology comes home: The American dream in Union City, N.J.* Editorial Projects in Education. In CAST, *The role of online communications in schools: A national study* (October 16). Peabody, MA: CAST. http://www.cast.org/.

Duncan, B. (1988). Media beat. *Forum: magazine of the Ontario secondary school teachers' federation* (April/May), 8–15.

Duncan, B., D'Ippolito, J., Mcpherson, C., & Wilson, C. (1996). *Mass media and popular culture* (version 2). Toronto, Canada: Harcourt Brace.

Dwyer, D. C. (1994). Apple classrooms of tomorrow: What we've learned. *Educational Leadership, 51,* 4–10.

Dwyer, D. C. (1996). *Changing the conversation about teaching, learning & technology: A report on 10 years of ACOT research.* Cupertino, CA: Apple Classrooms of Tomorrow.

Educational Video Center. (1995). *Yo! television production handbook.* New York: EVC.

Eisemon, T. O., Hallett, M., & Maunda, J. (1986). Primary school literature and folktales in Kenya: What makes a children's story African? *Comparative Education Review, 30*(2), 232–246.

Eisenstein, E. L. (1979). *The printing press as an agent of change: Communications and cultural transformations in early modern Europe.* Cambridge, England: Cambridge University Press.

Eisenstein, S. (1944). Dickens, Griffith, and film today. In Sergei Eisenstein, *Film form and the film sense* (pp. 195–255). Jay Leyda, Trans. and Ed. Cleveland, OH: Medidan Books. (Reprinted, 1957)

Ellsworth, E. (1987). Educational films against critical pedagogy. *Journal of Education, 169*(3), 10–26.

Ellsworth, E., & Whatley, M. J. (1990). *The ideology of images in educational media: Hidden curriculums in the classroom.* New York: Teachers College Press.

Escobar, G., & Swardson, A. (1995). From Monroe doctrine to MTV doctrine. *Washington Post Weekly* (11–17 September), p. 17.

Estrada, K., & McLaren, P. (1993). A dialogue on multiculturalism and democratic culture. *Educational Researcher, 22*(3), 27–33.

Fairclough, N. (1989). *Discourse and social change.* Cambridge: Polity Press.

Family & Community Critical Viewing Project, a partnership of the American Academy of Pediatrics, American Medical Association; Cable in the Classroom, National Cable Television Association (1997). *Taking charge of your tv.* VHS. Washington, DC: HBO.

Farmer, D. W., & Mech, T. F. (Eds.). (1992). *Information literacy: Developing students as independent learners.* San Francisco, CA: Jossey-Bass.

Febvre, L., & Martin, H.-J. (1990). In G. Nowell-Smith & D. Wootton (Eds.), *The coming of the book: The impact of printing 1450–1800* (pp. 302–303). New York: Verso.

Federman, J. (1996). *Media ratings: Design, use and consequences.* Century City, CA: Mediascope.

Ferguson, E. (1977). The mind's eye: Nonverbal thought in technology. *Science,* 197.

Ferris, S. P., & Montgomery, M. (1996). The new orality: Oral characteristics of computer-mediated communication. *The New Jersey Journal of Communication, 4*(1), 55–60.

Finnegan, R. (1988). *Literacy and orality: Studies in the technology of communication.* London: Basil Blackwell.

Fish, S. (1980). *Is there a text in this class? The authority of interpretive communities.* Cambridge, MA; Harvard University Press.

Fitzgerald, J., & Spiegel, D. (1983). Enhancing children's reading comprehension through instruction in narrative structure. *Journal of Reading Behavior, 15*(2), 2–17.

Ford Foundation (1975). *Television and children: Priorities for research.* Reston, VA: Ford Foundation.

Foucault, M. (1966). *The order of things.* New York: Random House.

Foucault, M. (1969). *The archaeology of knowledge.* New York: Random House.

Foucault, M. (1985). *The Foucault reader.* P. Rainbow (Ed.). New York: Pantheon.

Foxfire Fund (1990). The foxfire approach: Perspectives and core practices. *Hands-on: A Journal for Teachers,* (Spring/Summer).

Freire, P. (1970). *Pedagogy of the oppressed.* New York: Seabury Press.

Freire, P. (1973). *Education for critical consciousness.* New York: Seabury Press.

Freire, P. (1985). *The politics of education.* South Hadley, MA: Bergin & Garvey.

Freire, P., & Macedo, D. (1987). *Literacy: Reading the word and the world.* South Hadley, MA: Bergin & Garvey.

Freund, E. (1987). *The return of the reader: Reader-response criticism.* London: Methuen.

Fry, G. W. (1981). Schooling, development and inequality: Old myths and new realities. *Harvard Educational Review, 51,* 107–116.

Fulton, K. (1996). *Future visions: Education and technology* (September). Washington DC: Office of Technology Assessment, Congress of the United States.

Gadbury, S. (1980). Effects of restricting first graders' tv viewing on leisure time, i.q. change and cognitive style. *Journal of Applied Developmental Psychology, 1,* 161–176.

Gagne, R. M. (1965). *The conditions of learning.* New York: Holt, Rinehart & Winston.

Gantz, W. (1993). Introduction. In B. S. Greenberg & W. Gantz (Eds.), *Desert storm and the mass media.* Cresskill, NJ: Hampton Press.

Gardner, H. (1991). *The unschooled mind: How children think and how schools teach.* New York: Basic Books.

Gardner, H. (1993). *Multiple intelligences: The theory in practice.* New York: Basic Books.

Gauthier, G. (1976). *The semiology of the image.* London: British Film Institute/Open University.

Gee, J. P. (1991). The legacies of literacy: From Plato to Freire through Harvey Graff. In M. Minami & B. P. Kennedy (Eds.), *Language issues in literacy and bilingual/multicultural education, Reprint Series No. 22* (pp. 266–285). Cambridge, MA: Harvard University Press.

Gee, J. P. (1996). *Social linguistics and literacies: Ideology in discourses.* London & Bristol, PA: Taylor & Francis.

Gerbner, G., & Gross, L. (1976). Living with television: The violence profile. *Journal of Communication, 26*(2), 173–199.

Gibson, J. J. (1954). A theory of pictorial perception. *Audio Visual Communication Review, 2,* 2–23.

Gibson, J. J. (1982). *Reasons for realism: Selected essays of James J. Gibson* (pp. 225–293). E. Reed & R. Jones, Eds. Hillsdale, NJ: Lawrence Erlbaum Associates.

Gilbert, J. (1986). *A cycle of outrage: America's reaction to the juvenile delinquent in the 1950s.* (See reference to Gorman, P. R., 1996).

Ginsburg, M. (1996). Library to 'bury' old card catalog. *San Francisco Examiner* (13 November), A-12.

Giroux, H. (1988). *Schooling and the struggle for public life.* Minneapolis, MN: University of Minnesota Press.

Giroux, H. A., & Simon, R. L. (1989). *Popular culture, schooling & everyday life.* Toronto, Canada: Ontario Institute for Studies in Education Press.

Gitlin, T. (1994). Imagebusters: The hollow crusade against TV violence. *The American Prospect.* Winter, *16,* 42–49.

Gitlin, T. (1995). *The twilight of common dreams: Why America is wracked by culture wars.* New York: Metropolitan Books/Henry Holt.

Gitlin, T. (1996). An interview with Todd Gitlin. *San Francisco Examiner* (12 May), B-1.

Glenman, T. L., & Meldmed, A. (1996). *Fostering the use of educational technology: Elements of a national strategy.* Washington DC: The RAND Corporation.

Goffman, E. (1974). *Frame analysis.* New York: Harper & Row.

Gombrich, E. H. (1960). *Art and illusion: A study in the psychology of pictorial representation.* A. W. Mellon Lectures in Fine Arts, 1956. Princeton, NJ: Princeton University Press.

Gombrich, E. H. (1992). *Topics of our times: Twentieth-century issues in learning and in art.* Berkeley, CA: University of California Press.

Goodman, N. (1976). *Languages of art: An approach to a theory of symbols* (2nd ed.). Indianapolis: Hackett.

Goodman, S. (1996). Media, technology & education reform. *Video and Learning,* Fall/Winter, 1–2.

Goody, J. (Ed.). (1968). *Literacy in traditional societies.* Cambridge, England: Cambridge University Press.

Goody, J. (1973). Evolution and communication: The domestication of the savage mind. *British Journal of Sociology, 24.*

Goody, J., & Watt, I. (1988). The consequences of literacy. In E. R. Kintgen, B. M. Kroll, & M. Rose (Eds.), *Perspectives on literacy* (pp. 3–27). Carbondale, IL; Southern Illinois University Press.

Gorman, P. R. (1996). *Left intellectuals and popular culture in twentieth-century America.* Chapel Hill, NC: The University of North Carolina Press.

Gopinathan, S. (1987). Cross-cultural transfer of print media. In R. Murray Thomas & Victor N. Kobayashi (Eds.), *Educational technology: Its creation, development and cross-cultural transfer* (pp. 177–195). Oxford/New York: Pergamon Press.

Gough, K. (1988). Implications of literacy in traditional China and India. In E. R. Kintgen, B. M. Kroll, & M. Rose (Eds.), *Perspectives on literacy* (pp. 44–56). Cabondale, IL; Southern Illinois University Press.

Graff, H. J. (1979). *The literacy myth: Literacy and social structure in the nineteenth-century city.* New York and London: Academic Press.

Graff, H. J. (1987). *The legacies of literacy: Continuities and contradictions in western culture and society.* Bloomington: Indiana University Press.

Graff, H. J. (Ed.). (1995). *The labyrinths of literacy: Reflections on literacy past and present.* Pittsburgh, PA: University of Pittsburgh Press.

Graff, H. J., & Arnove, R. F. (1995). National literacy campaigns in historical and comparative perspective. In H. J. Graff (Ed.), *The labyrinths of literacy: Reflections on literacy past and present* (pp. 270–298). Pittsburgh, PA: University of Pittsburgh Press.

Gramsci, A. (1971). *Prison notebooks.* London: Lawrence & Wishart.

Guerrero, E. (1993). *Framing blackness: The African-American image in film.* Philadelphia: Temple University Press.

Hall, S. (1977). Culture, the media and the 'ideological effect'. In J. Curran, M. Guravitch, & J. Woollacott (Eds.), *Mass communication and society.* London & New York: Edward Arnold.

Hamilton, E., & Cairns, H. (1989). *Plato: Collected dialogues.* Bollinger series LXXI. Princeton, NJ: Princeton University Press.

Hanschen, A. (1994, August). *The Caddo village* (VHS, 6 minutes). Dallas, TX: Media, Analysis and Practice Workshop with Deborah Leveranz.

Harper, D. O. (1987). The creation and development of educational computer technology. In R. Murray Thomas & Victor N. Kobayashi (Eds.), *Educational technology: Its creation, development and cross-cultural transfer* (pp. 35–63). Oxford/New York: Pergamon Press.

Hart, A. (Ed.). (1998). *Teaching the Media: International Perspectives.* Mahwah, NJ: Lawrence Erlbaum Associates.

Harty, S. (1979). *Hucksters in the classroom: A review of industry propaganda in schools.* Washington, DC: Center for the Study of Responsive Law.

Harty, S. (1985). *The corporate Pied Piper: Ideas for international consumer action.* Malaysia: International Organization of Consumers Unions.

Hatfield, L. D. (1996). State's dropout rate sinks but Oakland's rises sharply. *San Francisco Examiner* (4 June), A-5.

Havelock, E. (1963). *Origins of western literacy.* Toronto: Ontario Institute for Studies in Education.

Havelock, E. (1986). *The muse learns to write: Reflections on orality and literacy from antiquity to the present.* New Haven, CT: Yale University Press.

Healy, J. M. (1990). *Endangered minds: Why children don't think and what we can do about it.* New York: Simon & Schuster.

Heath, S. B. (1978). Social history and sociolinguistics. *American Sociologist, 13,* 84–92.

Herrnstein, R. J., & Murray, C. (1994). *The bell curve.* New York: The Free Press.

Herrera, M., & Miller, B. *Maria Herrera* (1989, VHS, 6 minutes). From the I-Eye-I Workshop of the Henry Street Settlement and Young People's Resource Center, Bronx, NY. Chicago, IL; Video Data Bank, Art Institute of Chicago.

Hibbits, B. J. (1996). The interface is the message. *Wired* (September 1996), 130.

Hirsch, E. D., Jr. (1987). *Cultural literacy.* Boston: Houghton Mifflin.

Hobbs, R. (1994). Teaching media literacy—are you hip to this? *Media Studies Journal,* (Winter).

Hochberg, J. E. (1983). Pictorial functions in perception. *Art Education,* March, 15–18.

Hochberg, J. E. (1984). The perception of pictorial representations. *Social Research, 51*(4), 841–862.

Hodgkinson, A. W. (1964). *Screen education: Teaching a critical approach to cinema and television.* Paris: UNESCO.

Homan, R. (1992). *Introduction to visual literacy* (16 April). A presentation to Media Alliance at Fort Mason, San Francisco, CA.

Honey, M., & Henríquez, A. (1993). *Telecommunications and K–12 educators: Findings from a national survey.* New York: Center for Technology in Education, Bank Street College of Education.

Honey, M., & Henríquez, A. (1996). *Union City Interactive Multimedia Education Trial, 1993–1995 Summary Report.* New York: Education Development Center, Inc., Center for Children & Technology. http://www.edc.org/CCT/union-city/.

Horton, F. W. (Ed.). (1982). *Understanding U.S. information policy: The infrastructure handbook* (Vols. 1–4). Washington DC: Information Industry Association.

Horton, F. W. (1983). Information literacy vs. computer literacy. *Bulletin of the American Society for Information Science, 9,* 14–18.

Horton, J. (1982). A need for a theory of visual literacy. *Reading Improvement, 19,* 257–267.

Houston, R. (1985). *Scottish literacy and the Scottish identity: Illiteracy and society in Scotland and northern England, 1600–1800.* Cambridge, England: Cambridge University Press.

Hunter, B. (1997). Learning in an internetworked world. *The internet as paradigm: Annual review of the Institute for Informations Studies* (pp. 103–121). Queenstown, MD and Nashville, TN: Nortel North America and The Aspen Institute.

Innis, H. A. (1951). *The bias of communication.* Toronto: University of Toronto.

Intelliquest, Inc. (1995). *National computing survey* (April). Austin, TX: Microsoft/Intelliquest.

Ivins, W. (1969). *Prints and visual communications.* Cambridge, England: Cambridge University Press.

Johnson, B. D. (1977). Visual literacy, media literacy, and mass communications for English instruction. *Dissertation Abstract International, 38,* 6581A. (University Microfilms No. 78-5287).

Jordan, B. (1987). *Modes of teaching and learning: Questions raised by the training of traditional birth attendants* (Report No. IRL87-0004). Palo Alto, CA; Institute for Research on Learning.

Kaestle, C. F. (1991). Studying the history of literacy. In C. F. Kaestle, H. Damon-Moore, L. C. Stedman, K. Tinsley, & W. V. Trollinger, Jr. (Eds.), *Literacy in the United States: Readers and reading since 1880* (pp. 3–32). New Haven and London: Yale University Press.

Katz, E. (1988). On conceptualizing media effects: Another look. In S. Oschamp (Ed.), *Television as a social issue* (pp. 361–374). Newbury Park, CA: Sage.

Kennedy, J. M. (1984). How minds use pictures. *Social Research, 51*(4), 885–904.

Kilbourne, J. (1989). Beauty and the beast of advertising. *Media & Values, 49,* 8–10.

King, J. (Ed.). (1990). In search of African liberation pedagogy: Multiple contexts of education and struggle. Special Issue. *Journal of Education, 172*(2).

Kipper, P. (1990). *A new interpretive strategy for television's changing visual world.* Paper presented at the Fourth Annual Visual Communication Conference, Northstar, California.

Kress, G. (1985). *Linguistic processes in sociocultural practice.* Oxford, England: Oxford University Press.

Kubey, R. (1997). *Obstacles to the development of media education in the United States: A cross-national perspective.* Unpublished paper. Department of Communication, Rutgers University.

Kubey, R., & Csikszentmihalyi, M. (1990). *Television and the quality of life: How viewing shapes everyday experience.* Hillsdale, NJ: Lawrence Erlbaum Associates.

Kwasnik, B. H. (1990). Information literacy: Concepts of literacy in a computer age. In V. Blake & R. Thomas (Eds.), *Information literacies for the twenty-first century.* Boston: G. K. Hall & Co.

Lamb, G. (Ed.). (1994). *LA freewaves catalog of southern California youth media programs.* Los Angeles: LA Freewaves.

Lasn, K., & Schmaltz, B. (1993). Re-booting the north American mind. *Adbusters Quarterly 11*(2), 2.

Lave, J., Smith, S., & Butler, M. (1988). Problem solving as an everyday practice, *Learning mathematical problem solving* (Report No. IRL88-0006). Palo Alto, CA: Institute for Research on Learning.

Lazarus, W., & Lippert, L. (1994). *America's children & the information superhighway.* (September). San Francisco, CA: The Children's Partnership and the Tides Foundation.

Learning Channel (1995). *Know TV: Changing what, why and how you watch.* Bethesda, MD: The Learning Channel.

Leavis, F. R., & Thompson, D. (1933). *Culture and environment.* London: Chatto & Windus.

Lee, C. D. (1995). A culturally based cognitive apprenticeship: Teaching African American high school students skills in literary interpretation. *Reading Research Quarterly, 30*(4), 608–630.

Lehman, N. (1995). The great sorting, part II. *Atlantic Monthly, 276*(3), 84–100.

Leveranz, D. (1996). *The English language arts essential knowledge and skills viewing strand.* Dallas, TX: Media Analysis & Practice.

Lévi-Bruhl, L. (1910). *Les fonctions mentales dans les sociétés inférieures* [The mental functions of inferior societies]. Paris: Alcan.

Levine, K. (1986). *The social context of literacy.* London: Routledge & Kegan Paul.

Lloyd-Kolkin, D., & Tyner, K. (1991). *Media & you: An elementary media literacy curriculum.* Englewood Cliffs, NJ: Educational Technology Publications.

Lloyd-Kolkin, D., Wheeler, P., & Strand, T. (1980). Developing a curriculum for teenagers. *Journal of Communication, 30*(3), 119–125.

Lockridge, K. A. (1974). *Literacy in colonial New England.* New York: Norton.

Loveless, T. (1996). Why aren't computers used more in schools? *Educational Policy, 10,* 4.

Los Alamos National Laboratory, Department of Education Regional Laboratories. (1996, April). *Model nets: A nationwide study of computer networks in K–12 schools.* Paper presented to the American Educational Research Association. http://www.lbl.gov/Education/Compact/CaseStudies.html/.

Lull, J. (1985). The naturalistic study of media use and youth culture. In K. E. Rosengren, L. A. Wenner, & P. Palmgreen (Eds.), *Media gratification research: Current perspectives* (pp. 209–224). Beverly Hills, CA: Sage.

Macdonnel, D. (1986). *Theories of discourse: An introduction.* Oxford: Basil Blackwell.

Making choices: Kids of the 90s (1990) (VHS: 18 min). Denver, CO: Denver Public Schools.

Manguel, A. (1997). *A history of reading.* New York: Viking Press.

Marchand, P. (Ed.). (1989). *Marshall McLuhan: The medium and the messenger.* New York: Ticknor & Fields.

Martin, H.-J. (1994). *The history and power of writing.* Chicago and London: University of Chicago Press.

Masterman, L. (1985). *Teaching the media.* London: Comedia Books.

Masterman, L. (1990). Media education's eighteen principles. *Strategies, 2*(2), 8.

Masterman, L., & Mariet, F. (1994). *Media education in 1990s Europe: A teachers' guide.* The Netherlands: Council of Europe Press and Croton; NY: Manhattan Publishing.

McCaffrey, B. R. (1996). *Reducing drug use and its consequences in America* (16 August). Washington, DC: Office of National Drug Control Policy.

McClure, C. R. (1993). Network literacy in an electronic society: An educational disconnect? In *The knowledge economy: The nature of information in the 21st century.* Queenstown, MD: Aspen Institute.

McClure, C. R. (1994). Network literacy: A role for libraries? *Information technology and libraries, 13*(2), 115–125.

McCrank, L. J. (1992). Academic programs for information literacy: Theory and structure. *Research Quarterly,* (Summer), 485–495.

McGee, M. (1996). *On television.* VHS. New Brunswick, NJ: Rutgers University and San Francisco: California Newsreel.

McLaren, P. L. (1988). Culture or canon? Critical pedagogy and the politics of literacy. *Harvard Educational Review, 58*(2), 213–234.

McLaren, P. L. (1989). *Life in schools: An introduction to critical pedagogy in the foundations of education.* New York: Longman.

McLaren, P., & Hammer, R. (1992). Media knowledges, warrior citizenry, and postmodern literacies. *Journal of urban and cultural studies, 2*(2), 41–64.

McLuhan, M. (1960, June). *Report on project in understanding new media.* Washington, DC: National Association of Educational Broadcasters.

McLuhan, M. (1962). *The Gutenberg galaxy: The making of typographic man.* Toronto: University of Toronto Press.

McLuhan, M. (1964). *Understanding media: The extensions of man.* New York: McGraw-Hill.

McLuhan, M. (1966). Letter to the editor. *Life* (18 March).

McLuhan, M., Fiore, Q., & Agel, J. (1967). *The medium is the massage: An inventory of effects.* New York: Bantam.

Means, B. (1994). Using technology to advance educational goals. In B. Means (Ed.), *Technology and education reform* (pp. 1–21). San Francisco: Jossey-Bass.

Media Awareness Network. (1996). *http://www.schoolnet.ca/MediaNet/.* Ottawa/Ontario, Canada: The Media Network.

Mertes, C. (1996). *Signal to noise: Life with television.* VHS. New York: Mixed Media.

Messaris, P. (1994). *Visual literacy: Image, mind & reality.* Boulder, San Francisco, & Oxford: Westview Press.

Metz, J. M. (1996). Balancing act: The struggle between orality and linearity in computer-mediated communication. *The New Jersey Journal of Communication, 4*(1), 61–70.

Meyrowitz, J. (1985). *No sense of place: The impact of electronic media on social behavior.* New York: Oxford University Press.

Meyrowitz, J. (1995). Instructional technology and the bifurcation of the university. *Telematics and Informatics, 2,* 75–84.

Michigan Department of Education (1996). *Inventory of instructional telecommunications systems.* Grand Rapids, MI: Michigan Department of Education.

Miller, B. and the students from the Henry Street Settlement. (1989). *Birth of a candy bar* (VHS, 3 min). From the I-Eye-I Workshop of the Henry Street Settlement and Young People's Resource Center, Bronx, NY. Chicago, IL; Video Data Bank, Art Institute of Chicago.

Minami, M., & Kennedy, B. P. (Ed.). (1991). *Language issues in literacy and bilingual/multicultural education* (Reprint series no. 22). Cambridge, MA: Harvard University Press.

Minneapolis Public Schools. (1996). *Information media and technology content standards.* Minneapolis, MN: Minneapolis Public Schools.

Minton, T. (1996). Card catalog saved—but S.F. library is not sure where to put it. *San Francisco Chronicle* (5 September), A-13.

Molinaro, M., McLuhan, C., & Toye, W. (Eds.). (1987). *Letters of Marshall McLuhan.* New York: Oxford University Press.

Moody, K. (1980). *Growing up on television: A report to parents.* New York: McGraw-Hill.

Moore, D. M., & Dwyer, F. M. (Eds.). (1994). *Visual literacy: A spectrum of visual learning.* Englewood Cliffs, NJ: Educational Technology Publications.

National Teleconference on Media Literacy (1996, October). Washington, DC: PBS & Rutgers University. Distributed by California Newsreel, San Francisco.

NBC Today. (July 15, 1992). *Video segment: A production approach for elementary school children.* New York: NBC.

Negroponte, N. (1995). *Being digital.* New York: Random House.

The New London Group. (1996). A Pedagogy of multiliteracies: Designing social futures. *Harvard Educational Review, 66*(1), 60–92.

Newman, D., Griffin, P., & Cole, M. (1989). *The construction zone: Working for cognitive change in school.* Cambridge, England: Cambridge University Press.

Newspaper Association of America (1993). *An informal history and purpose of the newspaper in education program.* Reston, VA: NAA.

Nolker, P., & Tyner, K. (1991). Photographic discourse: Strategies for media literacy guide to understanding photographs. *Strategies, 4*(2), 1–8.

Oakland Unified School District (1996). *Adopted policy on standard American English language development* (December 18). Oakland, CA: Oakland Unified School District. See also: http://ousd.k12.ca.us/oakland.standard.html#app.3.

Olsen, J. K., & Coons, B. (1987). Competencies for the information literacy program: Encompassing goals & subordinate objectives. *LOEX-89* (12 September). Cornell University: Albert R. Mann Library.

Olson, D. (1977). The language of instruction: On the literate bias of school. In R. C. Anderson & W. E. Montague (Eds.), *Schooling and the acquisition of knowledge* (pp. 75–86). Hillsdale, NJ: Lawrence Erlbaum Associates.

Ong, W. J. (1958). *Ramus, method, and the decay of dialogue.* Cambridge, MA: Harvard University Press.

Ong, W. J. (1982). *Orality and literacy: The technologizing of the word.* New York: Metheun.

Ontario Ministry of Education. (1989). *Media literacy resource guide: Intermediate and senior divisions 1989.* Toronto: Ontario Ministry of Education.

Ontario Ministry of Education. (1995). *The common curriculum: Provincial standards language, grades 1–9.* Toronto: Ontario Ministry of Education.

Oppenheimer, T. (1997). The computer delusion. *Atlantic Monthly, 280*(1), 45–62.

Osborne, L. N. (1989). Teaching in American academic libraries. *International library review, 21,* 9–27.

Owens, M. R. (1976). State government and libraries. *Library Journal, 101,* 27.

Pacific Mountain Network (1993). *Creating critical viewers* (VHS). Denver, CO: Pacific Mountain Network and the National Academy of Television Arts and Science.

Palinscar, A. S., & Brown, A. L. (1984). Reciprocal teaching of comprehension-fostering and monitoring activities. *Cognition and Instruction, 1,* 117–175.

Pea, R. D. (1989). *Socializing the knowledge transfer problem* (Report No. IRL89-0009). Palo Alto, CA: Institute for Research on Learning.

Pearce, J. C. (1992). *Evolution's end: Claiming the potential of our intelligence.* San Francisco: HarperSanFrancisco.

Pearl, D., Bouthelet, L., & Lazar, J. (1982). *Television and behavior: Ten years of scientific progress and implications for the eighties* (Vols. 1 & 2). Washington DC: U.S. Department of Health and Human Services, National Institute of Mental Health and U.S. Government Printing Office.

Pearson, P., & Dole, J. (1987). Explicit comprehension instruction: A review of research and a new conceptualization of instruction. *Elementary School Journal, 88*(2), 151–165.

Pescovitch, D. (1996). Reality check. *Wired* (September), p. 80.

Pinker, S. (1989). *Learnability and cognition: The acquisition of argument structure.* Cambridge, MA: MIT Press.

Pinker, S. (1994). *The language instinct: How the mind creates language.* New York: William Morrow.

Postman, N. (1971). The new literacy. *The Grade Teacher, 40,* 26–27.

Postman, N. (1982). *The disappearance of childhood.* New York: Delacourte Press.

Postman, N. (1992). *Technopoly: The surrender of culture to technology.* New York: Alfred A. Knopf.

Powell, G. J. (1982). The impact of television on the self-concept development of minority children. In G. L. Berry & C. Mitchell-Kernan (Eds.), *Television and the socialization of the minority child* (pp. 105–131). New York: Academic Press.

Powgrow, S. (1990). Learning dramas: An alternative curricular approach to using computers with at-risk students. In C. Warger (Ed.), *Technology in today's schools.* Alexandria, VA: Association for Supervision and Curriculum Development.

Public Agenda Foundation. (1995). *Assignment incomplete: The unfinished business of education reform* (October). New York: Public Agenda Foundation.

Pungente, J. (1987). Media education in Europe: An overview of several countries. *Asociacion Mexicana de Investigadores de la Comunicacion. Medios de informacion y recepcion critica.* Mexico City: Universidad Iberoamericana.

Pungente, J. (1993). The second spring: Media education in Canada's secondary schools. *Canadian Journal of Education, 22*(1), 47–60.

Quin, R., & Aparici, R. (Eds.). (1996). Media education. *The Australian Journal of Media & Culture, 9*(2).

Quin, R., & McMahon, B. (1993). Evaluating standards in media education. *Canadian Journal of Educational Communication, 22*(1), 15–25.

Real, M. R. (1977). *Mass-mediated culture.* Englewood Cliffs, NJ: Prentice-Hall.

Real, M. R. (1989). *Super media: A cultural studies approach.* Newbury Park, CA: Sage.

Reich, R. (1991). *The work of nations: Preparing ourselves for the 21st century capitalism.* New York: Vintage Books.

Resnick, D. P., & Resnick, L. B. (1977). The nature of literacy: A historical exploration. *Harvard Educational Review, 47,* 370–385.

Riel, M. (1990). Computer-mediated communication: A tool for reconnecting kids with society. *Interactive Learning Environments, 1*(4), 255–263.

Riley, R. W. (1995). *Media literacy for America's young people.* Remarks at Julius West Middle School (December 13). Rockville, MD.

Robertson Stephens & Company (1993). *Educational technology: A catalyst for change.* (13 January). San Francisco, CA: Robertson Stephens & Company.

Robson, J., Simmons, J., & Sohn-Rethel, M. (1990). A media education policy across the curriculum. In D. Buckingham (Ed.), *Watching media learning: Making sense of media education* (pp. 171–193). London: The Falmer Press.

Rosengren, K. E., Wenner, L. A., & Palmgreen, P. (Eds.). (1985). *Media gratification research: Current perspectives.* Beverly Hills, CA: Sage.

Safford, S. (1990). *Self protection: Teen moms expand their options* (VHS, 12 Min). New York: Brooklyn Perinatal Network.

San Francisco Examiner. (1996). Jackson assails 'ebonics' policy. *San Francisco Examiner* (December 23), A-2.

Sandalow, M., & Lochhead, C. (1993). Historic global trade pact. *San Francisco Chronicle* (15 December), B-1.

Schofield, R. S. (1968). The measurement of literacy in preindustrial England. In J. Goody (Ed.), *Literacy in traditional societies* (pp. 311–325). Cambridge, England: Cambridge University Press.

Schramm, W. (1977). *Big media, little media: Tools and technologies for instruction.* Beverly Hills/London: Sage.

Schramm, W., Lyle, J., & Parker, E. B. (1961). *Television in the lives of our children.* Stanford, CA: Stanford University Press.

Scribner, S. (1988). Literacy in three metaphors. In E. R. Kintgen, B. M. Kroll, & M. Rose (Eds.), *Perspectives on literacy* (pp. 71–81). Carbondale & Edwardsville, IL: Southern Illinois University Press.

Scribner, S., & Cole, M. (1978). Literacy without schooling: Testing for intellectual effects. *Harvard Educational Review, 48,* 448–461.

Scribner, S., & Cole, M. (1981). *The psychology of literacy.* Cambridge, MA; Harvard University Press.

Scribner, S., & Cole, M. (1988). Unpackaging literacy. In E. R. Kintgen, B. M. Kroll, & M. Rose (Eds.), *Perspectives on literacy* (pp. 57–70). Carbondale & Edwardsville, IL: Southern Illinois University Press.

Seidman, S. A. (1992). An investigation of sex-role stereotyping in music videos. *Journal of Broadcasting & Electronic Media, 36*(2), 209–216.

Seiter, E. (1987). Semiotics and television. In R. C. Allen (Ed.), *Channels of discourse: Television and contemporary criticism* (pp. 17–41). Chapel Hill: University of North Carolina.

Seligman, K. (1996). Educators stick by ebonics. *San Francisco Chronicle* (22 December), C1, C7.

Sherarts, K. (Ed.). (1996). *The directory of the national alliance of media educators (name)*. Oakland, CA: The National Alliance of Media Arts and Culture.

Shor, I. (1982). *Empowering education: Critical teaching for social change.* Chicago: University of Chicago Press.

Silber, K. H. (1981). Some implications of the history of educational technology: We're all in this together. In J. W. Brown & S. N. Brown (Eds.), *Educational Media Yearbook 1981* (pp. 18–28). Littleton, CO: Libraries Unlimited.

Silverblatt, A. (1995). *Media literacy: Keys to interpreting media messages.* Westport, CT: Praeger Publishers.

Silverblatt, A., & Eliceiri, E. M. E. (1997). *Dictionary of media literacy.* Westport, CT: Greenwood Press.

Singer, J., & Singer, D. (1976). Can tv stimulate imaginative play? *Journal of Communication, 26*(3), 74–80.

Singer, J. L., Singer, D. G., Desmond, R. J., Hirsch, B., & Nichol, A. (1988). Family mediation and children's comprehension of television: A longitudinal study. *Journal of Applied Developmental Psychology, 9*, 117–140.

Singer, J. L., Singer, D. G., & Rapaczynski, W. S. (1984). Family patterns and television viewing as predictors of children's beliefs and aggression. *Journal of Communication, 34*(2), 73–89.

Smith, A. (1982). Information technology and the myth of abundance. *Daedalus, 4*, 1–16.

Soltow, L., & Stevens, E. (1981). *The rise of literacy and the common school in the United States.* Chicago: University of Chicago Press.

Sossel, S. (1997). The man who counts the killings. *Atlantic Monthly, 279*(5), 86–104.

Speech Communication Association (1996). *Speaking, listening, and media literacy standards for K through 12 education.* Annandale, VA: Speech Communication Association.

State University of New York (1992). *College expectations: The report of the SUNY task force on college entry-level knowledge and skills* (October). Rochester, NY: SUNY.

Steiner, G. (1997). Ex libris. *The New Yorker,* March 17, pp. 117–120.

Stephens, W. B. (1987). *Education, literacy and society: 1830–1870.* Manchester, England: Manchester University Press.

Stevens, E. (1985). Literacy and the worth of liberty. *Historical Social Research, 34*, 65–81.

Stone, L. (1969). Literacy and education in England, 1640–1900. *Past & Present, 42*, 69–139.

Surgeon General's Scientific Advisory Committee on Television and Social Behavior (1972). *Television and growing up: The impact of televised violence.* Washington, DC: United States Public Health Service and U.S. Government Printing Office.

Sutton, S. A. (1994). *Information literacy initiative. Part I: Problem analyses and statement of purpose* (September 30). San Jose, CA: The San Jose State University Library, The School of Library and Information Science, and The Alquist Center.

Takanishi, R. (1982). The influence of television on the ethnic identity of minority children: A conceptual framework. In G. L. Berry & C. Mitchell-Kernan (Eds.), *Socialization of the minority child* (pp. 81–104). New York: Academic Press.

Texas Education Agency (1997). *Texas Essential Knowledge and Skills (TEKS).* Austin, Texas: Texas Education Agency. (http://www.tea.texas.gov/teks)

Tharp, R., & Gallimore, R. (1988). *Rousing minds to life: Teaching, learning and schooling in social context.* Cambridge, England: Cambridge University Press.

Thomas, L. G., & Knezek, D. G. (1993). *Technology literacy for the nation and for its citizens.* Eugene, OR: International Society for Technology Educators (ISTE) and Intel Corporation.

Thomas, R. M. (1987). Educational radio and television: Their development in advanced industrial societies. In R. M. Thomas & V. N. Kobayashi (Eds.), *Educational technology: Its creation, development and cross-cultural transfer* (pp. 105–123). Oxford/New York: Pergamon Press.

Thornburg, D. (May 9, 1997). *Town Hall Meeting Speech for the Peoria Unified School District.* Glendale, Arizona.

Turbayne, C. M. (1970). *The myth of metaphor*. New Haven, CT: Yale University Press.

Tyner, K. (1992). The media education elephant. In C. Bazalgette (Ed.), *Proceedings of the 1992 UNESCO conference on media education*. London & Paris: British Film Institute and CLEMI.

Tyner, K. (1993). Sunrise in New Mexico. *Strategies, 6*(2), 1.

Tyner, K. (1994). Video: A tool for reform. *Arts Education Policy Review, 96*(1), 18–26.

Tyner, K., & Leveranz, D. (1996). *The Media Literacy Institute Guide*. San Francisco, CA: Strategies for Media Literacy and Southwest Alternate Media Project.

UCLA Center for Communication Policy (1995). *The UCLA Television violence monitoring report*. Los Angeles, CA: UCLA Center for Communication Policy.

U.S. Congress, Office of Technology Assessment. (1995). *Teachers and technology: Making the connection*. OTA-EHR-616. Washington DC: U.S. Government Printing Office.

U.S. Department of Education National Commission on Excellence in Education. (1983). *A nation at risk: The imperative for educational reform* (April). Washington DC: U.S. Government Printing Office.

U.S. Department of Education. (1995). *Advanced telecommunications in U.S. public schools, K–12*. Washington DC: Office of Educational Research and Improvement.

U.S. Department of Education (1997). *Building knowledge for a nation of learners: A framework for educational research 1997* (January). Washington DC: Office of Educational Research and Improvement. http://www.ed.gov/offices/OERI/RschPriority/plan/index.html/.

U.S. Department of Education (1996). *Getting America's students ready for the 21st century: A report to the nation on technology and education*. Washington DC: Office of Educational Technology. http://www.ed.gov/Technology/Plan/.

U.S. Department of Health and Human Services & Weekly Reader Corporation (1996). Media Literacy skills as a substance abuse prevention strategy. *Weekly Reader Teacher's Guide: Extra Supplement, 5*, 1–21.

Valenti, J. (1992). *The contribution of the movie industry to GNP*. Speech to the Commonwealth Club, May 29, San Francisco, California.

Vygotsky, L. S. (1962). *Thought and language*. Cambridge, MA: MIT Press.

Vygotsky, L. S. (1978). *Mind in society: The development of higher psychological processes*. Cambridge, MA: Harvard University Press.

Wagner, V. (19xx). Ebonics' uproar overlooks L.A. program. *San Francisco Chronicle*. (22 December), C7.

Wahlstrom, B. (1989). Desktop publishing: Perspectives, potentials and politics. In G. E. Hawisher & C. L. Selfe (Eds.), *Critical perspectives on computers and composition instruction* (pp. 162–186). New York: Teachers College Press.

Wallach, L., Dorfman, L., Jernigan, D., & Themba, M. (1993). *Media advocacy and public health: Power for prevention*. Newbury Park, CA: Sage.

Ware, M., & Stuck, M. F. (1985). Sex-role messages vis-a-vis microcomputer use: A look at the pictures. *Sex roles, 13*(3/4), 205–214.

Wartella, E., Heintz, K. E., Aidman, A. J., & Mazzarella, S. R. (1990). Television and beyond: Children's video media in one community. *Communication Research, 17*(1), 45–64.

Webb, R. K. (1955). *The British working class reader*. London: Allen and Unwin.

Wessels, M. (1990). *Computer, self, and society*. Englewood Cliffs, NJ: Prentice-Hall.

Wheeler, P., Lloyd-Kolkin, D., & Strand, T. (1981). *Formative review of the critical television viewing skills curriculum for secondary schools: Final report* (Vol. 1). San Francisco: Far West Laboratory for Educational Research and Development. (Eric Document Reproduction Service, pp. 215–669).

Wiley, P. B. (1996). *A free library in this city*. San Francisco: Weldon Owen.

Williams, L. (1996). Wilson undercut TV ads on smoking: 2 say state asked them to 'falsify' data. *San Francisco Examiner*, December 22, A-1.

Williams, M. T. (1980). *Griffith: First artists of the movies*. New York: Oxford University Press.

Williams, R. (1961). *The long revolution.* London: Chatto and Windus.

Williams, R. (1976). *Keywords.* London: Fontana.

Williams, T. (1995). *Always there* (VHS, 6 min). With M. Ma, J. Meltzer, & C. Saalfield (Producers). *Divas in training.* Los Angeles and New York: Eagles Center and Hetrick-Martin Institute.

Winick, C. (1988). The functions of television: Life without the big box. In S. Oscamp (Ed.), *Television as a social issue* (pp. 217–237). Newbury Park, CA: Sage.

Winn, M. (1987). *Unplugging the plug-in drug.* New York: Viking Penguin Books.

Wisconsin Educational Media Association (1993). *Information literacy in action.* Washington DC: National Forum for Information Literacy.

Wollen, P. (1969). *Signs and meaning in the cinema.* Bloomington, IN: Indiana University Press.

Woronov, T. (1994). Six myths (and five promising truths) about the uses of educational technology. *The Harvard Education Letter, X*(5), 1–9.

Worsnop, C. (1994). *Screening images: Ideas for media education.* Mississauga, Ontario: Wright Communications.

Worsnop, C. (1996). *Assessing media work.* Mississauga, Ontario: Wright Communications.

Wright, J. C., & Huston, A. C. (1983). A matter of form: Potentials of television for young viewers. *American Psychologist, 38*(7), 835–843.

Zancanella, D. (1994). Local conversations, national standards, and the future of English. *English Journal, 83,* 24–28.

Zettl, H. (1990). *Sight, sound motion: Applied media aesthetics* (2nd ed.). Belmont, CA: Wadsworth.

Zillman, D. (1991). Empathy: Affect from bearing witness to the emotions of others. In J. Bryant & D. Zillman (Eds.), *Responding to the screen: Reception and reaction processes* (pp. 135–168). Hillsdale, NJ: Lawrence Erlbaum Associates.

Zurkowski, P. G. (1974). *The information service environment relationships and priorities.* Washington DC: National Commission on Libraries and Information Science.

Author Index

Subject Index